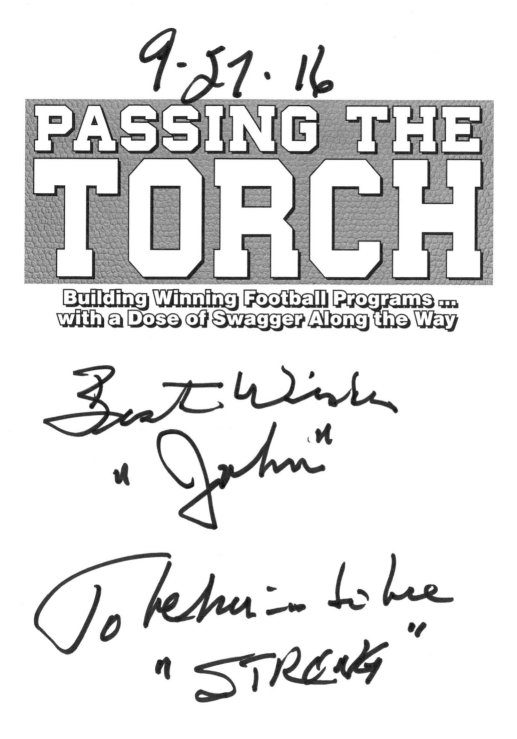

9-31-16

PASSING THE TORCH

Building Winning Football Programs ... with a Dose of Swagger Along the Way

Best Wishes
"John"

To Katherine to bee
"STRONG"

"Of all the coaches I've known, Howard is the closest I've seen to being like Bryant. There's a reverence about him. Kids can't help but give their best for him. He builds a great aura of confidence."

      – Bobby Bowden, *Florida State head coach 1976-2009*

"He took something from all the great coaches. He has a lot of charisma. He walks into a room and you know he's there. He has the ability to inspire. I can see him as a great general or a top CEO. He can look people in the eye and make them think this endeavor is the most important thing in the world. He can pull that off."

      – Billy Reed, *Lexington Herald sports editor*

"Howard was like our dad; he was always looking after us. He was the boss. We looked up to him. He was like a 25-year-old as a senior in high school. He had a coach's mentality even then."

      – Paul Hornung, *teammate at Flaget High School, Heisman Trophy winner at Notre Dame and nine-year NFL veteran*

"He was a classroom teacher and game planner. He showed us various blocking schemes. He used the chalkboard. He was very knowledgeable about who to match up with on the opposing side and what you needed to do to have the best opportunity to run the ball and to pass the ball."

      – Lee Roy Jordan, *two-way player at Alabama and Dallas Cowboys linebacker for 14 years*

"Coach Schnellenberger took me under his wing. He worked with me on meeting organization and meeting presentation. He took me through the whole process of how he did things. He helped me with grading the players on their performance. He helped me with technical things. He was like a graduate professor of X's and Q's to me."

      – Dick Vermeil, *assistant coach in L.A. and head coach of Philadelphia, St. Louis and Kansas City teams*

"Howard Schnellenberger was always about calling the right play at the right time and that was right up my alley offensively. I didn't call plays in college and when I got to Miami, I'd call a play and it had no meaning; it was rag-tag. Schnellenberger picked up on this. We would study film together and he would have me work on checking things off at the line."

— **Bob Griese,** *Dolphins quarterback for 14 years*

"Howard came in and was the first true coach I had who understood receiver play. Everything I was learning up to that point was from other players. He solidified what I was doing and instilled a work ethic. He pushed us to be better athletes."

— **Nat Moore,** *Dolphins receiver*
and 13-year NFL veteran

"He is always thinking how to handle the game, how to work it. He knows how to get young men to believe in themselves. He doesn't leave any stones unturned. He finds the right way."

— **Earl Morrall,** *Dolphins quarterback during 21-year*
NFL career and assistant coach at University of Miami

"He wasn't just offense. He knew defense. Execution was the main thing. He understood physical mistakes, but he would not tolerate mental mistakes on where you were supposed to be in a defense or in your assignment. He would chide me for lining up inside on the split formation. He was big on special teams, too. Special teams were a big part of his game."

— **Ted Hendricks,** *Baltimore linebacker*
and 15-year NFL player

"I was one of the first quarterbacks who started Quarterback U. And the reason I stayed at the University of Miami was Howard Schnellenberger. He is a class individual. When many guys are growing up in high school, they are All-Americans or All Everything. But they need coaching. I needed this man to settle me down. He was like my mom and my dad."

— **Jim Kelly,** *University of Miami quarterback*
who played 11 years with the Buffalo Bills

"Howard Schnellenberger was my mentor, my coach, my father figure. He taught me to know the system, to take command of an offense and audible into the right call. I assumed that was how it was everywhere, but it wasn't. It got me a national championship and into the NFL."

— **Bernie Kosar,** *University of Miami*
quarterback and 12-year NFL veteran

"When we held up four fingers it meant something. He made us brothers in pain. At times you were just trying to survive. His idea was to push us as far as possible and not break us. It wasn't enough to run gassers, then we'd run Super Bowl gassers. You think you can't do any more and then you hear coach saying "On the line" and you'd do it all over again."

— **Browning Nagle,** *Louisville quarterback*
who played in the NFL for five years

"When I got to the NFL, I was on teams with players from Florida, Alabama and USC. They didn't always transition well to the NFL. They were on such good teams that their issues were hidden. A guy from Louisville getting an NFL tryout was better equipped mentally and physically than they were. My work ethic was better than theirs. They hadn't had to push themselves."

— **Roman Oben,** *Louisville offensive lineman*
who played 10 seasons in the NFL

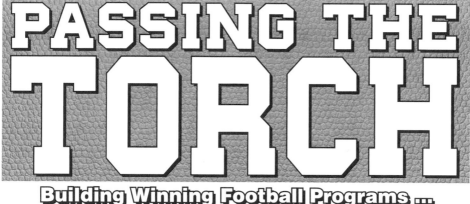

PASSING THE TORCH

Building Winning Football Programs ... with a Dose of Swagger Along the Way

HOWARD SCHNELLENBERGER

with Ron Smith
Foreword by Don Shula

Requests for permission should be addressed to: Ascend Books, LLC, Attn: Rights and
Permissions Department, 12710 Pflumm Road, Suite 200, Olathe, KS. 66062

10 9 8 7 6 5 4 3 2

ISBN: print book 978-0-9912756-7-0
ISBN: e-book 978-0-9912756-8-7

Library of Congress Cataloging-in-Publications Data Available Upon Request
Publisher: Bob Snodgrass
Editor: Katie Hoffman
Publication Coordinator: Christine Drummond
Sales and Marketing: Lenny Cohen and Dylan Tucker
Dust Jacket and Book Design: Rob Peters

All photos courtesy of Howard Schnellenberger unless otherwise indicated.

Every reasonable attempt has been made to determine the ownership of copyright.
Please notify the publisher of any erroneous credits or omissions, and corrections will be made
to subsequent editions/future printings. The goal of Ascend Books is to publish quality works.
With that goal in mind, we are proud to offer this book to our readers. Please note however,
that the story, the experiences and the words are those of the authors alone.

Printed in the United States of America

www.ascendbooks.com

TABLE OF CONTENTS

DEDICATION

My role as head coach for five teams was to choose the best assistant coaches and then coach the assistant coaches. I did my best work in selecting my chief assistant, my wife, Beverlee, who supported me through every minute of my coaching career. Beverlee was a very seasoned and outstanding coach's wife. I really considered her an assistant head coach. She understands the game of football, especially the challenges of the college game: the demands of the recruiting process and developing fan support. And she knows the importance of being a mother away from home for players. She understood my requirements from a time and commitment standpoint. She has been an absolute companion and help throughout the years. In order to be comfortable putting so much time in as a coach, you have to feel good about how things are at home. Beverlee has been mother and father, counselor, accountant, banker, mechanic, cook and housekeeper, and she has done it all in a loving way that allowed me to be free to do my thing in football without feeling bad about time spent on the job. I want to dedicate this book to my beautiful wife, who also successfully raised three wonderful boys, Stuart, Stephen and Timothy.

FOREWORD

GAME BALL PRESENTED BY DON SHULA

After a lifetime of coaching football I am more comfortable giving out game balls than I am offering a toast or writing a foreword to someone's book. If I were to present a game ball to Howard Schnellenberger here at the end of his hugely successful career, it would be for doing things the right way—for teaching and coaching the way it should be done. Howard had success in the NFL with the Rams and the Dolphins, but his greatest accomplishment is building up three communities and three college football programs, and he did it while playing by the rules.

We got to know each other while working as assistant coaches on Blanton Collier's University of Kentucky team in 1959. It was the first year of married life for each of us and we were very close. We spent a lot of time on the road together recruiting. Mostly we were just two young, dedicated guys trying to learn all we could. I left after that season to start my NFL coaching career in Detroit and then became head coach in Baltimore at age 33. I followed Howard's career as he stayed in Kentucky for two years, had a great run at Alabama with Bear Bryant and then joined George Allen in Los Angeles.

My Colts and Howard's Rams were in the same division, so we played each other twice each season for four years. We had Johnny Unitas. They had Roman Gabriel. We engaged in some classic battles in a day when only the division winners got to play in the post season. Twice they went on to the playoffs and twice we did. I was well aware of what Howard was doing on the other sideline as he helped the Rams become the highest scoring team in the NFL. When I left Baltimore to take over the Dolphins in 1970, I was focused on hiring a staff of winners. I thought that was crucial because I was intent on transforming an expansion team that had never enjoyed a winning season. Howard was a winner everywhere he had been, and I was fortunate to get him to join forces with me. Once I knew he was interested, it didn't take me long to come to a decision to hire him. I believe in letting the assistant coaches coach. You hire good people like Howard and you can do that.

I'll never forget showing him his new office in Miami. We were in the 23-story Bell South building downtown at that time. Howard looked out over Biscayne Bay at the sailboats and cruise ships. He sat down, put his feet up on his desk and said, "I wish my parents could see me now." He was proud of what he had accomplished, and he wished they could be a part of it. He had come a long way from Shively, Kentucky. And he has gone much further since then.

Howard coached with me for another seven seasons, and he helped me give the Dolphins that winning edge that culminated with our perfect 17-0 Super Bowl season.

Howard was always searching for another challenge, and eventually he found a massive one just down the road at a struggling University of Miami. When we were coaching Miami's two leading teams, we shared the Orange Bowl, and some people saw us as competitors. I didn't consider us to be in competition with each other. I hated that mentality. We lived in the same neighborhood. We were still friends. His youngest son, Tim, and my son, Michael, went to school and played football together at Columbus High. I wanted Howard to win it all and he did.

What I didn't know about Howard when he left the Dolphins was that there was a P.T. Barnum inside him. That didn't reveal itself until he took on the Hurricane challenge. When we sat down to talk about this book recently, I told Howard he hadn't shown that side of himself to me as an assistant, and Howard told me he became a showman out of necessity. That may be true, but it suits him well, and it has served him well. Howard never ceases to amaze me. The guy thinks big thoughts and the next thing you see is that they happen.

He made the University of Miami team into a national champion. He took his hometown school in Louisville to the Fiesta Bowl and established them as a big-time program. He started from scratch at Florida Atlantic and fought his way to two bowl victories and built a fabulous stadium that will stand as a lasting tribute to his vision and determination.

I know firsthand that it wasn't an accident that he accomplished the things he has. I know what kind of football tutor Howard was because I was on the receiving end of his pipeline to the pros. I drafted many of the athletes he trained and developed at the college level. I am even more impressed with the way he shaped young men's lives and the contribution he made away from football.

Miami, Louisville and Boca Raton owe much to the man. He and his wife, Beverlee, have invested their lives in those communities and made them better places. On behalf of all of them, in recognition of his moral strength and integrity, and for passing the torch to another generation, I give this game ball to Coach Howard Schnellenberger.

– Don Shula

CHAPTER 1

THE LEARNING TREE

"He would tell you he had good teachers, but he also had a gift. He knew football. He knew how to teach it, how to talk it, how to walk it, how to explain it to people. The job of a coach, of a leader, is to serve and give and not ask anything in return. By doing that, he's passed on those life skills and coaching skills. He'll live forever through others."

— **Marc Trestman,** *assistant to Schnellenberger at the University of Miami and hired as Head Coach of the Chicago Bears in 2013*

Mount Rushmore is rightly reserved for statesmen, but if we could honor just four leading football legends on a similarly magnificent scale I am certain the shrine would include two of the men who taught me my trade.

Paul "Bear" Bryant retired after winning more games than anyone in college football history. Don Shula remains the winningest head coach in professional ball. Both men molded me and embedded philosophies that carried me through my memorable lifetime in college and professional football.

I played college ball under Bryant and coached at his side while he won the first three of his six national championships at the University of Alabama. I joined Don Shula's Miami Dolphins staff for a meteoric ride that included two trips to the Super Bowl and the only perfect season in National Football League history. I have the rings to prove it and another favorite piece of jewelry that commemorates the college title for my 1983 University of Miami Hurricanes team.

During my last year as a football coach, in 2011, boosters at Florida Atlantic University (FAU) honored me for my career and taking their neophyte football machine from zero to 60 miles per hour, from inception to Division 1 bowl game, in just six years. No one has ever done it faster, but they overwhelmed me by erecting a life-size statue of me outside the new $70 million, 30,000-seat stadium we built there.

The designer of my bronze impression was Susan Cochran, but there are really five men who were the chief sculptors of the coach that the FAU community wished to honor. Bryant had the greatest influence on my thinking and the way I do things, but Shula was not far behind. Three others shaped me as well.

I might not have had a football career if it wasn't for my high school coach, Paulie Miller. Blanton Collier gave me my first coaching job as an assistant at Kentucky. And George Allen lifted me into the NFL fraternity.

Each of those five men freely shared their life's work with me. They lectured, they preached, they taught, and they demonstrated football techniques, strategies and philosophies. Instead of treating the keys to their success like it was copyrighted information, each one opened his personal vault to me.

I had a unique preparation in serving as an apprentice to all of them. No one else in the world can make that claim. No one else studied under or was mentored by these five Hall of Fame coaches.

I knew from the time I was in high school that I wanted to be a coach, and I know I was the most fortunate guy in the world to have learned from those five people. My dad told me that if I wanted to coach, I had to hook up with the best. It is no accident that I served under such great coaches.

I didn't study these five football greats like a scientist would. Much of what I assimilated was by osmosis. I was an area of low concentration coming in contact with areas of high concentration. They were all different. They all stressed different things. My mind is not five times as big as theirs. I couldn't use everything. I had to pick and choose. I didn't do it on paper. I saw what worked and what didn't work. It just came to me that this is the way I want to do it. My experiences with each of them in some disorganized way formed my way of doing things.

When you play and work for five of the best at their trade, it's really hard to quantitatively say which one did what for you. I don't know if I can say I got this from this coach and that from another coach. I think it's just a collection of the good that I've seen from every coach that I've worked with. You could say Bryant was the ultimate recruiter, Collier the master teacher, and Shula the great organizer. None of them was limited to one skill. All of them taught me multiple lessons.

The playbook that I carried with me all through my career has contributions from each of them. It grew along the way, but it is still in a binder that goes all the way back to my days in Alabama. What outsiders might not know is that it's more than a collection of play diagrams. It's really a coaching manual handed down to me by five football geniuses.

Each of my mentors passed his personal, professional light to me. It was done without ceremony but with as much meaning as there is in the unity candle lighting at many weddings. Two distinct flames merge into one light that will move forward. Five men generously poured their passion into me. I have tried to tend their legacies as carefully as the Olympic organizers mind their flame. These men passed me their torches. And I have tried to pass my unified version to the players and coaches who have walked with me.

BEAR BRYANT TAUGHT ME RECRUITING FIRSTHAND

Let me start with the mentor who did his most memorable work in a houndstooth hat.

I played in the first college football game that I ever saw. Paul Bryant was my coach. This was at the University of Kentucky in 1952. Bryant was on the second of his three head coaching stops before returning to his alma mater. He liked to say he went home to Mama in 1958 and, in doing so, he forever merged his identity with the University of Alabama football program.

I was 17 the first time I met the now iconic coach. He was standing in the living room of my family's home in Louisville, Kentucky and inviting me to come play for his University of Kentucky Wildcats. I was an All-State end on a well-traveled Bishop Flaget High School team that made it to the 1951 state championship game. That was my senior year and we featured Paul Hornung at quarterback. Yes, the same Paul Hornung who made his name at Notre Dame, who was the first pick in the NFL draft in 1957, and who kicked and played halfback and safety for the Green Bay Packers. Still, I didn't attract Bryant's attention until I committed to play college ball for Indiana.

In my first encounters with Bryant he taught me things about recruiting that would one day help me land Joe Namath and Kenny Stabler for him at Alabama. He also inspired my metaphorical fence around Miami that kept local talent home and led us to national success in my first college head coaching opportunity.

I was surprised to find Bryant knocking on my door. One of his assistants had recruited me a little bit, but nothing was really happening. I had already gone down to Miami to see Andy Gustafson, who left Army to go there and had quite a bit of success. I went down with a buddy from my high school team. That was a hell of a trip. It was my first flight out of Louisville. It was in a DC-3 that hadn't even been reconditioned for passenger service. It was designed for military use with the benches on the side like the paratroopers would use. It took off from Louisville, landed in Nashville, and stopped over in Atlanta. Then we went through Birmingham and Tampa and ended up in Miami. We got in late. It was about 8 at night. Nobody met us.

I had $2 in my pocket. My friend, Red Wilson, had $10; his family was a little better off financially than mine. We asked where the University of Miami was and they told us it was a couple miles away. So we started walking to Coral Gables. When we got tired, we looked across the street and there was a sign flashing on and off that said rooms to let $2.50 nightly or $1 an hour. That met our bankroll, so we went over there, spent the night and got educated.

The next morning we called the coach's office and we reached someone who came and got us. When we got to campus, they gave us uniforms and we started practicing. They had about 50 people in there and before long they had us scrimmaging. At the end of the workout they put us in two bunches. One group to go home and one that they offered scholarships. They offered me a scholarship. I said, "What about my buddy, Red? I can't come all the way from Louisville to Miami by myself." They said, "All right, we'll take him, too." Then I thought, "If we're down here, how are we going to get around?" I told them that and they said, "Well, we have some cars you can use." I asked how many of us get cars and they said just a couple of you. I thought that was a pretty good deal.

They had this big lake, Lake Osceola. There was a walkway going out to a big gazebo in the middle of the lake. There were swans. This was in January and the weather was beautiful. At 7 that night, after supper, I sat out there and thought, "This is pretty nice. This is where I want to go to school."

I was all set to go to Miami. Then later that winter a guy from Indiana came down and talked to my dad. We were from Saint Meinrad, Indiana, and my father took me up to the university for a visit. Lo and behold, I get up there and my dad thinks I should go to Indiana because that's where all our relatives live.

So I committed to them, too.

I didn't give Miami another thought. Miami believed they were all set, but they probably overbooked anyway. My moment in the University of Miami spotlight would have to wait another 27 years.

After I committed to Indiana, the Louisville paper picked up on my plans and Bryant took note. He decided to make a home visit to this local boy who was All-State and headed out of state. He didn't come by himself though. He brought the governor of the state of Kentucky, Lawrence W. Wetherby. We were sitting in the living room of this two-bedroom house with my mom and dad. I told Bryant I couldn't change my mind. I had already committed to Indiana because that's what Mom and Dad said. He didn't know anything about Miami. He said that was fine, he just wanted to visit with us. After about 10 minutes the governor said to my dad, "Mr. Schnellenberger, will you step into the kitchen with me?" So the governor and my father went into the kitchen. A few minutes later my dad came out and said, "Son, this is your state and you probably should go to your state school." Mom said, "No, he's already committed to Indiana, and that is where he should go."

A week later, I got another call. Coach Bryant wanted to come back and talk to us again. This time he came not with the governor, but with the Archbishop of Louisville, John Alexander Floersh. Needless to say, my mother went into the kitchen with the Archbishop, who was midway through a 30-year tenure as the head of our church. When they returned, my mother said, "Howard, God wants us to do what is best for you. He will understand if you change your mind."

I was on my way to Kentucky with Coach Bryant.

Notre Dame never called me, but Catholic boy that I was, I probably would have committed to them, too, if they had asked. They did give Hornung a scholarship, and I never forgot the slight I felt. I relished every matchup I ever had against their program.

My third college commitment would be my final answer. As it turned out, it was the right choice. There would still be a trial by fire in an off-campus boot camp, the likes of which the NCAA has long since banned, but I was meant to be one of Bryant's soldiers. Eventually, I would be one of his trusted lieutenants and develop a relationship that would last until his death in 1983.

Though I didn't have the rural upbringing that motivated Bryant all his life, I was from the same scrappy kind of environment. Bryant liked to say he grew up pushing a one-sided plow behind the family mule, and he was driven by the desire not to ever go back and stare that mule in the ass again. I moved to Louisville with my parents when I was two years old. They were the children of German immigrants, and I didn't speak English until I was seven years old. The football I learned in grade school was the kind you played with no helmet, just pads and cleats. It was full-speed tackle in a stocking cap so as not to tear your ears off. That was grade school. High school ball was better equipped and a mean enough brand that it would prepare me for my Bear encounter my freshman year at Kentucky.

When I reported to the University of Kentucky in July 1952, I didn't have a scholarship yet. There were 140 of us in that boot camp. None of us had a guaranteed scholarship. You didn't sign papers like you do today. What we had was an invitation to come to Millersburg, Kentucky. Some of us would make it through and go to Lexington to get ready for the season.

Bryant took us to training camp and pushed us until we didn't think we could have been put through a more intensive workout and survive. He drilled us three times a day. He really beat us up. It was just like the Marine Corps. That's what they do; they make the weakest recruits quit. Once he eliminated the shakiest in the group, those who didn't quit developed a special bond. The survivors are the few, the proud, the football team.

I made it through Bryant's program because my high school coach, Paulie Miller, was so tough. It didn't take long for those who were without a similar high school preparation to fall out.

We had a three-story dormitory at Millersburg Military Academy. No players on the first floor; that was for coaches. At about 11:30 on the third night of camp, I could hear suitcases dropping out of windows and people sliding down rainspouts. They would hit the ground running, going as hard as they could for town. There was a Greyhound bus from Cincinnati to Louisville that ran through Millersburg at midnight. They would run to the stop and get a ticket. Some of the coaches were hiding and watching. They'd see Billy and let him go. Then they would see Bobby and jump out there and grab him. It ended up after six weeks that 140 players dwindled to 40 by attrition. Bryant stopped then because 40 was what he wanted going into the freshman class.

There was no rule back then on how many he could invite to camp. That was a better system than what we have today because all those guys who quit went to Eastern Kentucky and Western Kentucky and Murray and Morehead. It was the same evolution we have now. It got us to the same point, but everybody had a free choice. If they wanted to fight and make it, then they could play at Kentucky or Alabama or Texas A&M. If you couldn't run the 40-yard dash in 5 seconds, but you made it through that torture period, then you were one of us.

Years later I still relied on the same concept, but the numbers were milder. We might try to get the weakest 10 percent to leave, but it brought the rest of the group closer.

Bryant's rules were simple enough: Be on time or meet him in his office. You could never be late to one of his meetings again because you would

Before I could play for Bear Bryant at the University of Kentucky, I had to survive his boot camp. This is from my freshman season in 1952.

already have been invited to leave the team if you didn't like the way things were run. Miss curfew and you were gone. Earn poor grades and you were suspended until they improved. Set a bad example off the field and you were no longer with the team. Work as hard as he and the coaches asked and never give up, and you would get your chance to play.

He told us, "Work as hard as I demand of you and you will be successful." That was the bedrock he built on. He only wanted players he could count on. Bryant tested our mettle every chance he could get. He would tell us, "The first time you quit, it's hard. The second time, it gets easier. The third time you don't even have to think about it."

He preferred "little rascals" he could motivate over self-satisfied stars. And he was a master motivator. For every time he would kick you in the pants on the practice field, he would hug you twice in the locker room.

If we didn't play well, he would appeal to our pride and tell us we were disgracing our mothers and fathers. He'd say, "You're playing for your school, for your parents, and for your home town."

He wanted players who were committed and not simply content. He wanted you to get better every single day. He worked us hard enough that we could feel ourselves getting stronger and better prepared for competition.

He was forever telling us how tough life could get; life is not easy. He did it to instill mental and physical toughness. "Don't give up. Stay with it. When life gets tough, how are you going to respond?"

Coach could have driven 225 miles mostly down I-65 to Nashville and written lyrics for the singers on stage at the Grand Ole Opry. "What are you going to do when you lose your job, when your dog bites you and your wife leaves you?" He had a dozen versions of that mantra, though I don't recall any involving a pickup truck.

He would tell us that if we stuck with the team in practice we would never give in to everyday stresses in life. Someone that quit on the team might quit on the wife and baby, but we wouldn't.

Coach Bryant placed a high value on not being outhustled. He appreciated players who would give an all-out effort more than he appreciated great athletes. But he didn't think the two were mutually exclusive. It is a mistake to think he didn't want the most talented players. He knew he needed four or five super players. His process was to work it so hard that only the right kinds of players stayed. He needed to evaluate the next tier of players on heart and guts and toughness. He would homogenize the group down to a core that would make a football team. There would be some chiefs in there, and you need them to throw and catch and rush the passer. But you need people to protect the chiefs and to do it without recognition or fanfare. You have got to have those guys who will play for personal pride and for the team with selflessness. If you get that with enough talent and it comes down to the fourth quarter against a team with more talented players, you will prevail.

Bryant cherished team chemistry over everything else.

"I'm just a plow hand from Arkansas," he would say, "but I have learned over the years how to hold a team together—how to lift some men up, how to calm down others, until finally they've got one heartbeat, together, a team."

I would play for Bryant for only two years before he moved to Texas A&M. By the time I joined him as a freshman, he had already made good on a promise to win a conference championship for Kentucky within five years. He did that in 1950, winning his first 10 games and the school's first ever title.

My two years playing for Bryant were the last of his nine years at Kentucky, all of them winning seasons. I would continue at Kentucky under another special coach, Blanton Collier, who came to us from the Cleveland Browns. I played left end on offense and left end on defense. I caught a lot of passes and earned All-American status my senior year.

My relationship with Bryant had just begun, though. After brief stints in the Canadian Football League, the U.S. Army and as an assistant coach at Kentucky, I would reunite with Bryant eight years later for a heck of a ride at Alabama. We would win 49 and lose only 5 from 1961 to 1965 as he wrote his name across the college football sky.

I would be there with Bryant as he went through his own trial by fire during twin national scandals in which he was maligned for supposedly encouraging a brutal form of football and then accused of fixing a college game. I watched him emerge shaken but stronger for the ordeal. He would make a final statement, winning three more national championships clustered near the end of his Alabama tenure.

Bryant died January 26, 1983, just one month after retiring. Much has been made over the years of the comment Coach once made that he couldn't retire because he wouldn't live a week if he gave up football. It was his life, but he didn't die because there was no more football. He had a family he loved and a legion of people devoted to him who would have continued to fill his life with purpose. He had suffered a stroke in 1981 and died of coronary heart disease.

Television covered the memorial services and funeral live with the solemnity and respect reserved for our greatest statesmen.

I was among thousands of people who loved this man and marched past Coach as he laid in state at the Memorial Coliseum. His closed casket was covered with red and white carnations.

Coach Bryant was buried at Elmwood Cemetery in Birmingham. Eight players were selected to carry the casket. The entire 1982 football team was named as pallbearers. They rode in three buses and traveled the 60 miles to Birmingham in a 300-vehicle motorcade that drew emotional crowds to overpasses and any other spot where there was access along the interstate. Police estimated that more than 100,000 people paid their respects. Each life touched in a different way.

This man had recruited me as a player. Coached me to play the same position he had played. Hired me to work on his staff. He launched me on my own independent career but never lost touch with me over the next two decades. One of the many emotional thoughts that worked their way to the surface for me during the services was the conviction that Coach Bryant could never have achieved more by leaving college football. He would not have added to his legacy by showcasing his leadership in professional football or in elected office. His life's work was complete as a college coach. He lives on in me and so many others. Fifty-four of his players or assistant coaches went on to become head coaches, ensuring that his influence will last for generations.

DON SHULA AND THE GREATEST SEASON EVER

Don Shula was the second great influence on me. He is to pro football what Bryant was to the college game. His record of 347 wins against 173 losses and 6 ties as a head coach will never be broken. The way the professional game is played, I can't imagine anyone ever coming close.

I was with Shula in Miami for a total of seven years. I was there when he collected his 100th career win in just his 10th season as a pro boss. No one else had ever done that. I joined him for two Super Bowls, including the victory over the Redskins that completed our perfect season.

The undefeated season is a signature Shula achievement that had never been accomplished before and is unmatched more than 40 years later. I think it is the greatest team accomplishment in all of sports history.

There wasn't room for anything but winning with Shula, and he taught the rest of us how to do it. He had a mindset and he preached that everyone he worked with needed to strive to be the best in the business at what they did.

While Bryant was twenty years my senior, Shula was a contemporary. He was born in 1930 and I came along in 1934. We are both children of immigrant families. My grandparents came to the U.S. from Germany, his parents from Hungary. I was a Catholic boy, an acolyte who rang the Angeles bell and raised and lowered the flag daily at St. Helen's Church in Shively, a village west of Louisville. Don was also Catholic and he was equally devout. We each played football on both sides of the ball in college. My opportunity came at Kentucky while his was at John Carroll University. I played end while he was a back. We both served brief stints in the military where we learned some lasting tips about leadership. I put in two years as a receiver in the Canadian Football League, starting out at $9,000 a year. Don played seven years in the NFL as a defensive back, happy to make $5,000 on his first contract.

One of the things that gave Don a leg up on his football career was that his college coach, Herb Eisele, adopted and taught his players the Cleveland Browns offensive and defensive schemes. Cleveland coach Paul Brown drafted Shula and one of his college teammates, Carl Tassef. They would be roommates in camp and both eventually made the team. They were even traded as a package to the Baltimore Colts after two seasons. I would eventually coach alongside both of them.

Shula would remain a disciple of Paul Brown throughout his career, and he was a teacher at heart, though he never tested players the way Brown would. Don was detail-oriented and communicated whatever was on his mind. He rightly considered himself to be as subtle as a punch in the face.

Shula and I would come together for one college season very early in our careers and bond for life. We were both assistants under Blanton Collier at the University of Kentucky in 1959. We were young, newly married and new fathers starting our coaching careers. I was 25 and in my first year as an assistant. Don had finished his career as a Redskin and put in one year as an assistant at the University of Virginia before moving to Kentucky. I was destined to coach at Kentucky for two years before heading to Alabama to join Coach Bryant. Don stayed with us just one year before jumping back to the NFL as a defensive assistant to George Wilson in Detroit.

By 1963 Shula would become the youngest head coach in the NFL. He was just 33 when he took over the Baltimore Colts in the prime of Unitas. He spent seven years there before we reunited in Miami with the considerable challenge of making winners out of an expansion team that had never won more than five games.

That year in Kentucky is when we got to know and trust each other. His wife, Dorothy, and my wife, Beverlee, became fast friends. They were nearly football widows, and they would go down to Belknaps discount store and buy furniture together as they set up their households.

I tried to keep up with Shula, and for a while we competed to be the first to get to the office. I eventually gave up. He'd be up at 5 and go to church at 6. He'd have communion, then breakfast and be at the office by 7. I finally had to just let him be first.

That season in Lexington was the only time I was an equal to Don Shula. Bill Arnsparger, who would later coordinate the Dolphins defense while I ran the offense, was on that Kentucky staff, too. Our time together that year gave the two of us an undeniable edge as Don's chief assistants when we came back together in Miami. We had all been peers at the start of our careers.

For one year I had the privilege to play Shula even-steven on the tennis and handball and squash courts. It was the only time I ever had a chance to win a judgment call on whether a ball was in, on the line or out. Once Don became head coach, he made all the calls and everything went his way. You'll never hear me say an unkind word about Don Shula, but for the rest of my career with him, he was the boss and the boss got all the calls.

PAULIE MILLER INSPIRED ME TO BE A COACH

If it wasn't for my high school coach, Paulie Miller, I never would have gone to college. He convinced me I could handle the academics, but I didn't exactly apply myself right away. Kentucky is known for fast horses and beautiful women. Growing up in Louisville, I had noticed the horses. Now I was fascinated with the women. I was placed on probation when the first grades came out. When I didn't pass enough hours by the end of the year, I was nearly expelled. I thought my football days were over. It took special dispensation from Bryant and Cecil B. Carpenter, the dean of the College of Commerce, to let me continue. They gave me another opportunity with a lot of special conditions involving study halls and tutors. I thanked my God and returned to school in a different frame of mind. I became a good student and graduated with a degree in business. It took a second chance, but I managed not to embarrass my parents or my high school coach.

Paulie is also the one who taught me to love football. Like any kid growing up in Kentucky, I liked to play basketball. It didn't matter if it was a game or a shoot-around, it was enjoyable. Baseball practice had the same quality. Football practice is just hard work. It has its own reward, and I learned that from Paulie. The value of the game is it teaches manhood. The hard work gives you discipline. Your ability is constantly tested.

My parents gave me a good work ethic and Paulie reinforced it. My father, Leslie, hauled freight and worked other odd jobs. My mother, Rosena, worked as a waitress and at a munitions factory to help pay the bills. Paulie demanded the toughness and commitment that made me a successful athlete.

Paulie set high goals and those goals were to be the best in the state and perhaps the nation. If there was a team in another region ranked No. 1, he'd call and say we want to play you. He took a new school and athletic program through the growing pains of inexperience. He developed a fight song, a mascot, and esprit de corps.

He was also an innovator at the high school level. He had us run the split-T offense that was developed by Missouri coach Don Faurot during World War II. Paulie learned it under Faurot while he was with the Iowa Pre-Flight team. Jim Tatum and Bud Wilkinson learned it in the same place and used it at Oklahoma to win national titles.

Instead of lining up in a tight group, the offensive line would spread out over twice as much space, and one receiver would split off to the sideline. This forced the defense to move out and it created gaps. The blocking schemes were simplified with little need for pulling guards or trap blocking.

Depending on how the defense reacted, the ball could be handed to a halfback diving inside, or the handoff could be quickly withdrawn to allow the quarterback to keep the ball and go outside with the second halfback trailing. Faurot said he got the outside idea from the two-on-one fast break in basketball.

Paulie had already convinced us we could run through walls or leap eight-foot-high fences. Now he convinced us that our offense was unstoppable.

On defense it wasn't exactly bounty gate, but we were rewarded for gang tackling. Paulie taught us the value of pursuit, and the football boosters, known as the Flageteers, paid us a dollar for every tackle. We chased down opposing ball carriers like a pack of dogs. Back in those days a dollar was worth something, and you didn't have to be the first one there to earn it. You got paid as long as the hit didn't get you an unnecessary roughness penalty.

Paulie helped us believe in ourselves and believe we would win if we gave the maximum effort. He taught us that if you did the best your training, your talent and your physique allowed, then you won on or off the field. He talked about and instilled what he called "a burning desire to win."

Paulie Miller installed a split-T offense and turned us into a high school power. With Paul Hornung throwing to me, I managed to get behind the defense a few times.

Hornung says Paulie was as tough as Vince Lombardi. Since he played for both of them, Hornung should know.

By the time I was a senior, Phil Schweri and I were co-captains of the football team, and we were an extension of the coach. We made a pact with each other to set an example by running five extra laps after every practice. We kept the vow, but sometimes while we were running we would cuss each other for being dumb enough to announce our leadership concept.

It is really Paulie Miller who inspired me to want to be a coach. I thought about trying to work for him at Flaget High School after I completed my military obligation and ended my playing career. But I wanted to coach at a higher level. I had seen Paulie get rejected for college jobs despite winning state titles and guiding one of the top prep school programs in the region. So Paulie gave me confidence and drive and determination, but it was Blanton Collier who gave me my first coaching job.

THE GREATEST COLLEGE FOOTBALL STAFF EVER ASSEMBLED

It was Collier, of course, who put in the pro-style offense at Kentucky my junior season and then developed me into an All-American end. In 1959 he gave me my first coaching job, inviting me to join his staff and work with the receivers.

What a staff that turned out to be. There were eight of us and all eight would later have successful NFL careers. Five of us would become NFL head coaches. Two would win NFL championships. Collier, of course, would go on to coach the Cleveland Browns and win an NFL title there. Shula was on the staff. So was Bill Arnsparger, who would become head coach of the New York Giants, and John North, who later coached the New Orleans Saints. Bob Cummings became an assistant to North in New Orleans. Ermal Allen made his mark as an assistant for the Dallas Cowboys. Ed Rutledge became an NFL scout. Chuck Knox, a future NFL coach of the year, didn't join Collier's staff until 1961 when he replaced me.

I was in a very good place to learn the coaching trade.

Collier had been an assistant under Paul Brown in Cleveland, and he installed Brown's offense while he was at Kentucky. That is where I learned the NFL passing game that has been associated with me throughout the years.

Collier was a classroom-style teacher. Under Brown he learned to put things on a blackboard and have the players write everything down. His locker room was like a one-room schoolhouse. He taught everything in a very logical fashion. He would outline things step by step. One, two, three. A, B, C.

He was the best I ever saw at teaching football players technique. This was before we had all the film we use today. We would diagram the play, then walk people through it and then jog our routes. We would get even more basic than that. He wanted you to know how to do a crossover step, how to make a fake, how to get the defender's mass moving backward. He showed players that a combination of force and balance goes further.

He would have you get down in your stance against your man and make sure you fired out with short steps. The toe of your trailing foot had to be inside the heel of the lead foot and the first step couldn't be more than 6 inches. If you take a long step and you are right in the middle of it and the defender moves, you can't adjust. He wanted your head up with your belt buckle in the middle, and he wanted you to explode right at contact.

To Howard –
with affection and respect –

Blanton Collier

Photo courtesy of University of Kentucky Athletics

Blanton Collier introduced a pro-style offense at Kentucky in my junior season and then developed me into an All-American end. He also gave me my first coaching job.

Then Collier would reverse the order. He would say let's start here at the block with your head past the defender's hip and with a flat back. Let's walk backward all the way to that first step. He wanted you to understand the technique so you could repeat it the way a major league pitcher can repeat his motion or a golfer can repeat his swing.

Collier was more of an NFL coach than a college mentor. He put me and everyone else on that staff on a path to pro ball.

AN OPPORTUNITY IN THE NFL

It was George Allen who first lifted me into the NFL. He did that after my five sensational years at Alabama. He called when he left the Chicago Bears to take the head coaching job with the L.A. Rams. Allen said he wanted to place one college coach on his staff, and he wanted me to work with his offense. He wanted a young, enthusiastic coach to teach technique. I had never gotten to play in the NFL, and I was intrigued with another incredible learning opportunity. I joined Ted Marchibroda and Jack Patera, two more future NFL head coaches, on Allen's staff.

Allen had been tutored by George Halas for eight years, and he was obsessed with winning. He showed me winning is the science of being totally prepared. And preparation can be defined in three words: leave nothing undone.

I thought I worked extremely hard. He worked harder. He believed your leisure time is that 5 or 6 hours when you sleep at night.

Allen showed me what it meant to be in complete control. He demanded better equipment and better facilities, anything he thought would help him win. He had no patience with mistakes, and that led him to value veterans and shun even talented rookies.

Allen was a defensive-minded coach and he left the offense to others. He put me in charge of the offensive book and we had something special there. My book now merged three great lineages. Paul Bryant to me. Paul Brown to Blanton Collier to me. And George Halas to George Allen to me.

Allen was always scribbling in a notebook and he would write six books on coaching. I was lucky enough to learn from him first hand. The same way I learned from all of my Hall of Fame mentors.

CHAPTER 2

RECRUITING JOE NAMATH

"Passing the torch refers to the coaching life and his passion as a teacher. He passed a torch to me and many others. He inspired us with his leadership and style and coaching with his tough love. You needed to listen to him and his discipline. I'd have gotten sidetracked if it wasn't for him."

– Joe Namath, *University of Alabama recruit and Super Bowl winning quarterback of the New York Jets*

Coach Bryant assigned me a critical task shortly after I joined his University of Alabama staff. Before we began our 1961 season, he got a call from Tom Nugent, the head coach up at Maryland. Nugent and Bryant were great drinking buddies. Just as we were starting our training camp, Nugent told Bryant he had this quarterback up there that was the greatest thing to ever come through. Lee Corso, then Maryland's quarterback coach, thought this fellow, Joe Namath, was the best high school quarterback in the country. They believed the kid was a sure thing, but the president of the school had looked at his transcripts and test scores and didn't think he was of the yolk that was needed for student athletes at the University of Maryland. They had Namath retake the SAT battery, but he couldn't get above their self-imposed 750 standard. Nugent couldn't keep him but didn't want to see him on any team Maryland would face. He told Bryant, "Send somebody up here and get his ass out of the area—get him down to Dixie."

It didn't take much to convince Bryant there was an opportunity here. He already knew about Namath. Joe was All-State as a 6'1", 175-pound leader of the Pennsylvania state championship football team.

Before Namath chose Maryland, Bryant had sent Clem Gryska, his top recruiter, to Beaver Falls. Gryska and Dude Hennessey made that trip. They visited Joe's high school, met with Joe's coach and watched film of Joe. Namath, though, declined an early invitation to visit Tuscaloosa. He made seven other official visits. He chose Maryland after seeing Notre Dame, Arizona State, Minnesota, Iowa, Indiana and Miami.

Now given a second chance, we knew the big thing was getting Joe out of Beaver Falls before the other eastern schools got wind that he was free. It was almost on a lark. Maybe we could do something before Notre Dame and Penn State and the rest of those people descended on Beaver Falls.

Well, Bryant looked around at his staff. Somebody had to go to Pennsylvania and try to win Joe over. Bryant remembered that in 1952, when he recruited me to come to the University of Kentucky, there was another prospect in that same class named Frank Namath. Joe's older brother and I were on the team together for that whole football year. The truth is that I wasn't particularly close to Frank, but we had the same bond that all teammates share. So coach thought I might have the best chance. He decided I should go up there, get Joe out of Pennsylvania and get him down to Tuscaloosa. I accepted the order and told Bryant I would bring Joe to him.

Photo courtesy of University of Alabama Athletics

I went straight to Carney Laslie, our assistant athletic director. I told Carney, "I got to get out of here. Coach wants me in Beaver Falls as quickly as I can get there, so please give me some money." This

I was all smiles working for Bear Bryant for five years. My first big assignment was to go to Beaver Falls, PA and convince Joe Namath to come south.

conversation took place in a tiny back office. So Carney reached down into a drawer and pulled out a big metal box. He took out a corn sack and in the sack was a lot of money, cash. He reached in and gave me a handful of bills. Some of them were twenty dollar bills and some of them were ones and some were fives. I stuck it all in my pocket. I don't know how much it was. I eventually got it all straightened out and put it in my wallet. As it turned out, Carney didn't dig deep enough. There weren't enough twenties.

I headed out to Beaver Falls immediately. I flew up there, got off the plane in Pittsburgh, got a car and drove 50 miles into the coal-mining countryside. I got to this little town and started looking for Joe Namath. I didn't even have an address for him. I found him at one of his favorite hang-outs, a pool hall called The Blue Room. It was a converted bowling alley with a dozen or so tables. You could rent a table for as little as 60 cents an hour, but the newer ones up front cost you 90 cents to control. You got in there through the back of a lunchroom. It was a popular spot for the young people in town. They didn't serve alcohol in the pool hall, but there was a bar right next door.

The first time I laid eyes on him, Joe was wearing one of those one-button roll jackets. He was wearing real loose pants, and he had a key chain that he swung kind of like the Fonz, the character Henry Winkler portrayed on the "Happy Days" television show.

Joe was a teenager approaching that kind of popularity as the top local high school athlete. He had grown up in the Lower End, a neighborhood populated mostly by minorities and wedged between the Beaver River to the east and the Pennsylvania Railroad to the west. His best friend was a black neighbor named Linwood Alford, who was from Eufala, Alabama. Joe was the only white starter on the Beaver Falls basketball team that featured his friend Alford and three others from the same Lower End neighborhood. Joe had big hands. He loved to dunk the basketball, occasionally backward. I found out while I was up there that he was also a star on the baseball team, the best golfer at the school, and the girls really liked him, too.

All the Namath boys played sports while the family was intact in the Lower End in a white, two-story frame house with its only bathroom in the basement. Joe's older brothers drilled him hard and pushed him to excel at sports. Joe was able to start his academic and athletic career at the local Catholic school, St. Mary's. But when he was in the seventh grade, Joe's parents divorced. The family struggled. Joe's father would attend his games and pay for some of his clothes, but he had to be sued by Joe's mother for support. Joe's brother, Frank, left the University of Kentucky after his freshman season and came home to help the family finances. He became Joe's keeper and eventually my ally in getting Joe to Alabama.

Frank thought that Coach Bryant's disciplinarian style might help mature his maverick younger brother. Frank was very, very helpful. If it weren't for Frank, I doubt seriously that I would have been able to convince Joe to come south with me. But nothing was going to happen until I won over his mother, Rose, too.

Once I found Joe swinging that key chain and introduced myself, I tried to hang with him all week long. I hustled around town with him. I would take him over to the school and talk with his coaches. I took him to a movie palace called the Granada. I just wanted to make sure he couldn't get a telephone call from Notre Dame or get located by anybody else that wanted to swoop in like a vulture and pick up the dead meat.

I spent every moment I could with Joe, but I couldn't stay with him all the time. So if he was in town with friends, I would spend time at the house with his mother. As I learned from Bryant, mothers are the key. You get the mothers on your side and you are all right. She was going to be the one Joe listened to.

I had taken up residence at a hotel, and I wasn't leaving until Joe agreed to come to Tuscaloosa, but money was starting to get short. I needed to get back home. On the eighth day, Joe's mother finally asked me to come to dinner. When I got there, Joe said to me, "Boy, you must have really impressed my mom because she's got chicken and dumplins."

This was my chance. I asked him about coming down for an official visit even though it was late and we were already in practice for the fall. Our season opener was less than 30 days away.

Joe was still sitting on offers to sign a baseball contract with the St. Louis Cardinals or the Chicago Cubs. Mom really wanted him to go to college though. She finally said, "Take him," and sent him upstairs to pack. He didn't commit to enroll, but he did say he would make the trip back with me. Coach Bryant would have to close the deal.

Now all I had to do was get him to Alabama. I was out of money. I was smart enough that I brought a checkbook with me. So I wrote a bad check to Delta Air Lines. It was all right, I guess. Back in those days they didn't put you in jail for that.

So I got him on that plane and we headed down south. We only got as far as Atlanta. We were supposed to get on Southern Airlines and go over to Tuscaloosa. Then Southern cancelled. I had to put Joe in a hotel. So I wrote another bad check.

All I had left was a quarter and two dimes. We got up and I said, "Hey, Joe, you want to get some coffee?" He says, "Yeah," and I find a coffee machine and use my last quarter. I was happy he didn't ask me for some breakfast.

We got on the plane and flew into Tuscaloosa. They met me at the airport with a nice car. It had been 10 days since I left with two shirts and that handful of cash. I came down the steps in a white shirt that had turned yellow. I looked like a rag. I was carrying Joe's bags. The staff must have thought I was the player and he was the coach coming off that plane. So we got him in the car and took him to the school. The team was already working out, and we took Joe out onto the practice field. I think some of the players were wondering if Bryant had fired me because I had missed the first week of practice. It got around, eventually, that I was trying to get that big quarterback down here. So they started sizing up this player as we were walking out there.

Joe was wearing sunglasses, a checkered sport coat and a snap-brim hat with a pearl in the band. The hat was tilted just a little to the right. He was chewing on a toothpick. He looked like someone from another country.

Bryant was up in his famous coaching tower, and we heard this voice blasted out of a bullhorn. "Is that Namath? Send him up here. I want to talk to him."

Nobody had ever been up there with Bryant. The governor would eventually go up there, and the president of the university would get up there, but certainly no player was ever going to go up there.

Namath climbed the 39 stairs and stayed up there for 15 minutes. Bryant appeared to do most of the talking.

Finally, Joe wound his way back down the spiral staircase. Then we heard the bullhorn again. "The boy wants to come with us."

Drama and championships would follow.

Joe said later he only understood one word the coach drawled: "Stud." The rooster in Joe liked the word. If that was what the coach thought of him, it sounded like he would be a big man on the team and a big man on campus.

I don't know exactly what Bryant said to him up there, but I would recruit others with Bryant, and I am sure he closed with the same thing he always did. He must have asked Joe, "Can I count on you for the next four years?"

But now we had another problem. You can't pay for a student to come to enroll. You can only pay for him to come for an official visit. So we were required to put him on a plane and send him back to the place I had worked so hard to get him away from.

Well, we put him on a plane at the direction of Coach Bryant. He had to stop in Birmingham, and the plane went on to Atlanta and up to Beaver Falls. But Joe got off in Birmingham. I have a feeling there may have been some of Bryant's people there. I know Joe showed right back up on campus, and we turned to the business of the 1961 season.

Photo courtesy of University of Alabama Athletics

Once I convinced Namath to visit Tuscaloosa, Bryant closed the deal during a 15-minute visit in his famous coaching tower.

CHAPTER 3

CRIMSON TSUNAMI

"I was down from New York working with Bryant on a series for Sports Illustrated that led to my book on Bear. We played golf at the Tuscaloosa Country Club, and Bear played craps in the locker room with guys at the club. That night, as we headed back to his house, we drove by the athletic complex and there was a light on in an upstairs room. I remember Bear saying, 'It must be that damn Schnellenberger making me look like a genius.' Howard did more than his due diligence and Bryant thought the world of Howard and with good reason."

— **John Underwood,** *award-winning writer for the Miami Herald and Sports Illustrated. Author of eight books, including Bear: The Hard Life & Good Times of Alabama's Coach Bryant*

Getting Namath on board guaranteed us exciting times lay ahead, but Joe was destined to spend his first year learning our ways on the freshman team. We had a veteran squad and high expectations without him in 1961.

Bryant had come to Tuscaloosa in 1958, inheriting a club that had posted a 4-24-1 record over the previous three years despite a proud history. He had put up five wins in his first season and followed that with seven and then eight victories.

The Southeastern Conference had been a national powerhouse for years, so the quick turnaround for the Tide captured plenty of attention. The SEC had produced national championships out of Auburn in 1957 and Louisiana State in 1958. Ole Miss had been runner-up in the AP poll in 1959 and 1960. The conference and the country were about to hear from Alabama again.

A savvy quarterback by the name of Pat Trammell would return as the leader of the offense. Linebacker Lee Roy Jordan and All-America tackle Billy Neighbors, two future professional stars, anchored a stunningly good defense. We opened the season ranked third in the nation.

After an opening win over Georgia, Bryant did something I had never seen him do at Kentucky. He decided to take it easy on the team. Despite our lopsided win over the Bulldogs, we were a little beat up. Bryant decided unilaterally to leave the pads in the locker room and take chairs to the practice field for a concentration drill.

This was a senior team and he recognized that. He believed the best way to reward players is to take it easy on them. So we did. The offensive and defensive teams set up across from each other in chairs.

Photo courtesy of The Paul W. Bryant Museum, University of Alabama

Bryant went home to Alabama in 1958. He is shown here in 1961, the year I joined him as an assistant.

We had seats for the first team and the second team. Everyone was in shorts and T-shirts and we went through our drills. We had a ball and we would call a play and break like we were in the huddle.

"Thirty-six power trap, on two, ready, break." Everybody would stiffen up. Then, on the snap count, "Set, hut," everyone would point to their assignment. If the linebackers are stacked, my center has to know his responsibility. Each man has an assignment. Coaches are standing there watching all these hands declare their responsibility. And then we would audible out of the trap play. The quarterback would shout, "Red" and if that was our live color, all the other colors are dead. "Red, 19 straight" meant we were changing the play. We would adjust and players would check to their men and commit with their hands. That would be the only contact.

We got every mental benefit out of the practice but cut down the physical wear on the team. It worked well enough that we returned to it throughout the year.

The defense would post a mind-boggling seven, yes seven, shutouts over the course of the season. This was a unit that included future Clemson and Florida head coach Charlie Pell at defensive tackle and defensive back Ray Abruzzese, who would play professionally with the Buffalo Bills and the New York Jets.

It should be obvious what that meant for our offense. Ball protection was everything. As Bryant's offensive coordinator and line coach, that's what I preached. I organized our football lessons and made many of our off-the-field presentations to the team. Trammel, a pre-med student, was our poster boy for taking care of the football. He was a smart play caller, who rarely threw the ball to people in the wrong color jersey.

We didn't wag in plays the way they do today. The quarterback called most of the plays, but if we did our job right, he knew what was needed in each situation.

A few years before this, you weren't even allowed to coach from the sidelines. You had a captain that talked with the referee and accepted or declined all penalties. The coaches were organizers. Any game planning was done in advance.

My job was to give the quarterback a solid game plan. We put him on a conservative track and let him execute it from there.

Trammel would throw just 133 times in 11 games. He would complete 75 passes for 1,035 yards. He had 8 touchdowns through the air and a 56.4 percent completion record. Trammel knew how to win games. He couldn't run any faster than I could, but he was the man we needed to run our offense. He was a natural leader, and the players lined up behind him like they were following their mamas.

One of the ways I tried to build on that strength was to recognize the best efforts of the offensive line. That's an eternally underappreciated crew, and I had an incentive for them if they did the job I wanted inside the five-yard line. Tickets to one of our games were hard to come by, but coaches could always get them. If you got one for $10 you could sell it for $40. If we were inside the five and a lineman blocked his man into the end zone, I gave him the opportunity to buy one $10 ticket. They had to get their fanny in the air and come off the ball and move their man into the end zone where he was not a factor and couldn't prevent a score. I had them really blocking when we got down close and I was proud of that.

We took advantage of our scoring opportunities all year, but it was our defense that dominated. Bryant had them convinced that it was a sin to give up a point, and most weeks they played like saints.

A shutout was something to brag about, and we didn't let too many teams score on us. If we had the second and third team defense in the game and an opponent moved too deep in our end, Lee Roy Jordan and a few of our other top defenders would sneak back in there and try to keep them from scoring.

In our fourth game, Roman Gabriel's North Carolina State team would score the second and last touchdown we would give up all season. We would win easily, 26-7.

Next up was Tennessee. We hadn't beaten them since 1954, but we hadn't fielded a defense like this one either. We held the Vols to five first downs and a total of 61 yards of offense. Trammel passed for one touchdown and scooted for another. The quarterback would run 75 times for 279 yards on the season and wind up our second leading rusher. We won easily, 34-3.

Then we started pitching a string of shutouts. We scored 17 against Houston and 24 versus Mississippi State. Neither club scored a point. After we put up 66 points against zero for an overmatched Richmond, we entered the final two weeks of the season ranked number two behind only Texas.

We headed back to Georgia, this time to play Georgia Tech. Darrell Royal and his Longhorns would host Texas Christian in Austin. We kept the ball on the ground in a very physical game at home. We would win 10-0, running our record to 9-0.

We didn't know it at the time, but one devastating play would cause us headaches for the next few years.

Our team, like all of Coach Bryant's clubs until then and forever, carried a reputation for hard hits and gang tackles. Setting up a punt return, one of our players, Darwin Holt, shattered the jaw of Tech captain Chick Graning.

I didn't see what happened on the play. I was busy complaining that Billy Richardson was interfered with while catching the punt. When we watched the film, we could see Holt reared up and hit Graning with a forearm shiver as Holt ran Graning out of bounds. Somehow the elbow got through his face guard and Graning was badly hurt. Holt was apologetic after the game, but by Tuesday there was no climate for forgiveness.

There was no penalty called on the play, but the visitors viewed it as dirty and the newspapers howled. The play would drive a rift between the schools. Over the next couple of years it resulted in scandalous accusations and lawsuits. It even prompted Georgia Tech to pull out of the Southeastern Conference.

The Atlanta papers and then the *Saturday Evening Post* accused Bryant of condoning and coaching a style of football both brutal and cruel. Under a Post headline "College Football Is Going Berserk," his methods and character were questioned. His brand of hard-nosed football was depicted as devoid of values. Fair play and sportsmanship were being sacrificed to win at all costs.

Bryant responded by suing for $500,000. The battle would grow uglier over the next two years.

We would have to resolve that unpleasantness at another time over the horizon. Texas couldn't keep up with us. TCU played the spoiler in their match, winning for just the third time on the year. We were now alone at the top of the Associated Press rankings. Immediately ahead was a 6-3 Auburn team and our shot at clinching a national championship in Birmingham.

Cue the defense. In the opening minutes Holt, yes that same Darwin Holt, recovered a fumble. Billy Richardson rushed 11 yards into the end zone. Trammell ran for a touchdown and passed for another in the second quarter. We were up by three touchdowns at the half. We stretched that to 34-0 late in the game.

A defense that was certainly among the most miserly ever, outdid itself. They stopped Auburn on downs inside the one-yard line in the fourth quarter. They extinguished Auburn's final threat with an interception in the end zone to preserve a fifth straight shutout.

We were undefeated and untied, 10-0 in the regular season. The AP took its final poll of the year, as was the custom at the time, and crowned us national champions.

We were not ready to celebrate just yet. Four other national champions had faltered in a bowl setting in the last decade. We were determined not to join them. We still craved perfection and that would require a Sugar Bowl victory against 8-2 Arkansas on the last day of the year.

It wouldn't come easy.

As he did all year, Mike Fracchia (130 rushes for 652 yards on the season) would lead the ground attack. Midway through the opening period he chugged 43 yards to the Arkansas 12-yard line. Trammel rolled into the end zone one play later. We got a 10-0 lead and we turned it over to the defense.

The Hogs made it to our 7-yard line in the third quarter and kicked a field goal. We were in our closest match all year. Arkansas moved to our 40-yard line late in the game. A deep pass try from George McKinney to Lance Alworth came inches from tying the game. Moments later, defensive back Butch Wilson put the matter away for us with an interception near the goal line. The final score was in the books at a heart-stopping 10-3.

Alabama was back on top of the college football world.

It was a year for the ages. We had allowed just two touchdowns all season. The defense gave up 25 points in 11 matches. The average score of our games was 27-2.

We tasted perfection. We savored the championship. Bryant had played on the 1934 unbeaten, untied Alabama team that won the Rose Bowl, so he knew what that felt like. Now I did, too. We knew what it took to reach the summit and we both wanted to live there the rest of our football lives.

There were bows to take by all the key players. Pat Trammel would finish fifth in the Heisman voting behind Syracuse halfback Ernie Davis. Trammel would skip a football career and achieve his dream of becoming a doctor, but he would die of cancer in 1968 at the age of 28. Tackle Billy Neighbors would be drafted by the Washington Redskins but opt for the upstart American Football League and play eight years with the Patriots and the Dolphins. Bryant would be named coach of the year for the first time as he wrapped up his seventeenth season as a head coach.

DEFENDING OUR CHAMPIONSHIP

The 1962 season opened with our team third in the polls. We would quickly climb to the top and stay there for most of the season in an effort to defend our title. We would again feature Lee Roy Jordan, now a senior.

Bryant and I had played both ways at end when we were in school, but the college game was increasingly moving away from that. Lee Roy Jordan was one of the last greats to play both ways. He was a center on our offense, and then he would turn around and chase opposing quarterbacks from the linebacker position.

This was another team loaded with leaders. Charlie Pell and Richard Williamson were back. Both of them would one day be coaches along with end Bill Battle, guard Jimmy Sharpe and backup quarterback Mal Moore.

Sophomore Joe Namath was about to take Trammel's place behind center. Namath didn't arrive as Broadway Joe, but he had confidence when he was out on the playing field, and he was quickly becoming a leader. We knew what we had in Namath after a season of freshman contests and from his showing in the spring game.

Bryant was well-known for poor-mouthing his teams to the media, but he took a radically different approach when he set the stage for the coming season. He knew we weren't going to sneak up on anyone any longer. The newly confident coach called his new quarterback the best player he had ever seen. He christened him Joe Willie Namath, putting a Southern face on the street smart Yankee.

Bryant knew how to motivate his young quarterback, and he was willing to jump start the legend. What he wasn't ready to do was change his offensive scheme. At least not yet.

Even with the great passing potential of Namath, we continued to work out of a tight T formation but gave our quarterbacks an option that preceded the wishbone and the veer. Depending on how the defense reacted, the ball could be handed to a halfback diving inside or the handoff could be quickly withdrawn to allow the quarterback to keep the ball and go outside with the second halfback trailing.

Although the offense wasn't designed to showcase his throwing arm, Namath prospered in it because he had fleet feet, too. He succeeded because he generally made good choices with the ball.

Joe Willie's debut on the big stage came between the privet hedges in Athens and he did not disappoint. He faked to the fullback and hit Richard Williamson in stride for a touchdown on the first play from scrimmage. Namath ran for one touchdown and threw for two. He had 215 total yards of offense before being pulled in the third quarter of a 35-0 show.

We continued to build on our undefeated championship season working our way through the schedule. We put another whipping on Tennessee, this time 27-7 with Namath throwing TD passes of 32 and 45 yards.

This one was special to me. Bryant liked to assign each of his assistants a team to scout and keep up with all year long. Tennessee was always my team. Bryant remembered I had some of my best games as a player against Tennessee. We were 5-0-1 against them when I was a player and then assistant coach at Kentucky. We would go 4-0-1 against them while I was at Alabama.

After this particular dismantling of Tennessee at their place, the players tried to carry Bryant off the field. I still treasure a picture taken when he got down off their shoulders and tried to put me up on his shoulders.

We followed that up by closing down Mississippi State 20-0. Then we went to 8-0 with our 19th straight win as we beat a 6-1 Miami team.

Which brought us to Atlanta for a rematch with an emotional Georgia Tech. The furor from the game the year before was revisited. The lawsuits over the scandalous allegations growing out of the injury to the Georgia Tech captain would eventually bring Bryant back to an Atlanta courtroom. And he would win at least partial vindication in the form of cash. But that was the next summer's drama. At hand was a more familiar battle on the football field.

Photo courtesy of University of Alabama Athletics

I was assigned to scout Tennessee. When we beat them in 1962, Bear tried to lift me onto his shoulders as we celebrated on the field.

Georgia Tech surprised us with a shotgun offense. Namath was intercepted early and Tech returned the ball 26 yards to the 14. That set up their one touchdown, but we couldn't do much offensively.

Namath missed most of the game after injuring his leg when tackled in the first period. They limited us to 78 yards rushing on the day, and we were staring at a shutout on our side. We caught a break in the fourth quarter when they turned the ball over to us at their 9 on a freak play. Their punter accidentally touched down his knee while trying to kick. Cotton Clark quickly converted the TD, but backup quarterback Jack Hurlbut's 2-point run failed. We fell 7-6.

Tech Coach Bobby Dowd met Bryant at midfield saying, "I believe that was the cleanest game I've ever seen." Bryant responded, "It certainly was. But I didn't expect anything different."

Tech had its revenge, and it had to be as sweet for them as it was sour for us. They snapped our streak and they cost us a national championship. We would play them just twice more before they left the Southeastern Conference.

We would rebound with a 38-0 thrashing of Auburn and finish fifth in the final poll with an undefeated Southern Cal getting the nod over an undefeated Mississippi team.

In the Orange Bowl, we enjoyed a 17-0 win against Bud Wilkinson's Oklahoma team. Jordan made 24 tackles and played his best game as a collegian in the bowl after we freed him up to play only defense.

With those two closing shutouts we had outscored our opponents 289-39 in 11 games.

Jordan was a consensus All-America who finished fourth in the Heisman voting behind Oregon State QB Terry Baker. Jordan would

Photo courtesy of University of Alabama Athletics

The staff presented me with a victory cigar after one of our wins over Tennessee. We were 4-0-1 against them in my five years at Alabama.

go to the Cowboys as their number 1 pick in the NFL draft and play linebacker for them for the next 14 years.

SCANDALOUS TIMES

In 1963, we had more drama than a Shakespearian play both on and off the field.

The trouble with the Atlanta media continued to fester. What started with allegations of brutality after the Georgia Tech player was injured spiraled into charges of Bryant conspiring to fix the first game of the previous season, our 35-0 whitewash of Georgia at Legion Field.

The *Saturday Evening Post*, a news magazine with a circulation of 6.5 million copies, paid an Atlanta insurance man for notes he said he took of a conversation overheard on a crossed phone line. He said he heard Bryant and Georgia Athletic Director Wally Butts discussing Georgia football secrets. Some banter about a former Georgia quarterback inadvertently telegraphing his plays by positioning his feet differently if he was preparing to drop back for a pass was misinterpreted to be a plan to tip plays in advance at the upcoming game.

The allegation was sensational and career-threatening. It came at us like a thunderbolt. I remember the day the call came and coach got an advance copy of the story. He let us know right then. He realized the importance of talking to the team and he called everyone together. He was distraught, angry. He raised his voice a little while speaking directly to us. He was in a very serious mood, but he made it clear the whole thing was ridiculous.

Bryant took the time to read us the article. One of the claims in the piece was that we were able to hold Georgia to 37 yards rushing because we knew their plays in advance. When he got to that part of the article, Bryant stopped. "Hell, that's too many yards to give them regardless."

We never thought it would amount to anything, but we knew it wouldn't go away anytime soon.

After he met with the team, Bryant held a press conference to deny any wrongdoing. Once the article appeared in print, he went on statewide TV to deny the accusations and demand justice.

Bryant sued for $5 million in damages. Butts asked for $10 million.

The Butts case would go to trial first, in August 1963. The attorney for the Post would grab headlines by equating the charges to the Black

Sox scandal involving payoffs to throw the World Series. Bryant would testify. When he did, he showed contempt for his accusers. He called the suggestion of a fix preposterous. He acknowledged he and Butts did talk for over an hour six days before the game, but explained there was nothing unusual about that.

Asked on the witness stand if he was corrupt, Bryant responded, "Absolutely not. If we did it we ought to go to jail. And if we didn't, anybody who had anything to do with this story ought to go to jail. Taking their money is not enough."

Butts was awarded $3.6 million by the jury, but the award was reduced to $300,000 after an appeal. Bryant agreed to settle his suit shortly after the trial and received $360,000 and a retraction.

Bryant later defended himself, writing in *Sports Illustrated* that the tough reputation he had preceded his Alabama years.

Bryant defended what he called helmet-cracking football. He wanted his players to gang tackle, to get up and hit the opponent again, but it had better be legal. He wouldn't tolerate a guy who draws penalties. He believed three 15-yard penalties in a game will beat you.

"I doubt that the Holt-Graning incident would ever have reached the proportions it did if I had not had that reputation. Then there probably would never have been that first story in the *Saturday Evening Post* claiming I was an advocate of brutal football. I wouldn't have sued the Post over that, and if I hadn't sued the Post, I doubt that there would have been the second story, the real filthy, malicious one that said Wally Butts and I fixed a football game. The whole thing just snowballed, but, looking back on it all, if it meant changing my methods, my program, to avoid the heartaches that followed, then I'd just as soon have the heartaches."

The settlement was a lot of money, and it helped make Bryant a businessman and eventually a wealthy man. But he was always going to be a football man first, and there was another season about to start. While the media storm raged, the team pulled together. We had a siege mentality. It would be a season of living dangerously.

DEVELOPING THE PASSING GAME

Bryant and I were ready to unleash Namath. That spring we had put in a drop back passing game with two wide receivers. Before he would agree to let me do that, though, Bryant extracted a promise. I had to give him my personal word that I wouldn't let us get soft on the line, that we'd maintain the same toughness.

We started strong. The first points of the season came on a 47-yard pass from Namath to Charlie Stephens, but we still ran a lot out of the option. We beat Georgia, Tulane and Vanderbilt by a combined score of 84-7.

But then we stumbled badly against Florida. It was the only time I ever saw us lose in Tuscaloosa. Bryant would lose only one other in those confines in 25 seasons. Our problem this day was turnovers. We lost three fumbles and Namath threw two interceptions. We were behind 10-0 before Namath scored on a sneak late in the game. We couldn't convert two and lost 10-6.

We bounced back with three wins to set up a game with Georgia Tech. We scored twice in the last three minutes to secure a 27-11 victory. We would play it conservatively, while Tech waited for the aerial explosion. With Namath calling all but one play in the game, we put the ball in the air only four times. One of those resulted in a pass interference call on our last drive. Namath had just one completion in three recorded attempts, an eleven-yard jump pass to Butch Henry. He ran 13 times for 53 yards.

Namath would even make an appearance at safety in this game to help us protect against a long pass from Tech's Billy Lothridge. Their senior quarterback was a big enough threat to force that type of radical deployment. Lothridge would finish second in the Heisman voting behind Navy quarterback Roger Staubach.

Bryant told the press after the game that this was Namath's finest hour. It was a magical day, but the coach's sentiment may have had something to do with winning what was now a heightened rivalry game. The line in the Alabama fight song bidding the Crimson Tide to "send the Yellow Jackets to a watery grave" never had more meaning.

We were 7-1 and ready to face an 8-1 Auburn team. It would be a matchup of Top 10 clubs, but we had no more magic and soon we would lose Namath, too. They smothered our offense all day long and prevailed 10-8.

That was followed by a disciplinary crisis. Bryant had always let Joe know what he expected. During his sophomore season, Namath got a stern lecture after throwing his helmet. If it happened again, he would be off the team. Now Namath was caught out on the town in violation of well-established team rules. We met as coaches to talk about the infraction, and while some of us waivered, Bryant insisted Joe would have to be suspended.

When Namath was called in before all the coaches, Bryant delivered the news. "How many days?" Joe asked. "Forever," came the answer. "Or until you prove something to me." Bryant offered to let Namath transfer. He said he'd help him try to catch on with a Canadian football team if he didn't want to stick around.

Namath was crushed, but he accepted the punishment and decided to stay. He asked Bryant to call his mother before she heard it from anyone else.

Fans would send in petitions with 6,000 fans demanding Namath be reinstated, but we would finish the season without him.

When we teed it up against Miami in the final game of the regular season, we had Jack Hurlbut at quarterback, and we came out on top 17-12.

Our regular season 8-2 record earned us a spot in the Sugar Bowl. We pushed sophomore Steve Sloan out into the spotlight for the first time. He managed just enough forward progress to set up four field goals by senior kicker Tim Davis. One kick set a bowl record from 48 yards out. Leading just 12-7, the defense stopped the Rebels at the 2-yard line on the final play of the game.

NAMATH REDEEMS HIMSELF

Namath would show some humility in his winter of shame. He stayed in school and kept his head low for several months. Bryant would reinstate him for spring practice and let him regain his pride with a championship season.

Now a senior, our quarterback returned to grace. Joe would become our career leader in touchdown passes in the second game of the season.

Then, at home against North Carolina State, while rolling right with all his receivers covered, Namath turned upfield and crumbled to the ground. There was no contact on the play. The crowd groaned. While trainer Jim Goostree worked on him, Joe moaned, "It's my knee." Joe struggled to the locker room under his own power and came back to the sideline in the third quarter with an ice wrap on his leg.

After a weekend in the hospital with what was described as a twisted right knee, the swelling remained and blood and fluid had to be drained.

That ritual would become part of Joe's routine as he continued to play despite what would later be diagnosed as torn cartilage.

In the first quarter against Florida, Namath called his own number, pushed forward for a first down and fumbled. He reinjured the knee as he scrambled for the loose ball. Namath would become a relief pitcher for the rest of the season.

It was unfortunate how it happened, but it was one more sign of Joe's growth in his time with us. Four years earlier, while on the freshman team, Joe lost a fumble and made no further effort on the play. Bryant went out on the field in that game to tell Namath it wasn't his job to lay on the ground and disown the play. By now Namath knew what kind of effort was expected and he always gave it.

Namath's knee was on everyone's mind. Bryant told the Tuscaloosa News, "Namath moves like a human now. He did move like a cat." Namath was now playing on heart as he would for 13 years in the NFL.

We were 8-0 and Georgia Tech (7-1) and Auburn (6-3) were all that remained on our schedule.

After playing Tech every year since 1902, this would be our final faceoff for a while. With bad feelings between the schools still stewing, we would take a 15-year sabbatical from each other. We would say our goodbyes in Atlanta. Bryant would take the field wearing a helmet. It was more than a safety precaution. It was a statement of defiance and a shaming of the crowd for throwing things at us the last time we were at their field.

Namath wouldn't get into the match until the second quarter. It was still scoreless when he threw a 48-yard bomb to David Ray. Fullback Steve Bowman ran it in from the one. After an aggressive onside kick, Namath threw 45 yards to Ray Ogden who made it to the 3. A couple plays later Namath found Ray in the end zone for a 14-0 lead. Two touchdowns in 78 seconds and Namath could sit for the rest of the day. We needed to preserve the resource. The final was 24-7.

Namath's disciplinarian now sounded more like his publicist or his agent with a perfect season intact and the draft looming.

"If a pro team needed a quarterback and didn't take Namath, they ought to go out of business," Bryant told the media. "This boy is great. If he doesn't sign one of the biggest professional contracts ever, I'll be awfully surprised."

Auburn came to Birmingham on Thanksgiving that year. We would call on Namath in the third quarter after Sloan came up lame. Namath's 22-yard touchdown pass to Ray Perkins turned out to be the 21-14 game winner.

Southern Cal took the drama out of the final AP poll of the season by beating Notre Dame and Heisman winning quarterback John Huarte 20-17, spoiling their perfect season.

We were 10-0 for the second time in four years. We had lost by one point to Georgia Tech in 1962 and by two to Florida and four to Auburn in 1963. We deserved our bows as national champions when the final poll came out in early December. Even if it would be the last time anyone crowned a champion before the holiday bowl games.

Our Orange Bowl matchup with Darrell Royal's 9-1 Texas Longhorns would prove unforgettable. It was the first Orange Bowl played at night and turned the college bowl celebration into an all-day, all-night affair. The television bonanza helped bowl games to multiply rapidly in the next few years.

We would have Namath coming off the bench again. The Alabama partisans in the crowd came alive when he trotted onto the field down by two touchdowns. By now he was properly diagnosed with a cartilage tear and knew he would need surgery before going professional. His knee was heavily wrapped. He wore white sneakers instead of cleats. They were not the fashion statement some perceived but an attempt to protect the knee.

Namath completed touchdown passes to Wayne Trimble and Ray Perkins, but we still trailed 21-17 late in the fourth quarter. We marched down to first and goal at the 6 with time running out. Namath handed off to fullback Steve Bowman three times, but we could only get to the one-yard line.

Now we had just 20 seconds left on the clock. Time out. Namath came to the sideline. "Hey, what play should we run?" I looked at Bryant. Bryant looked at me. I guess we hesitated too long. So Joe said, "Well, I'll take a quarterback sneak." I said, "Great call, Joe." Bryant nodded, "Yeah, that's okay."

So Joe went out there and got set. We practiced on the goal line all the time. We made it all the time. We'd pick them up and throw their ass backward. We'd practice tightening our gaps so nobody could get any penetration. Instead of taking a three-point stance, we would take a four-point stance. Instead of having a flat back, we put our head down and our ass up, so that we could go down underneath them. The lowest guy always wins. But they had been practicing, too. They had their asses up and their heads down. We had the tight ends and the receivers come in and the backs cheating up. Everything was keyed, ready to go.

Joe said, "Hike." He took the ball and made a step back like he should to make sure to control the ball. If you take it and go forward, a lot of the time you will fumble the snap. Joe got the ball and made it secure. You have to take that time to let your two backs get up there and stymie those linebackers. The center can never get to them. Our guys were down there snorting and groveling. The defense was doing the same thing there at the goal line. Tommy Nobis was their middle linebacker. He was a future first-round pick of the Atlanta Falcons. He would play that position for them for 11 years. He was 6'2" and 240 pounds. Joe was 6'2", 198. And they vaulted. They met face to face right over the top of the goal line and they dropped straight down.

The two wing officials came running in. This one was looking at that one and that one was looking at this one. Each one was waiting for the other to put his hands up. As soon as you see one guy put his hands up, the other is supposed to reinforce him. They came running in but nothing happened. It seemed like forever. The referee walked up there and turned his back to the goal line and pointed downfield and said first down Texas.

So that's the play calling I did while I was at Alabama. And that's the only bowl game we lost the five years I was there. It was by the thinnest of margins.

As he left the field, Namath told Bryant that he believed he had scored. Bryant responded quietly and sent him away. Bryant told a reporter he ordered Namath to get inside the dressing room. "It didn't make any difference. If you can't jam it in from there without leaving any doubt, you don't deserve to win."

Bryant didn't mean it as a criticism of Namath. Joe had made a supreme effort on his one good leg. Though it meant nothing to him, Namath was voted MVP of the game.

The very next day Namath signed a record $427,000 contract with the New York Jets. He was just four years from the Super Bowl performance that would immortalize him in the football universe. Jets owner Sonny Werblin said he met with Namath prior to the bowl game, but Namath would not even drink the soda he offered because Bryant had warned him not to accept anything before the game. An eligibility scandal deftly avoided.

NO SHORTAGE OF QUARTERBACKS

Life after Joe Namath meant lower expectations for Alabama in the media, but we hadn't exactly run out of quarterbacks. In fact, we already had two more future NFL passers on campus.

Bryant believed every outstanding team had two distinct characteristics: a fighting spirit and a great quarterback. He could instill the spirit, but we had to go out and find the quarterbacks.

We recruited Steve Sloan out of Cleveland, Tennessee, practically in the shadow of Neyland Stadium. The University of Tennessee wanted him. They just didn't want him as bad as I did. On one recruiting trip, I carried his golf bag around a municipal course and we talked football for hours. He was the smart and capable kid every coach is seeking.

But when it comes to quarterbacks, one is never enough. Coming along behind Sloan we had another special talent, one we found closer to home. Fellow by the name of Kenny Stabler. He was a three-sport star in Alabama. Like Namath, he entertained offers from major league baseball teams, but decided to pitch footballs. At Foley High School, his football teams were 29-1. He had already earned his lifelong nickname "the Snake" for his long, winding touchdown runs. Bryant gave him the loyalty talk and convinced him to stay at home, with his state university.

Stabler was a left-handed thrower with the confidence of a riverboat gambler. The kind of confidence that inspires others. The kind that wins games when it is married to preparation. He was a maverick to rival Namath and would go on to play 15 years in the NFL, most of it with the Oakland Raiders.

So, naturally, we handed the reins of our 1965 offense to Sloan. Working behind Namath for two years, he had already shown us he was another solid citizen and dependable leader like Trammel.

Stabler would start in the defensive backfield in his sophomore season. We did think he was good enough to spell Sloan at quarterback. He would play enough to be the second leading rusher on the team.

Even opening to lower expectations, we somehow managed not to live up to them. We lost our opener 18-17 in Athens.

Coach Bryant responded by calling a 5:30 a.m. practice. Any player who was late would be off the team. Any coach who was late would be fired. Everyone showed up on time. Despite the bad break, Bryant believed we had not given our best. He told the players they should be ashamed to hold hands with their girlfriends.

We would walk over Tulane 27-0, and then come from behind to beat Ole Miss. We would win three games but then stumble again and settle for a tie with Tennessee. It was a humbling day for our quarterbacks. Despite moving the ball fairly well, Sloan lost fumbles in the third and fourth quarters. Stabler came in and moved us downfield. He gained a first down just inside the 10-yard line in the final minute. A bad pitch on second down set us back. After Stabler ran 14 yards, the ball was at the four. Believing he had just scrambled for a first down, Stabler rushed to set up and then threw the ball out of bounds. He meant to stop the clock and bring on the field goal squad. Instead, we turned the ball over on downs with six seconds left.

The tie left us 3-1-1. It could have crushed all of us. We were unranked and seemingly irrelevant in the national picture. Instead, Bryant started a rally right then. When we went to the locker room, the door was locked. Bryant lowered his shoulder and knocked the door off its hinges. Once inside, Bryant took the blame for the end-of-game confusion. He told the team they would have won the game if he had stayed home.

Then he told them something even more remarkable. He said they could still win another national championship if they wanted it badly enough. They did and we began to play like it.

Bryant paced the sidelines with me in 1965 wearing his trademark houndstooth hat.

We would win five straight and climb in the polls. We trailed only three unbeaten teams: Michigan State, Arkansas and Nebraska. With the bowl games to be played before the final vote, all things were still possible.

No. 1 Michigan State was slated to play UCLA in the Rose Bowl. No.

2 Arkansas drew LSU in the Cotton Bowl. We would need help from UCLA and LSU to make it really meaningful, but we would have the chance to dispatch No. 3 Nebraska ourselves in a prime-time Orange Bowl that counted in the polls for the first time.

We were proud of a defense that gave up just 79 points in 10 regular season games. We were led by end Gilmer Creed, tackle Jim Fuller and linebacker and future coach Jackie Sherrill. But to do our part on this most meaningful of bowl days, we were going to have to win an offensive showdown.

Nebraska had outscored its opponents by 23 points a game. They outweighed us by 35 pounds a man on the lines. The Nebraska line featured two future NFL draft picks, Walt Barnes at 240 pounds and Tony Jeter at 230. We had an All-America center in 212-pound Paul Crane and a very scrappy offensive guard, John Calvery, who weighed 178 pounds.

This would not be your ordinary Alabama game plan. We met with Sloan and asked him to play the whole game like we were behind by two touchdowns. It was going to be fun.

The Cotton Bowl was first up and LSU won that one 14-7. The Rose Bowl was competitive when we kicked off.

Nebraska coach Bob Devaney expected a conservative ball control approach from us. With his club concentrating on our top two receivers, Ray Perkins and Dennis Homan, we ran a tackle eligible pass on our first play from scrimmage. The play calls for the offensive tackle to report to the official as an eligible receiver and then line up a few steps behind the line. Jerry Duncan, who set high school records as a running back and had good hands, made the unconventional catch for a 35-yard gain.

So we did something else no one would ever expect. We ran the same trick play again. On the very next play. The second pass brought us another first down and Nebraska was on its heels.

We meant it when we said we were going to play like we were behind. After going up 21-7 late in the first half, we tried an onside kick and recovered it. With Nebraska still in shock we moved down for a field goal and a 24-7 halftime lead.

In the locker room, Bryant told the team UCLA had won 14-12. All we had to do now was play 30 more solid minutes to win our third championship in five years.

It was a madcap second half. Nebraska would score three times, but we were good for two more touchdowns. Sloan wound up 20 of 28 passing for 296 yards with two touchdowns. Perkins hauled in 9 passes worth 159 yards.

In the middle of it all, Bryant turned to me on the sideline. "Isn't this the damndest way to win a football game? I promise you this will never happen again." I'm not sure he was enjoying our style of play, but it was all according to plan.

The final score was in our favor, 39-28.

With the change in the way the championship was decided, we became the fifth team in history to win back-to-back titles.

Sloan headed to the Atlanta Falcons. Ray Perkins joined the Baltimore Colts. After five seasons there, Perkins would climb the coaching ladder, lead the New York Giants and one day return as Bryant's successor at Alabama.

I was about to move on, too, but Stabler would be there to lead the team to an undefeated and untied record in 1966. The polls chose Notre Dame, but the Tide had a 17-game winning streak and bookend perfect seasons in a six-year run with only four losses and one tie. There has never been anything like it.

Bear would then run out of quarterbacks and suffer through a brief down period, including back-to-back six-win seasons, before reestablishing the school's dominance and marching toward the record for wins as a college coach.

Celebrating three national championships in 5 years (left to right: Dude Hennessey, me, Carney Laslie, Coach Bryant, Sam Bailey, Ken Donahue and Ken Meyer)

CHAPTER 4

GOING PROFESSIONAL

"When I was first with the Rams there was not a whole lot of discipline and Coach Schnellenberger brought it to us. He was in charge of our workouts and led us in calisthenics, and it was a new world. His passing offense was built on discipline, too. When you planted that back foot you had to already know where that ball was going. And you didn't run out of bounds and you didn't slide, you went for the first down. Howard was tough."

– Roman Gabriel, *Rams quarterback and 16-year NFL player*

Three years into my apprenticeship with Bryant, I was beginning to wonder if there were greater opportunities out there. I applied for a head coaching job at the University of Colorado. I waited to hear from them, but they never called. They ended up hiring Eddie Crowder, who had been an assistant to Red Blaik at Army and Bud Wilkinson at Oklahoma. He stayed 11 years and had some success in a 67-49-2 career.

We had circled the wagons in Alabama and survived the scandalous reporting of the *Saturday Evening Post*. It seemed to make Bryant all the more powerful and famous. He got that financial settlement, and it made him very comfortable with himself. We were 30-3 over my first three seasons, and I thought I should be a hot commodity. Yet I received no calls, no letters, no inquiries about what interest I might have in a college head coaching job. People usually send out feelers; I couldn't get a nibble.

Something was wrong, but I didn't see it right away.

Today it is clear to me what dried up the market for Alabama assistants for most of a decade. One of Bryant's disciples, Charlie Bradshaw, lost his mind up in Kentucky and tarnished the brand.

Bradshaw wanted to clone Bryant's magic when he left as our receivers coach and took over the University of Kentucky football team in 1962.

Bradshaw took only the demanding half of Bryant's philosophy north with him. He took the kick-them-in-the-butt trait, but forgot the hug-their-neck trait. He took practice and conditioning to an extreme level. Tragedy followed as two of his players died in as many years. He was left with only 30 healthy players that first season, and the surviving team was forever labeled "the thin thirty."

Sports Illustrated put Bradshaw's program in a shameful spotlight under the headline "Rage to Win." Bradshaw was fired and Bryant's magnificent coaching tree that eventually produced 54 head coaches would be stunted. Gene Stallings would be called home to Texas A&M, but nobody else in Bryant's camp would become a head coach for another seven years.

When Bradshaw left Alabama before the 1962 season, I took over his duties as receivers coach and continued as offensive coordinator. Everywhere I have worked as an assistant I have been the receivers coach except those first two seasons at Alabama when I directed the offensive line.

As we continued our dominance and won our third national championship in five years in 1965, I was seriously frustrated at the lack of opportunities. I was offensive coordinator for the best college team in America. I believed I was the most qualified assistant coach in the country. I helped send Joe Namath and Steve Sloan to the NFL, and Kenny Stabler was coming behind them.

With the success we were having, I probably could have stayed at Alabama forever. I loved the man I was working for, but he didn't pay anybody very much because everyone wanted to be on his staff. I had only managed a small raise when I came down from Kentucky, and after three championships, Bryant offered me another $1,000 raise.

At this point I was married with two young children and making just $13,000 a year.

Finally the phone rang. The call was from George Allen. He was leaving the Chicago Bears to take the head coaching job with the L.A. Rams. Allen said he wanted me to join him. The college market seemed to have nothing more for me at the time, but I was sitting in a very good position. I decided I would bleed Allen for every dime I could.

After some lengthy negotiations, I got Allen up to $16,000 a year. I kept dickering until I got him to give me a car. A car can tell you a lot about a man. In this case, it would eventually tell me more than I wanted to know about Allen and his business practices.

George Allen was shrewd. I think that is the best word for it. He didn't have the authority to give me the car he promised, but he arranged to get me one anyway.

We moved to an elegant area of Belmont Shores. I felt like I was in paradise with my wife and children. I was happy as could be. We had a little two-bedroom ranch, a swimming pool, flowers along the sidewalk. My nice new car.

After the first season, though, someone came to my home concerned about the car. He was from Hertz, and he said "You've been driving this car on a weekly rental agreement for about a year now, and we thought we ought to bring it in and change the oil." The bill for that first year was $8,000.

My experience with Allen was not unique. Dan Reeves, the owner of the Rams, once commented that he gave Allen unlimited budget authority and he somehow exceeded it.

Allen was quick to pay the higher salaries needed to bring in veteran players because he wasn't willing to let young players learn on his watch. He became well known for his tendency to trade draft picks for established, even aging talent.

He was a detail guy who was obsessed with winning now, and I was obsessed with learning from him. Allen would spend all day working in the capacity of general manager and all night working as head coach. He had a personal assistant who drove him everywhere so he could work while he was in the car. He had one of the first car phones and he was on it all the time. He was a workaholic and he worked everyone around the clock. His assistants sweated all day long to prepare, and after supper they would be there with Allen every night until 11, 12 or 1 o'clock and then be back at the office in the morning to scout teams and practice.

Allen was a defensive-minded head coach and a great one. He established himself as a turn-around artist with the job he did in L.A. He took a team coming off seven straight losing seasons and went 49-17-4 over five years.

We went to the playoffs twice in that period at a time when only four teams in each conference made it to the post season. We were in a division with the Baltimore Colts, who were led by Don Shula and Johnny Unitas, and only the division winner advanced.

Once again, I was on a staff for the ages and in a perfect position to master my trade. Five of the assistants who worked for Allen in Los Angeles became NFL head coaches. Two of them started with me in 1966: Ted Marchibroda and Jack Patera.

Marchibroda, who was beginning his coaching career, was in charge of the offensive backfield. He would stay with Allen and move to the Redskins before following me as head coach of the Baltimore Colts.

Jack Patera was the defensive line coach directing a group that became known as the Fearsome Foursome. He would eventually become the head coach of the Seattle Seahawks expansion team.

Dick Vermeil also got his first pro job when Allen named him Rams special teams coach in 1969. Vermeil was the first NFL assistant to devote full time to those units, taking over my responsibilities in that area. I still went to special teams meetings and offered what support I could because we were really trying to sell the team on the importance of those plays.

Vermeil, of course, would go on to coach the Eagles, Rams and Chiefs.

Marv Levy, who would become head coach of the Chiefs and the Bills, joined the Rams staff for the 1970 season as I moved to the Dolphins.

As a head coach, Allen believed good

1966 Los Angeles Rams coaching staff (left to right kneeling: Tom Catlin, Ray Prohaska, George Allen, me, Marion Campbell; left to right standing: Joe Sullivan, Ted Marchibroda) assistants make a great head coach, and he obviously had an eye for good help. He made his name as personnel director for George Halas' Bears when he brought in two straight rookies of the year (Mike Ditka and Ron Bull). His draftees made up more than half the 1963 Bears championship roster and included Gale Sayers and Dick Butkus.

There was no offensive coordinator under Allen, and he gave me a lot of freedom to plan. I was in charge of the offensive book, and he just let us do our thing on that side of the ball. The defensive manual made ours look skimpy. Allen had 300 variations of his defense and 150 audibles that might be called. He considered offense a necessary evil. He is the type of coach who is thinking about punting on first down. He considered it an offensive play.

We were the first team to incorporate computers into our game planning. We did it before anyone even thought of using computers to analyze football. We went out to Simi Valley one summer with two professors from the University of Southern California. It took them six weeks, but they wrote the first programs to help us scout opponents.

You had to rent the computer for an hour and it would print out the data from your project. This is back when the machine took up an entire air-conditioned room and computer operators sorted those cards that you could not spindle, punch or mutilate.

You've got 72 plays on offense per game and five games of data on an opponent, and each play is a line on one of those cards. We fed the cards into the computer on a trawl and it would grind and scratch.

Whomp, whomp.

You want to know the probability of each play being called on each down in each situation, third and short, third and long. What is the probability they will call a certain play if it is first and 10 on the minus 25-yard line and the opponent is in brown right or whatever defensive set up? What are they likely to do on the first play of the game when there is no score? What do they do in windy weather?

Whomp, whomp.

You get all the plays by formation and down and distance and hash mark.

Whomp whomp.

Then you print out three copies of everything on a dot-matrix printer. One copy for the head coach and one copy for the offense and one for the defense. Then you rush home and sit down and read the summary and then the detail. Then you study it and translate it and explain it to your team.

It's obviously simpler today, but this was the start of it all. The computer told us all the probabilities, how many times this play has been run in relation to all the plays they run. If they have a play that they usually run to the wide side of the field, and I know that's what they'll run in a certain situation, then I can bring the weak side end in.

This is what makes football such a wonderful game. To me it's like chess. There is an ability to use your intelligence, to use your skills and be able to study a defense and change a play. Your pre-snap read will tell you the defense is not what you were expecting because the strong safety is too deep, and you know you need to switch to another play.

To take advantage of all the information, though, you must have the right quarterback. We did. His name was Roman Gabriel. He was an Academic All-American at North Carolina State. He had a sharp mind, a great arm and tremendous athletic ability. Marchibroda and I worked with him and

Photo courtesy of the LA Rams

refined his game.

We installed Gabriel as the quarterback ahead of Bill Munson, who had started for the past two seasons. Munson and the Rams were 4-10 in 1965 and finished last in the seven-team Western Conference. Munson was traded to Detroit in 1968 and played 16 seasons in the league.

Gabriel passed for 10,232 yards in my four seasons with the Rams. He led the league with 24 TD passes and was the NFL's Most Valuable Player in 1969. The team was 40-13-3 in that period.

To jump start the offense in Los Angeles I moved Roman Gabriel into the starting quarterback job. With him behind center we quickly developed into one of the top offenses in the NFL. He was the league MVP in 1969.

Allen had been with Halas for seven-and-one-half years and there was some hard feeling on Halas' part when Allen left before his contract with the Bears was up. Allen wanted his own show and he quickly proved he could run one. The Bears' boss was not happy and he sued Allen for breach of contract. Halas prevailed in court, but then dropped the matter without collecting any penalty. He considered the point made. Today, though, leaving for a better job is widely accepted behavior by coaches.

All of that made for an emotional situation when the Rams hosted Halas' Bears in the second game of the 1966 season. Allen did better in the game than in the suit. The Rams won 31-17. Afterward Halas refused to have his picture taken with Allen.

We were thought of as a defensive team our first year. We had the Fearsome Foursome: Lamar Lundy at 6'6", 255 pounds; Rosey Grier at 6'5", 285; Merlin Olsen at 6'5", 275; and Deacon Jones at 6'5", 260 pounds.

Jones became known as the Secretary of Defense. He was famous for the head slap as a first move on an opposing lineman. Jones credited Grier with inventing the move and claimed his role was perfecting it.

Deacon had a head slap, a double head slap and a fake head slap. He looked like Muhammad Ali at a punching bag. He got so damn good at it, I am sure he was handing out concussions. The league eventually had to ban the move.

Photo courtesy of AP Images

The Rams defensive line may have been the best ever. They became known as the Fearsome Foursome. (left to right: Lamar Lundy, Merlin Olsen, Rosey Grier, Deacon Jones)

Our four intimidators stared opposing linemen in the eye before getting down in their stances. They were like brothers in arms, and they may have been the best defensive line ever.

Allen called them his rush men and they worked in concert with each other to create havoc every Sunday. Lundy would destroy the pocket and Grier would corral the quarterback. Or Jones would go outside and force the passer to step up and meet Olsen.

Of course, Roger Brown became a valuable fourth man on the line when Grier was injured and retired.

We were a bit erratic that first season, winning four of our first five, then losing four straight and rebounding to win four straight. We finished 8-6 and in third place. It was a good start and a quick turnaround.

Allen's creed was now firmly established with the team. His meeting rooms were kept at 64 degrees to keep players awake. His motivational slogans plastered the locker room walls. "100 percent is not enough;" "The harder I work, the luckier I get;" "The tougher the job, the greater the reward."

Allen was a disciplinarian, but he also dished out rewards. He did whatever it took to get people to do things his way. He had the strictest set of fines in the league. He dunned you $1,000 if you misplaced our playbook, $500 for breaking curfew and up to $100 a pound for being overweight. On the flip side, when we won, we would come in the next day and grade the players and give out 20 monetary inducements. There were televisions handed out to the top offensive and defensive players and the best special teams performer. Every week there were restaurant gift certificates passed out for big plays. After one game, he gave out 60 game balls.

He made people hungry to be recognized and they gave him their best effort.

Allen also had a craving for information about his opponents, and he believed every coach was as obsessed about it as he was. He bought into the theory that if you weren't spying, you weren't trying. It bought us some trouble in 1967.

Allen hired a retired Long Beach detective to provide security and do a little scouting. We all referred to him as 007. Ed Boynton was his real name and he had investigated the Black Dahlia case involving the butchering of a young movie extra in 1947.

Allen wanted Boynton to keep people from peeking in on our practices. There was a high school and some houses across from our practice fields, and anyone looking in our direction was suspect.

Our secret service man would also go out on covert operations. The goal was to get pictures of an opposing team's practice. He would climb a telephone pole in work clothes or get as close as he could for Allen and report back.

The Cowboys caught one of Allen's spies shortly before a game with Dallas. A custodian became suspicious about someone watching practice from a car for two straight days. He took down the license plate number, and the team traced the car to the Rams personnel director and one of our scouts.

That resulted in an official complaint to the commissioner. Allen tried to make light of it. He said there was no need to spy because we have film of each opponent and teams win with better execution.

I happen to agree with what Allen was saying in response to getting caught, but he was just trying to make the issue go away. I knew his real thoughts because he had sent me out to spy on one occasion. I drove around aimlessly for a while and came back. I had to tell him something, so I said I couldn't get close enough to see anything meaningful.

Allen believed there was no such thing as a surplus of information on an opponent. He insisted that George Halas was not above it and said everyone gathered what information they could.

When I was with Bryant, you couldn't send anyone to scout games and there wasn't any film, so a lot of what you knew about any new wrinkle a team was using came to you from friendly alumni.

My opinion, though, was that spying did not help us at this point. We were allowed to scout an opponent's games and we had the film swap. We could plot tendencies and all the probabilities with the proper study.

We were getting better, but 007 wasn't the reason.

Our defense made us competitive, and we started building our passing game our first season there. Gabriel and the offense broke out for good in 1967 when Allen brought in wide receiver Bernie Casey. The addition of Casey kept most teams from double teaming Jack Snow. Snow went to the Pro Bowl the first year we had two deep threats, and Casey went the following season.

We finished second in the league in points in 1967, moving up from 289 to 398. We improved from 50 to 75 percent on third down and short conversions.

We got the ultimate compliment from Allen, who pronounced us a complete team. The defense was as good as ever. The combination allowed us to boast a 106-38 fourth quarter scoring advantage.

We started the year 9-1-2 and somehow it didn't look like it was going to be good enough. We were facing a new league alignment. We were in a four-team Coastal Division, and we had to finish first to make the post season. Baltimore was in that division with us and they started the season 10-0-2. We were one game behind Shula and Unitas with two games to play, both of them in the Coliseum.

We had already met the Colts once and the game ended in a tie. We were set to play Baltimore in the final game of the season, so we still had a chance to finish with a better record.

It took a dramatic win the next week to make the final showdown meaningful. We trailed the Green Bay Packers with less than a minute to go, but blocked a punt and recovered the ball at their five-yard line. Gabriel hit Casey for a winning touchdown with thirty-four seconds left on the clock.

The blocked kick was not a fluke. Green Bay's punter, Donny Anderson, kicked with his left foot. We spent time that week practicing blocking that kick. Other weeks we practiced things like missed snaps. We had passing and running plays off of fake punts and field goals. We prided ourselves on our special teams play. We recognized the work the players did in that area, and they rewarded us with focused effort.

When Baltimore came to town, we were still sky high. Gabriel was a spectacular 18-22 passing. He put up 275 yards and three TDs that gave him the Rams' season record. The defense was in shut-down mode. The line battered Unitas, and we won the division on the back of a dominating 34-10 performance.

If I could, I would end the story of that season right there on a high note. Not to be. After two electrifying wins we had six days to prepare for a rematch with Green Bay in Milwaukee. It was the week before the championship game that has been popularized as the Ice Bowl and it was nearly as cold.

We couldn't beat Bart Starr and Vince Lombardi a second time in three weeks. After staying home and practicing in the sunshine all week, we shivered through a 28-7 beating. They would go on to win their second straight Super Bowl to launch that great tradition.

The league didn't give us a chance to lick our wounds. They marched us down to Miami for a Runner-Up Bowl with a Cleveland team that had fallen to Dallas in the new playoff format.

The fans gave a collective yawn to the idea of a bronze medal game declaring a third-place finisher, but Allen considered the match the first game of the next season, and he expected a full effort from everyone. This was a man who told his players that if they could accept defeat and open their pay envelopes without feeling guilty, then they were stealing. That attitude and his intensity rankled some players in this setting and in the two Pro Bowl games we coached together.

But we did beat Cleveland 30-6 and followed up by posting a 10-3-1 record in 1968. That wasn't good enough. Baltimore went 13-1 on the way to an embarrassing Super Bowl III loss to Joe Namath's Jets.

Allen had a five-year deal with the Rams, but he was fired by the owner, Dan Reeves, three years into that contract. Allen's spending habits and the Dallas spying incident were part of it, but Reeves said it was mostly a personality conflict. It was well known Allen had refused to shake hands with Reeves on the sideline following one late season win.

We had just gone 21-4-3 over two seasons and winning proved to be pretty good insurance for anything Allen did, especially in a place that hadn't won in a while.

The press and the fans predictably went nuts. That was followed by a player revolt. Thirty-eight players including Gabriel, Snow, Tom Mack, Jack Pardee, Olsen, Jones, Lundy and Eddie Meador attended a press conference and announced they would retire or seek to be traded if Reeves didn't let Allen keep his entire staff and finish his contract.

Gabriel told me he called all the offensive players and Meador called all the defensive players. I'm sure Allen's assistant, Joe Sullivan, helped orchestrate it all.

Reeves brought us back, but the situation was not good. Allen stayed his final two years before heading to Washington. I took an opportunity to join up with Don Shula after one more west coast season.

My last year in L.A. started spectacularly with 11 straight wins, but ended in another playoff disappointment. This time we had to play in Minnesota.

We thought we had learned our lesson in arriving late in Milwaukee two years earlier. We weren't going to make the same mistake we did against Green Bay. Turns out we made a new mistake.

We decided to spend Christmas week in St. Paul getting acclimated to the cold, the wind and the snow. There was so much snow at Macalester College, we had to use orange paint to line the white stuff and see the shape of our field. Every patch of land was under 6-8 inches of packed down snow. We tried using shoes with suction cups on the bottom so receivers could run a square-in route.

Our practices were less than ideal. Meanwhile, Bud Grant took the Vikings to Phoenix to work out and prepare without any weather difficulties.

We had a perfectly miserable holiday and then earned our Beach Boy reputation by giving up a halftime lead and losing the game 23-20.

Allen was certainly one of my mentors, but he wasn't perfect and I actually ran from him when I got the chance following that season. We accomplished a lot while I was in L.A., but he worked us like slaves.

It was incredibly hard to sustain the pace that Allen demanded of everyone. In one of the many books Allen wrote, he set out 10 commandments. The first rule was football comes first. There was no mention of God or family.

I learned attention to detail and Allen's philosophy that to win a championship you have to have everything going together, even the girl at the switchboard, but I needed to go someplace where being a mere workaholic was enough. I took that opportunity when it came up after the 1969 season. At that point Allen was a lame duck coach, even if he was being allowed to finish out the last year of his contract.

There is a line you have to recognize between what's fair and equitable and what's improper. I'm not sure Allen saw the line.

Allen and I would remain friends, and we would have more business with each other in the future. He would move to the Redskins, and we would meet in a Super Bowl in just a few years.

Long after we were both out of the NFL, I was able to pay Allen back a bit of the debt I owed him. He had been away from the sidelines for six years by 1990 when Long Beach State was looking for a football coach. An old friend, Corey Johnson, was the athletic director there, and I called him and suggested he hire Allen at age 71. The program was struggling when they gave Allen the job, but they wound up with a winning record his only year there. He was quoted in *The New York Times* as saying that his season there was the most rewarding of his career. Allen died of a heart attack that winter.

I'm sure I also learned something about self-promotion in my time with the Rams. The team was part of the popular culture and seemed to be drawn to Hollywood.

Bernie Casey left us after two seasons to start a long movie career. Jack Snow followed him a few years later. The Fearsome Foursome formed a singing group. They appeared on the *Tonight Show*. They made commercials together, including a memorable one for Miller Lite beer. Olsen, of course, went on to a television career as a broadcaster and an actor. Grier became a minister and was active in politics. He is well known for being at Bobby Kennedy's side during his assassination.

Before I left town, I got my one and only Hollywood credit. My favorite movie will always be M*A*S*H because I was in it. I was a technical adviser while with the Rams. They had a football game in the movie, as you may

*Joe Sullivan and I were hired as technical consultants for the movie M*A*S*H. We appeared as referees alongside stars including Donald Sutherland and Elliott Gould. I am flipping the coin in this picture.*

remember, and they needed somebody to get those guys lined up and able to run plays. So they hired me and Joe Sullivan to be technical advisers. To be able to get that done we put on referees' uniforms and appeared on the field in the film while doing our advising work.

Every time the movie shows on television I smile because I still get a small residual payment when it is shown.

CHAPTER 5

PERFECTION

"Schnellenberger and Shula had great chemistry. Shula oversaw everything, but Howard was the leader of our offense. He was a teacher who gave me help with my blocking. I enjoyed catching the ball and he created plays for me. He was an intelligent coach. He knew what he was doing and he was a big part of our success."

– Jim Kiick, *Dolphins running back and 10-year professional player*

Bear Bryant called first. He had an offer to become head coach in Miami. Dolphins owner Joe Robbie was attempting to lure him away from Alabama with a proposed contract that included an ownership stake in the four-year-old expansion team. Bryant had three college titles in the bank and was genuinely intrigued by the challenge of repeating his success at the professional level.

Bear asked me about the talent on the young Dolphins team. I gave him a favorable appraisal of the key players and told him he could win there. But I urged him not to leave the University of Alabama.

The way the people of Alabama felt about him and the impact he had on collegiate players was too important to Bryant and the players. I told him coaching college football is very different than coaching in the professional ranks, and he was meant to be in college football.

We talked about the influence of money in pro football. I said there is a real difficulty getting the attention of players who collect bigger paychecks than their coaches.

Bryant decided to stay at Alabama and would reinvent himself within two years using a triple option attack that put him back on top of the college game for another decade. He would win three more national championships before retiring.

Six weeks after I talked to Bryant, Don Shula called. Joe Robbie had just pried him away from Baltimore. It had been 11 years since Shula and I worked together as assistants to Blanton Collier in Kentucky. Don had gone directly to the NFL, working in Detroit under George Wilson before taking over as head coach of the Colts. After I joined George Allen's Rams, we spent four seasons on opposite sidelines in those twice-a-year battles for divisional supremacy.

Shula was the youngest head coach in the league when he took over the Colts in 1963. He was 33 at the time and would compile seven straight winning seasons and a 71-23-4 record there. The only real smirch on his resume was the shocking loss of Super Bowl III to Namath and the Jets. Somehow Baltimore owner Carroll Rosenbloom let that devastating loss unravel their previously strong working relationship.

Shula decided to move on when Robbie offered him the same ownership interest he dangled before Bryant. The Dolphins came into the AFL as an expansion club in 1966 and were desperate to move forward after winning only 15 games in their first four seasons.

We were joining the Dolphins the same year the AFL and NFL completed their merger. The two leagues agreed to a combined amateur draft and an end to their bidding wars for players in 1966 and followed that with an interleague championship game that became known as the Super Bowl.

The final step in the merger was realignment. Baltimore, Pittsburgh and Cleveland moved over to the new American Football Conference so the league could have two 14-team conferences, each with three divisions.

When it was all sorted out, we were in the AFC East and our competition featured Unitas and his Colts, Namath and his Jets, the Buffalo Bills with a rising O.J. Simpson and the New England Patriots, still a year away from grabbing Heisman winner Jim Plunkett with the first pick in the draft.

We wouldn't have a first-round pick in that draft because the league taxed Robbie his first selection and gave it to Baltimore as compensation for contacting Shula without the owner's permission. Robbie bemoaned the penalty in public, but he knew it was a tremendous trade. He got the greatest coach in league history.

Three things made Shula the best coach ever in pro ball. He is known for his fierce competitive determination and his organizational intelligence. Maybe the biggest edge he had, though, was his grasp of how players feel. I don't think a lot of coaches have that. Shula had played in the league for seven years, and he used that time to gain insights into the psyche of his peers. He knew what players wanted and how they reacted to everything.

So many coaches will make a decision and they'll come out and announce it. They don't spend a hell of a lot of time giving the background and talking about things that are important for the players to know. I think Shula had a genuine concern for his players and the way they felt about what's going on. He presented changes to the players in a way that made them feel good about things.

He wasn't afraid to make a decision, and he was about to make many changes in Miami. His special ability to communicate his purpose helped keep the team with us.

When he asked me to join him, Shula said he was putting together a staff of winners because it was crucial to changing the culture in a locker room that had never posted a winning season. That made perfect sense to me.

Shula assigned me the offensive book and primary responsibility for the receiving corps, so I was doing pretty much what I did for Bryant and Allen. He brought Bill Arnsparger, a future head coach, along from Baltimore to continue to run his defense. All three of us had been with Blanton Collier in

Photo courtesy of the Miami Dolphins

Don Shula recruited a group of winners to try to turn around the expansion Dolphins. I was his offensive coordinator for a total of seven seasons.

Kentucky, so we were very comfortable working together. Arnsparger and I would drive to the office together each day.

We had major support from assistants on both sides of the ball. Arnsparger had two assistants who won championships as players and had prior experience as coaches. Tom Keane, who won a championship with the Rams and then coached in Chicago, Pittsburgh and Miami, stayed on board to work with the defensive backs. Mike "Mo" Scarry, who was the first captain of the Cleveland Browns and had coached the defensive line for the Washington Redskins, held those responsibilities for us.

I had Carl Tassef to work with the offensive backs. Tassef had played with Shula in college and the pros and had been an assistant with the Patriots and the Lions. Shula also recruited Monte Clark to coach the offensive line. He had just retired from the Cleveland Browns as a standout tackle. Clark, another future head coach, helped me with the offensive book and brought tremendous energy to the staff.

The team put all the transplanted coaches up at the Jockey Club on Biscayne Boulevard while our spouses sold our homes and relocated. We were free to get to work, and we started by watching film and grading every player on every play from the previous season.

Arnsparger was the king of the film room. When he was working with players, they were always antsy, but he would rewind the film and run a play back 10 times or 20 times if he needed to make a point. He would rock the projector back and forth to show someone they were a step late with the ball in the air.

He spared us some of that in our season-in-review, but when we finished, we knew the abilities of every member of the team and we were ready to meet them.

There was some serious talent in place, even though the team had not come together in those first four seasons. The expansion draft was designed to create a doormat for the rest of the league and it did, but the college draft was a great equalizer over time.

The Dolphins also had a general manager, Joe Thomas, who had an eye for talent. Thomas started out as the director of player personnel for the expansion Minnesota Vikings. While there, he picked Fran Tarkenton to lead that young team. He did similarly savvy work for the Dolphins, drafting my entire backfield. He took Bob Griese out of Purdue with the fourth pick in the 1967 draft. He grabbed Larry Csonka from Syracuse and Jim Kiick of Wyoming in 1968. He plucked Mercury Morris from West Texas State in 1969.

Shula gave Thomas his due, but he wanted his coaches involved in the talent evaluation, too. From year one he sent us to see all the players we might have a chance to draft. That put us out on the road to college spring practices. I was to see as many of the receivers as I could, and each coach would eyeball his own position players. Then we would sit down with the scouts and the reports from the services that Thomas paid for and map out a battle plan with Shula as commander in chief. On draft day, we all sat at the training center and were connected to Thomas by phone. We had everyone rated there by position and by best player available. If we were six picks away, we would have seven names on our board, and if we were just two picks away, we had three names on the board. If we made a trade, we would reconfigure our lists.

Thomas was willing to improve by trade and free agency, too. He imported some serious veteran help for the offense just as Shula and the new staff arrived. He signed tight end Marv Fleming as a free agent when he played out his option in Green Bay. Then he traded the third pick in the 1970 draft for Paul Warfield, who I considered the best wide receiver in the game. Warfield made 215 catches in six years with the Browns and 42 of them went for touchdowns. We would never throw to him as much as they did in Cleveland, but he demanded double coverage and tremendously improved all our options.

Shula was on top of everything and he challenged everyone. On my side of the ball, he wanted to see Kiick work as a fullback. He wanted Larry Csonka to play at 235 pounds, not 249. He wanted Morris to prove he was durable. He didn't think Bob Griese was effective when he was scrambling.

We got to work with Griese and the Miami area players in April. Griese made it clear he wasn't running by choice. He told Shula to give him a line that can create a pocket and he would pass from it.

Shula was determined to make that happen. That is what he had in mind when he brought in Monte Clark to make the line over. Jim Langer, the future Hall of Fame center, was joining us as a rookie but he wouldn't start for a couple more years. Norm Evans and Doug Crusan were already there at the tackle spots, and Clark worked hard to make them better. We picked up Bob Kuechenberg as a free agent. He won a starting job and stayed on the line for the next 15 seasons. Larry Little had come over in a trade the year before and would become one of the all-time greats.

You could tell Langer and Kuechenberg were going to be good as soon as they picked up the offense. They were lifting barbells and working to get stronger long before sophisticated weight rooms were common.

In those spring practices at the University of Miami, we paid attention to cadence and pass routes. We were lucky to get those sessions. Our first camp was delayed until six days before the start of preseason games because of contract strife between the players' association and the league. We used the downtime to some advantage, working closely with the rookies while the veterans held out.

That extra time with the new arrivals was especially helpful to Arnsparger, who was going to count heavily on Tim Foley and Jake Scott to team with Dick Anderson in his defensive backfield. He also needed Mike Kolen and Doug Swift to step up and join the veteran Nick Buoniconti at linebacker.

While we waited for the virtual strike to end, Shula and I met in his office one night. He talked about trying to give the team a "winning edge." We batted the term around for a few minutes and decided we needed to turn the "edge" into an acronym that stood for something. Before we left the room, we came up with what we needed. The E stood for extra study. The D for determination. The G was for gassers and the final letter stood for extra effort. Gassers were sprints the width of the field the players ran at the end of practice.

The concept touched on the mental, physical and emotional investment everyone needed to make. The winning edge ended up on posters in our locker room and became associated with the team. Shula penned a book with that as the title.

Once the holdout ended and we had everyone in house, Shula had a message for all of us. "We are aiming for a championship and nothing else," he said. And he meant it.

He said he didn't care about the past, the past was for losers. And he made it known he was not interested in hearing any excuses. He expected everyone to give him their best.

Shula let his assistants do the teaching, but he oversaw everything. Now that the team was in camp, he immediately put his imprint on it.

He inherited a locker room where the black players sat on one side of the room and whites sat on the other. He integrated the room by seating players in their offensive or defensive units. He paired up roommates across racial lines and in a way he hoped would improve communication. He had the guards living together so they would talk more about their assignments. He put Griese with Warfield knowing they would dissect the passing game. He had coaches stay on the same floor as their players.

Shula banned the floating cocktail party that flourished under the previous coach, George Wilson. He doled out parking spaces. He assigned seats on the bench.

Everyone was on notice. This was a new world. The returning players had been beat up in those early years. They were hungry to win and they came along.

We had natural leaders on the team, and Shula made sure to involve them in some decisions before acting. He got Buoniconti's approval before instituting four-a-day practices for our one-week training camp.

We would go 4-2 in the preseason, including a home win over Baltimore in front of 76,712 fans, the largest crowd ever in Miami. There weren't many fans willing to suffer with the team those first four years, but once we won a few games, we didn't have any trouble selling tickets in a town with no other professional sports teams.

We jumped out to a 4-1 start in the regular season. It was all the more special because it included the team's first-ever wins over the long-dominant Oakland Raiders and Namath's Jets.

Our newfound faith would be tested when we lost the next three straight. We would be shut out twice, once in Baltimore. Griese threw eight interceptions in the losses, and the press was screaming for his head. He had a couple of bad games, but he was our quarterback now and for the future.

Shula realized Griese was learning a new system, and he was willing to stick with him. It was a crucial decision that started a long run of success. Griese broke out with a dominating performance against New Orleans. He showcased the balanced attack that would become our identity. He was 15 for 19 passing for 225 yards. The backs ran for another 181 yards and we won easily, 21-10.

When the defense concentrated on Csonka and Kiick, it opened up the passing game. If they tried to shut down Warfield and Howard Twilley, they were susceptible to the run.

With Griese starting to master the playbook and read defenses better, we rattled off six straight wins. We had another big crowd when we beat Baltimore 34-17 in Miami in week 10. The Colts only lost two games all season. They were on their way to a Super Bowl victory, but we were establishing ourselves as the team of the future.

Our winning streak gave us the second best record in the conference at 10-4 and put the team into the playoffs in just its fifth year of existence.

We drew Oakland for a first round matchup and had to travel there. We had beaten them in the third week of the season, but fell 21-14 the second time around. The loss stung, but we had arrived. We were young. We were talented. We knew we would be back.

The following season we would be even better. We had the benefit of a full camp. Csonka and Kiick created some controversy when they held out together for bigger contracts, but they came back strong. They would alternate as battering rams, blocking powerfully for each other and gaining extra yards by sheer will.

You had to love Larry Csonka. He brought a black lunch pail to work every day just like his daddy did. He really got beat up as a runner. He was like a college wrestler racing out onto the mat. He would just go right at the people trying to tackle him. He didn't need to dodge anyone. It might take six hits to take him down. Our second year there, Csonka would become the first Dolphin to rush for 1,000 yards in a season.

His buddy, Kiick, would establish himself as a superior receiver coming out of the backfield. We made a lot of first downs and Kiick made a living off of one particular pass play I put into our offense for him. He would get outside the tackle and then have the option of going left or right depending on who tried to pick him up. That play pumped up our third down efficiency and made Kiick the second leading receiver on the team.

We were more consistent now. Griese, who had not called plays while in college, became the master of this offense. He had set up a film room at his home and was studying defenses and their tendencies.

He read defenses well, and he had the poise and confidence to get out of a bad play. When the line moves over and they leave the linebackers stacked, they have two more people over there than you have; you are in a bad play and you need to get out of it. He did that. He was able to react properly because he was doing the kind of homework that Peyton Manning is known for today.

We would watch three to five game films on each opponent and he sometimes looked at up to 10. We both wanted to know what they were going to do in every situation.

Griese was not the physical talent that Namath and Gabriel were, but he was a great field general. His skill was to execute a game plan. I didn't feed him the plays during the game. My job was to work with him on a game plan, and we went over it so much in practice we both knew what he was going to do. During the game, I would keep him advised on what was happening after the snap. I was always upstairs. I knew the plays we were going to call in our first series and after every play, I'd call down to the sideline and talk about the defensive formations. After we saw some patterns, I could relay information to him. If they were disguising what they were doing and changing at the snap we would make adjustments.

The key was always Griese's take at the line of scrimmage. In our two-minute drill we didn't even call plays in the huddle. He called them at the line after he saw how they lined up.

The coverage on Warfield was always key. That determined everything else that happened. If they weren't going to let Paul go anywhere without two people covering him, Twilley was going to be in single coverage. And Twilley could also beat any one man.

Griese would lead the AFC in passing that year. Our second-year kicker, Garo Yepremian, would be the leading scorer in the league, booting 117 points through the uprights.

We started the season 7-1-1. Baltimore was 7-2 over the same stretch and we still needed to play each other twice.

The first meeting came the next week in Miami and it was a championship-level game in front of 75,312 delirious fans.

Unitas gave them an early lead with a long touchdown drive that held up until the third quarter. Jim Kiick got us on the board and after Swift intercepted Unitas, Griese put us ahead with a pass to Fleming. Earl

Morrall came on in relief of Unitas and tied things up, but Yepremian was good from 20 yards to put us on top, 17-14. Dick Anderson protected the lead by intercepting Morrall in the end zone late.

The players presented a game ball to Shula. He gave it to Csonka who rushed for 93 yards on 15 carries. Csonka gave it to Doug Crusan in thanks for the job the offensive line did. The willingness to pass the game ball on was a perfect representation of the team we had become.

We beat up the Chicago Bears on Monday Night Football the following week for our eighth straight win. Then we stumbled. We would let down against New England and lose up there 34-13, with Griese injuring his shoulder in the first half.

We were down to a half game lead in the division and had Baltimore again in their stadium. Unitas completed 12 of his first 13 passes and the Colts jumped out front 14-0. Our offense ran just six plays in the first 26 minutes of the game. Our defense was strong after giving up two scores, but we couldn't manage more than a field goal and left town in second place after a 14-3 loss.

We were down, but the season wasn't over. We were still assured of a playoff berth, and as it turned out, we would win the division as well. Jim Plunkett gave Baltimore the same treatment he had just given us, and New England upset the Colts in their final game. We took care of Green Bay in the Orange Bowl, turning a 6-6 third period tussle into a 27-6 statement win. Kiick capped a long drive with a one-yard run and then Csonka followed from the same distance two minutes later. A blocked field goal that resulted in a touchdown produced the final score.

We were 10-3-1 and headed to Kansas City for a playoff game on Christmas Day. They were a difficult matchup for us, and they were favored by the odds-makers. Their quarterback, Lenny Dawson, had a receiver, Otis Taylor, who presented big play possibilities and demanded double coverage.

We got a break from the weather. When we received the kickoff at 3 p.m. in Municipal Stadium, it was 63 degrees and felt more like Miami.

It was a game that seemed like it would never end, and for our fans it was something they might never forget. It would go into double overtime and feature plenty of heart-stopping turns on both sides of the ball. We came from behind three times to produce the tie at the end of regulation.

Griese hit Fleming for a game-tying touchdown with only 1:42 left. And the drama was just beginning.

The Chiefs nearly returned the ensuing kickoff all the way. Yepremian was the last man standing in front of Ed Podolak, and he slowed him just enough for Curtis Johnson to catch up and make the tackle from behind at the Miami 22.

Our defense would hold and their great kicker, Jan Stenerud, missed from 31 yards at the end of regulation. He also failed from 42 yards in the first 15-minute overtime.

We finally broke through in the second overtime. Csonka set up a field goal with a 29-yard run. It came off a play we called roll right, trap left. We had not used the play all day. Griese handed off and the entire backfield sold the misdirection. Griese moved with Kiick to the right, and Csonka made a step that way before heading back behind Larry Little and Norm Evans. That was enough for Yepremian to end the longest game in NFL history from 37 yards out. The kick came seven minutes and 40 seconds into the second overtime.

Our prize was another game against the reigning champion Colts with the winner going to Super Bowl VI. The contest would be the first playoff game ever played in Miami. The Colts had beaten the Browns the day after Christmas to get there.

We had already seen them twice and earned a split. The team that got out front won each time with a ball-control offense. With the luxury of a lead, they had been able to run the table with short passes. When we had the edge, we exhausted the clock with our running game.

This time we would get the early lead. Midway through the first period we were at our own 25-yard line with second down and five yards to go. They were focused on stopping the run. Griese faked the handoff and the corner and the safety came up just enough for Warfield to break past them. He caught the ball on the other side of the 50 and went the rest of the way untouched.

Csonka and Kiick took over along with our defense. Kiick ran 18 times for 66 yards. Csonka carried 15 times for 63 yards and a touchdown. Griese would only put the ball in the air eight times all day.

Arnsparger and the defense focused on shutting down the short passes and screens Unitas loved. He would attempt 36 passes and complete 20, but we intercepted him three times. Dick Anderson returned one of the picks 62 yards for a back-breaking touchdown. The defense was a full partner as we won 21-0.

We had two weeks until Super Bowl VI in New Orleans against Dallas. Tom Landry and his Cowboys had lost the big game by a field goal the year before.

The second time around, Roger Staubach and his crew seemed relaxed in the circus atmosphere. Shula tried to shelter our club from some of it. He had us studying film after a team meal each evening and put in an 11 p.m. curfew.

We were ready on Sunday, but we didn't play like it. We had prospered all season with a no-mistake offense. Now, for the first time all year, Csonka fumbled. That came early in the game and the Cowboys scored first. They were ahead 10-0 when we mounted our only successful drive of the day just before the half.

We had to do it all through the air. Playing from behind all day, Griese completed 12 of 23 passes for 134 yards with one interception. Csonka carried only nine times for 40 yards and Kiick ran 10 times for 40 of his own. We mounted a couple more promising drives but spit up the ball each time.

Staubach was the MVP of the 24-3 skunking. He was 12-19 for 119 yards and threw two touchdown passes. Duane Thomas rushed 19 times for 95 yards and the other touchdown.

It just wasn't meant to be for us on that day. We were morose in the locker room. Each coach and every player took the embarrassment personally.

It seemed like a giant waste not to capitalize on the emotional win in the longest game ever and the dominating performance against the Colts in the Conference Championship game.

Shula spared no feelings after the game. He told the team that the way they lost wiped out everything they had accomplished in the season. He said the only way something good could come of it was if it motivated us to get back to the Super Bowl and win.

When the city of Miami started to plan a parade for the team, Shula derided the idea of having a parade for a losing team. "Maybe next year we can have a winner's parade," he said.

None of us sent back the $25,000 post season share we got for playing in the Super Bowl, but we didn't feel like celebrating either.

Shula's stance wasn't a psychological ploy to motivate the team. He was hurting right along with the rest of us. The pain had purpose. I know now, the frustration we felt spawned the perfect season that followed.

Everything works out as it was intended.

We came back to camp before the 1972 season with the same emptiness and lack of fulfillment we had when we left New Orleans in January.

Shula laid out a series of goals, each a stepping stone to winning the next Super Bowl. He talked about giving the effort necessary to win every game, lock up a playoff spot, win the division, the conference and then the championship. We all bought in.

It is human nature to get a lead and relax, to run off a string of victories and then let down. That is not Don Shula's nature. All coaches have the goal of winning every time out. Only Shula hates losing with all his being. That's why perfection in the football world starts and ends with him.

Shula's quest for Super Bowl VII was helped by two bold preseason decisions.

The first critical personnel move he made was to take out an insurance policy on Bob Griese. Griese had missed a lot of time in 1969 and was beat up in the season we had just been through. George Mira, who starred at the University of Miami but was a professional journeyman, was our backup. We improved ourselves and lowered our risk factor with the acquisition of Earl Morrall.

We might have been willing to give up a draft choice or a player in return, but the Colts placed the 37-year-old veteran on waivers. That meant 24 other teams had to pass on the 38-year-old Unitas' young buddy before we had an opportunity to claim him. They all did. We would have to pay the last year of Morrall's sizeable contract, but no one knew his value as well as Shula.

Baltimore could start its youth movement; we were playing for this season. That was the thinking, too, in trading a future first round draft pick to Buffalo for All-Pro receiver Marlin Briscoe's services now.

A final infusion of offense came from our own stable when we decided to elevate Mercury Morris into a rotation with Kiick and Csonka. Morris' speed was lights out. We had been using him mostly in the kick return game and he was pushing for a bigger opportunity. He had rushed for over 100 yards in a game when Kiick was sidelined the year before, and he deserved a chance.

The move gave us a third gear. We used it mostly to run wide, but he showed us he could run inside occasionally, and he proved he could pick up the pass rush, too. The move wasn't popular with Kiick or Csonka, but they saw the value as Morris started to roll toward a 1,000-yard season. He and Csonka would both reach that mantle, the first teammates to do it in the same NFL season.

With three very different backs, we were able to make more situational substitutions. We did the same thing at tight end and with the wide receivers. Marv Fleming was the better blocker, but we liked Jim Mandich at tight end in some passing situations. Briscoe was a threat to go over the top, but Twilley was great across the middle. Warfield could do anything.

We were now loaded with star power on my side of the ball, but Arnsparger's defense was just as talented, even if his players had a lot lower profile.

That was in great contrast to what was happening with defenses around the league. While the Rams played up the Fearsome Foursome, and the Minnesota Vikings were celebrating their Purple People Eaters on the defensive line, we had an anonymous crew.

It was a ball-hawking eleven, though. They would come up with 26 interceptions on the year while Griese and Morrall threw just 11. Our defensive players had speed and they had brainpower. They always seemed to know where the ball would be thrown.

They became known as the No-Name Defense. It fit because Buoniconti was the only player with any kind of reputation at that point.

Our defense gave us a chance to go undefeated. They gave up less than 13 points a game that season, and you can win a lot of games with a defense like that.

If the perfect season were a movie, then the poster might advertise cameo roles by three of my old friends. Football is a small world after all. Appearances by Joe Namath, Deacon Jones and George Allen would make it all the more memorable for me.

We had to get past Namath and the Jets twice and once we had to rally to do it. Jones would create an offensive crisis for us, and Allen would be the last obstacle in our way, waiting with his Washington Redskins when we got to the Super Bowl.

We opened our 1972 season with three tough road games in the first month. Our multi-dimensional offense and four very strong defensive performances helped us get control of the division early.

Arnsparger had something new for the league to try to digest. He had a defensive scheme that disguised our coverages and kept opposing quarterbacks off balance. Linebacker Bob Matheson could show up as a defensive end in a four-man line or as an extra linebacker behind a three-man line. He wouldn't commit until the ball was snapped. We called it the 5-3 defense because that was Matheson's uniform number.

In Kansas City for a reprise of our Christmas marathon, we used the new defense to jump ahead 20-0 by the third quarter and won 20-10. We had closed their old stadium with a heartbreaking loss for the Chiefs, and now we christened the new Arrowhead Stadium with another loss for the home team.

Against Houston we led 27-0 and prevailed 34-13. Csonka, Morris and Kiick combined for 247 yards rushing and four touchdowns on the ground.

The following week in Minnesota our defense was even better than the Viking's high-profile brand. We sacked Fran Tarkenton five times and intercepted him three times. That gave us a chance to rally with 16 second half points. We trailed 14-6 before kicking a 51-yard field goal with four minutes left in the game. We got the ball again with 2:29 to go and won it with a six-play drive. Griese finished the comeback with a three-yard pass to Jim Mandich while the Vikings looked for the run.

We were 3-0 when we traveled to New York to play a second place Jet team that was 2-1. With Namath struggling to decode Matheson's intentions, Arnsparger added another twist, frequently deploying a fifth defensive back instead of the extra linebacker. Namath managed to pass for just 152 yards. Kiick led our attack with two touchdown runs for a 27-17 advantage. That gave us a two-game lead in the division four weeks into the season, but our resolve was about to be tested.

San Diego came to town with Deacon Jones now on their defensive line. Jones and tackle Ron East would clobber Griese while he was rolling out for a pass to Kiick early in the game. Jones hit high and East hit low. Griese went down with a broken leg and a dislocated ankle.

Enter Earl Morrall.

It was hard to believe at this point that the two of us were All-America college players the same year. He and Howard "Hopalong" Cassidy had gone at the top of the NFL draft. I had a military obligation to complete and played two years in the Canadian Football League. I worked with Bryant for five years and had been in the NFL for seven more. Morrall had been in the NFL all that time. He had won 15 games filling in for Unitas in 1968 and taken the Colts to the Super Bowl.

He was Shula's security blanket. He was about to become mine.

The team was nearly in shock as we carted Griese off the field. Morrall was perhaps the one man who could keep everybody on task. He was the consummate professional. He had the temperament, wisdom, understanding and congeniality that were needed in this situation.

He knew how to calm everybody down: mount a scoring drive. He came into the huddle and called a conservative pass play. He had the tight end delay and then slip into the flat. He hit Fleming for a first down and then continued to drive for the touchdown. We got our blood pressure back under control.

Don Shula (left) made a bold move when he picked up 37-year-old Earl Morrall (center) as quarterback insurance behind Bob Griese (right). When Griese suffered a broken leg in the fifth game of the 1972 season, Morrall held the team together for 10 games while Griese recuperated.

Morrall passed for two scores and Dick Anderson returned a fumble to give us a comfortable lead. The defense didn't give up a touchdown until the last period and we beat the Chargers 24-10.

We would have only two more close contests in the regular season with Morrall at the wheel all the way.

I love Earl Morrall and he steadied the ship, but he didn't win those final 10 games. The Dolphins did. Csonka and Kiick and Morris did. They led us to an NFL record 2,960 yards rushing that season. We ran the ball twice for every time we went to the air.

Morrall, though, made it possible for the others to shine, including our defense.

Buffalo would post the closest final score the very next week, but we led the entire fourth quarter and they put up the last points to get within one.

Namath would have the last real chance to derail our perfect regular season. We were 9-0 and coming off a 52-0 pasting of New England when the Jets came to Miami the week before Thanksgiving.

My old friend put the visitors ahead 17-7 in the second quarter before we climbed back into the contest. Mercury Morris would run for 107 yards on the day and give us the lead on a 14-yard run with 11 minutes to go. The defense held on for a 28-24 victory.

We closed the regular season at home against Baltimore, winning 16-0. The game was already won when we decided to let Griese get comfortable again without playoff pressure. Shula told Griese he was going in when we got the ball back in the fourth quarter, but Shula waited to send him in on second down. That allowed Griese to run onto the field alone and let the crowd acknowledge him.

In the locker room, Shula rejected another game ball. The Super Bowl was the only game that mattered to him. Getting there would prove difficult.

Griese wasn't ready to take over yet, even though he had been a part of our offensive meetings all season long and he never stopped working. Once the cast came off his leg, he walked backwards and then criss-cross until the ankle was solid. He had been throwing from a seated position all along and the arm was in shape, but he needed a couple more weeks of practice.

Morrall would have to lead us past Cleveland in round one at the Orange Bowl. We got ahead 10-0 and led most of the day, but they went on top 14-13 with 8 minutes left in the game. Morrall had only four completions to that point in the game and only 38 yards to show for it, but he found Warfield for 15 yards and then 35 yards on the winning drive. Warfield drew a pass interference penalty at the 8-yard line to set up the final touchdown by Kiick. Doug Swift sealed the 20-14 win with an interception.

Next up was Terry Bradshaw and the Pittsburgh Steelers in Three Rivers Stadium. The Steelers led 10-7 in the third quarter when we turned to Griese. For all that Morrall had done, it was really an easy decision. We hated to take the ball away from Morrall, but the offense had been struggling for three weeks. Griese was going to have to lead us the rest of the way.

We would march down the field twice, converting a key fourth down play on each drive. Griese would complete three of five passes for 70 yards and Kiick would run it in from 2 and 3 yards out to get us on top 21-10. Bradshaw would get the Steelers one more touchdown, but Buoniconti and then Mike Kolen would intercept him to preserve a 21-17 win.

Running the table in the other conference was George Allen. His veteran Washington Redskins team was now led by Billy Kilmer. They had trampled Green Bay 16-3 and Dallas 26-3 to get to Super Bowl VII.

They were favored. That was fine with us. Completing this mission as an underdog would make the achievement all the more respected. We would have 90,182 witnesses to our bid for football immortality in Los Angeles Memorial Coliseum.

The opposing coaches knew each other well, maybe too well. Shula was very much aware of Allen's reputation for spying, and I confirmed the behavior even as I argued it did Allen no good. Shula still played it safe. He decided to abandon the Rams practice facilities because the setting was too public. Instead, he bused the team to Orange County Community College. He posted an equipment manager on the perimeter and he stopped practice when helicopters flew over.

Maybe the more important insight to Allen was knowing he liked to plan his defense off the tendencies of his opponent. The general doesn't deploy his main force in the first skirmish. The boxer has to jab with the left and smash with the right. We plotted a little misdirection. We broke our own tendencies while they stuck to theirs.

Griese was the ultimate chess player. He knew what defense Washington would be in, and he knew what play they would expect us to turn to in every situation. And he was willing to adjust and gain an advantage.

Griese passed on first down and in a few other running situations. He worked with Twilley to turn a predictable down-and-out route into a deep pattern once the corner bit. That produced the first touchdown of the game on a 28-yard pass play while they defended against the first down.

Griese would complete 6 of 6 passes in the first half. Jim Kiick added a touchdown from the one and we led 14-0 when we went into the locker room at the half.

Larry Csonka would rush 15 times for 112 yards on the day and we were in our comfort zone, playing a mistake-free, ball-control game. We were all set to kick a late field goal from 42 yards and leave with a storybook 17-0 final score to match our perfect record.

Not so fast, said the football gods. Garo Yepremian picked up a bad snap and tried to pass for probably the first time in his life. Mike Bass picked off the ill-advised effort and ran it in for a touchdown to make it 14-7.

Kilmer would get the ball back one more time with a chance to tie it, but that merely gave our defense the opportunity to take a final bow. Three passes fell incomplete with everyone covered. On fourth down, Kilmer was corralled by Bill Stanfill and Vern Den Herder, and the television audience got to know the names of a couple more Dolphin defenders.

Jake Scott would be elevated out of the No-Name Defense and be celebrated as the Most Valuable Player of the game.

The entire team, though, won a place in football history. No one had done this before. No one has done it since.

I consider it the greatest accomplishment in the history of team sports. Our 17-0 run has been talked about for decades as the league's best teams try each year to repeat the feat. It stands out enough that President Barack Obama honored the one-of-a-kind team 40 years after the perfect season. I was proud to go to the White House last year with Shula and the boys.

With three straight trips to the playoffs, two Super Bowl appearances and a perfect season, Don Shula gave me the final credential I needed to become a head coach. He gave me the equivalent of a doctoral degree and it was like getting one from both Harvard and Yale.

Shortly after the perfect season, Shula also gave me and everyone associated with the team a Super Bowl ring he designed. It features a large diamond surrounded by 16 smaller stones, one for each game we won in that unparalleled season. The ring proclaims the Miami Dolphins 1972 World Champions. Shula also incorporated our "winning edge" theme on the side.

I have worn that ring proudly ever since, but I have always considered it Don's ring, and I set out almost immediately to get another one I could call my own.

CHAPTER 6

STANDING UP

"I have so much respect for Howard. He had his reversals but he never felt sorry for himself. He kept looking forward. He didn't worry about coulda, woulda, shoulda. He would start from scratch after each separation and rebound. He was an entrepreneur in the sports world. No challenge was too big. He did it the hard way, but he is a legend and he belongs in the College Football Hall of Fame."

– John Y. Brown Jr., *builder of the Kentucky Fried Chicken chain, Kentucky governor 1979 to 1983 and former owner of the Boston Celtics*

I was a head coach at last and I was due for a bit of a wardrobe change.

When I was in Tuscaloosa with Bear Bryant, my wife, Beverlee, bought me a pair of Italian half boots. That was a good shopping find in those parts and they were my Sunday best. I only wore them to church and football games. I wore them for five years in Tuscaloosa and had them half-soled. I wore them in Los Angeles while I was with the Rams and then had them re-soled. I was still wearing them when we got through our undefeated season in Miami.

Now, as I headed to Baltimore, I needed some new shoes. So I threw the boots in the trash, only to have them reappear four months later bronzed by Beverlee.

I had seen bronzed baby shoes before, but these were size 12½. I still have them in my office, though, because they cover a remarkable run. Tucked into the shoes is a tattered piece of yellowing paper with some notes made by my son, Stephen, as we prepared to move north.

That paper chronicles my record in three cities. It looks like this:

UNIVERSITY OF ALABAMA

1961   11-0 Sugar Bowl win over Arkansas (national champions)
1962   10-1 Orange Bowl win over Oklahoma
1963   9-2 Sugar Bowl win over Mississippi
1964   10-1 Orange Bowl loss to Texas (national champions)
1965   9-1-1 Orange Bowl win over Nebraska (national champions)

LOS ANGELES RAMS

1966   8-6
1967   11-1-2 Playoff loss to Green Bay
1968   10-3-1
1969   11-3 Playoff loss to Minnesota

MIAMI DOLPHINS

1970   10-4 Playoff loss to Oakland
1971   10-3-1 Playoff wins vs. Chiefs, Colts; Super Bowl loss to Cowboys
1972   14-0 Playoff wins vs. Browns, Steelers; Super Bowl over Redskins

Stephen totaled up the 12-year record this way:

Regular season totals: 119-24-5

Post season record: 9-5

Deep down I must have known better, but as I took over the Colts I will admit to having the thought: "Boy, this is easy."

I inherited a Colts team that had won the Super Bowl just three years earlier, but was now rebuilding. They suffered through a 5-9 season in 1972. It was the team's first losing campaign in 16 seasons. That was the year Robert Irsay purchased the Rams franchise for $19 million and traded that property to Carroll Rosenbloom for his Baltimore Colts. Twelve years later, in the early morning hours of March 28, 1984, the ever-erratic Irsay would move the Colts to Indiana, where they continue to play as the Indianapolis Colts under the direction of Irsay's son, Jim.

This is where my legacy in football is going to be that I was not very smart. Leaving Don Shula and the Miami Dolphins in 1972 to take the head job in Baltimore was stupid. I really wanted to be a head coach, but I wasn't smart enough to follow Coach Bryant's instructions and never go to any school or become coach anywhere that you didn't get hired by and report directly to the head man. I would make a similar mistake when I went to the University of Oklahoma later in my career, but when I was ready to leave the Dolphins I should have made sure to deal with the top guy. Irsay wasn't involved in the negotiations. All my business was done with the general manager, Joe Thomas.

That's the same Joe Thomas who helped assemble the Dolphins' roster. Robbie fired him after the 1971 season, and Thomas arranged Irsay's entry into the league through the bizarre franchise swap between L.A. and Baltimore. The Colts GM post was his reward.

The great Baltimore franchise was in disarray when I arrived as it tried to replace the legendary Johnny Unitas. When I got up there, I was invited to Irsay's home. It was only then that I found out what everybody else knew and I didn't: Irsay was a terrible alcoholic and impossible to work with.

I believe I could work with an intensely involved owner, someone like Cowboy-in-Chief Jerry Jones. I just have to know going in that this is the way it will be. Plus the owner would have to be honest, upright and sober more than one hour every day.

Photo Courtesy of Bill Mark, NY

My first head coaching job was with the Baltimore Colts in 1973. I was introduced in a press conference at the NFL league meetings. The team was just three years removed from the Super Bowl but was in rebuilding mode.

Unitas' disappointing swan song season earned the Colts the second overall pick in the 1973 draft. The face of the Colts dynasty was traded away and would wear a San Diego Charger uniform during the final act of his career. My new club would place its future in the hands of a pure passer out of Ruston, Louisiana, and LSU. Thomas picked Bertram Hays Jones, the son of former Cleveland Browns running back Dub Jones, as the heir apparent to Unitas.

But this wasn't the NFL of 2012, when five rookies could start and play at the highest levels. It was a different time. Quarterbacks didn't get the same level of preparation in college that they do now. Bert Jones had only started two games at LSU before his senior season when he led LSU into the AP's Top 10 with a 9-2-1 record. He threw into the end zone for a touchdown as time expired to beat Ole Miss 17-16 and beat an Auburn team ranked ninth at the time, 35-7. He was a consensus All-American and finished fourth in the Heisman Trophy voting.

Thomas moved out a lot of the veteran players that had been so good with Unitas. He handed me the youngest team in the league and not

Joe Thomas helped assemble the Dolphins' roster that went to two straight Super Bowls and was the general manager who hired me in Baltimore. We are shown here in front of Memorial Stadium.

enough experience on the line to protect Jones or any other quarterback. I went to camp hoping against hope that journeyman Marty Domres, who came over in the Unitas trade, could hold his own behind center and the young guys could get good enough fast enough.

After playing both quarterbacks in our preseason games it was apparent to me that Bert Jones was so much better. The standard thing would be to play the veteran and let the rookie be on the sidelines a while. But I had enjoyed all that success for the last 12 years. I thought I was indestructible. I believed I could coach up Jones and the offense well enough. I knew it would be hard for him and we might not win right away, but we would get better and he would get game experience. In my heart it was the right move, even if in my mind I knew it was wrong to throw the rookie in there.

Jones would be my field general on September 16, 1973, when I coached my first game in the National Football League. We opened on the road against the Cleveland Browns. It was my first game at any level as a head coach. I was 38 years old, the youngest coach in the league at that time. It had taken me seven years as a coach to get to the NFL and seven more years to become a head coach.

Jones was sacked five times. He managed to complete just 6 of 22 passes for 52 yards. After the sacks were deducted, we netted 4 yards with our passing game. The final score was 24-14.

We would come home to Memorial Stadium and fall to Namath's Jets the next week. Jones completed a more promising 12 of 23 passes for 176 yards and a TD, but he had four interceptions and we were battered 34-10.

Jones and I would notch our first NFL wins together in week 3 against Archie Manning and the Saints. We got a two touchdown lead and then hung on to win 14-10. Jones was 7-16 for 91 yards. He had one TD and 4 more interceptions.

We would lose twice more with Jones struggling before I turned to Domres, hoping he could give me a bridge to our future with Jones.

Domres had been a backup in San Diego for three years and had started nine games for the Colts in 1972. He would play 9 years in the league but start only 32 games with four teams over that span. He completed fewer than half the passes he threw in his career and managed just 27 touchdowns to 50 interceptions.

He would give us some hope, though, with an inspired performance against Greg Landry's Detroit Lions at Tiger Stadium. Domres was an efficient 9 of 13 passing for 177 yards with one TD on the ground and one through the air. Lydell Mitchell kicked in with 24 carries for 84 yards, and it looked like we had an offense now in a 29-27 win.

It was mostly an illusion. We lost six straight games after that, though Mitchell was an emerging star at tailback. In just his second year out of Penn State I rushed him 253 times for 963 yards. He would amass over 1,000 yards three times later in his career.

Included in what was an unprecedented and devastating losing streak for me would be a humbling trip to Miami. I smiled to myself as I looked across the field at Don Shula and the defending Super Bowl champions before that contest began. There aren't any good memories I can share of the game after the opening kickoff. Mercury Morris ran 12 times for 144 yards, breaking loose for touchdowns of 48 and 53 yards. Tim Foley blocked two punts and returned them for touchdowns. So much for knowing the other team well. The final score was 44-0. We were the ones with nothing.

Irsay was far from patient. He gave us a hint of my impending nightmare when he blew into the Colts locker room after a week 11 loss to O.J. Simpson and the Bills and began berating Domres in front of the team. Players thought it might be a joke, but Irsay ranted until Thomas dragged him away.

We would win only those two games against the Saints and Lions in our first 12 weeks. Then we would get a chance at redemption.

Our rematch with the Dolphins would be in Baltimore.

I was at my wits end as we got ready to play them again in week 13. They had lost only one game to that point in their follow-up to a perfect season. I thought to myself it would be crazy to do anything the same against them.

So we got creative. I decided I would take fullback Bill Olds and use him at halfback with Lydell Mitchell. I'd use them in tandem, substitute frequently, and have them act as one. I put a tight end in at fullback. I left another receiver out and brought in a third tight end. I took my biggest receiver and put him right outside the tight end and had us all bunched up in close. We were going to take the ball and jam it down their throat. And we did.

We had the philosophy that Nick Buoniconti was the key. We were ready for the 5-3 defense Arnsparger and Matheson had now made famous. But Buoniconti at middle linebacker was the key for us. We made it really simple with our running game. We set up our inside plays and our outside plays. Normally for each play called we said check with me. For this game, we called the play and said check with Buoniconti. If we were to run an inside play, we would check it to Buoniconti. If he was on our left, we would go with the odd side play, and if he was to the right side, the strong side, we would go to that side. We ran at him because he liked to pursue.

I told the team we were never going to punt. We went for it on fourth down four times. We used two running plays and made the yards we needed on each. Once we lined up in punt formation but ran out of it and made first down. Another time we lined up for a field goal but faked that as well. We made them all.

That was the game plan.

Lydell Mitchell picked up 104 yards on 35 carries. Olds would rush 11 times for 50 yards to give Mitchell a breather. Domres threw just eight times, completing five for 35 yards.

The final score was 16-3. The 16 belonged to us. To make up that many points in one game was special. My history with the Dolphins and Shula gave it extra meaning. It is still a highlight of my coaching career. It gave me the best record in football against Don Shula: 1 win and 1 loss. Heck, I'm the only guy with a 50-50 record against the greatest coach in NFL history.

Other than that memorable win over the defending world champions, we didn't have much to show for my first run of the gauntlet. We did win the following week with Domres throwing two TD passes as we came from behind to top the Patriots, 18-13.

Our two closing victories let us hold our heads up at the end of a 4-10 campaign. Still, there was an overwhelming mood of impatience all around as we headed into the 1974 season.

I was certainly as excited about Bert Jones' potential as anyone, but he was still not quite ready. We opened with a 30-0 loss to the Steelers at Three Rivers and Bert was sacked six times. He was 8-17 passing for 100 yards and had two interceptions. Even though we were in a hurry to succeed with Jones, I told Irsay I was going to rely heavily on Marty Domres for the next few weeks.

I knew I was playing with fire. I thought it was going to be tough, but I thought we could make more progress with Jones on the sideline. I didn't want to get him killed. They called him "the Ruston Rifle" in high school and I didn't want to make him gun-shy.

I didn't tell that to Bert. I started Domres against the Packers in week 2 and he struggled, completing just 8 of 20 passes for 72 yards and throwing three interceptions. Trailing 20-6, I put Jones in and he threw a late TD, but we fell 20-13. Jones was 7-16 for 88 yards with the one TD and one interception. He also scrambled 19 yards for a first down.

When we went to Philadelphia the next week, I stuck with Domres as planned, just to keep the pressure off Jones. He would be ready soon enough. We went to Veteran's Stadium badly needing a spark to ignite a change of direction and grab back the attention of our fans. We fell behind 20-3 when Joe Lavender intercepted Domres and ran it back 37 yards for a touchdown. I was beginning to realize the future was now.

Moments later, while Philadelphia had the ball, Robert Irsay marched down to the sidelines and demanded I replace Domres with Jones. Sparks flew, even if they weren't the kind I had in mind before the game. A few salty words were spoken. By each of us. My relationship with Irsay melted down in front of 64,205 fans during my 17th game as field boss of the Colts.

Irsay told me to change quarterbacks. I said, "No, I can't do that." He said, "God dammit, do it." I refused. I stuck with Domres when the ball changed sides. Then I walked over to Irsay and told him to get his fat ass back up to the box. A coach can't be ordered to make a change like that. My control of the team was on the line.

We exchanged a few more choice words. The last thing I recall saying is, "You can't fire me on the sideline. You can wait until the game is over and then you can fire me." It didn't matter. When I ordered him back upstairs that was, in effect, a resignation.

Robert Irsay threatened to fire everyone daily. I could have saved my job and said, "OK, I'll send Jones in," but I would have saved the job for the moment and lost a coaching career. I sent Jones in to mop up later in the game, but if I had done it when Irsay demanded, that would have been a poor trade of my dignity for a continuing paycheck. What registered was if I succumbed to that, I would be the losing general in this war. I would never lead troops again. My thinking was, even when you have superiors, you don't have to follow an illegal order. You have to do what is best for the people in your command. I think head coaches all feel that way.

Irsay beat me to the locker room after the 30-10 loss was in the books. While I shook hands with Philadelphia coach Mike McCormack and answered a few press queries on the stadium astroturf, Irsay told the team I was fired and Thomas was the new head coach. Thomas didn't find out until he ran into Irsay a few minutes later. I learned the details when I got to the locker room, which made me all the madder. That he told the team before he told me pissed me off worse. When I saw Irsay, I grabbed him by the lapel and shoved him against a locker. The players separated us.

My time in Baltimore was over prematurely. Bert Jones' time was coming.

Jones was a tremendous competitor. He would complete 22 of 41 passes for 215 yards in a 42-3 loss to the Patriots the following week. His season highlight probably came in a losing effort in the final game of the year. Jones gave fans a shining preview of better days, engaging in a slinging competition with Joe Namath. Jones completed 36 of 53 passes for 385 yards. He had four touchdowns and four interceptions in a 45-38 loss.

The Colts finished the 1974 season 2-12. Jones would start at quarterback for eight years and enjoy success. Jones and his teammates won three consecutive AFC East division titles from 1975-1977. He was the league MVP in 1976, but in each of those three peak years, the Colts lost in the first round of the playoffs. Jones missed most of the 1978 and 1979 schedules with a shoulder injury, and the Colts finished last each of those seasons.

After standing up to Irsay and choosing my coaching integrity over my job with the Colts, I didn't tell anyone for

Photo courtesy of the Baltimore Colts

Bert Jones was the second overall pick in the 1973 draft and replaced the legendary Johnny Unitas. Jones would blossom into a league MVP in 1976 and lead the Colts to three straight AFC East division titles.

years how unnecessary Irsay's sideline intervention was. That afternoon, down 20-3, I had already told Bert Jones that he was going in at quarterback on our next series. Irsay's meddling forced me to cancel that plan.

You can check that with Jones if you like. He now owns and operates a lumber yard and wood treatment facility in Simsboro, Louisiana.

I saw Bert Jones again when we were both on radio row at the Super Bowl game in New Orleans in February 2013. I hadn't seen him since that day Irsay and I went at it. The team went back to Baltimore on the train that night, and I went back in a car with three reporters from the Baltimore Sun. I recognized Bert easily despite the passage of 38 years. He was the same big, tall, good-looking guy. We sat there and embraced and talked for 10 or 15 minutes. He recalled the firefight, said there was a lot going on but he was standing right there when the two of us were separated. "I didn't really think I needed to grab you," he told me. But he is wrong. He really did need to grab me. I'm glad someone did, and I thank God it didn't get any uglier in that Philadelphia locker room.

Thomas struggled with Irsay for control of the team for five years before being chased away himself. Baltimore had five head coaches in that short period. The revolving door started when Thomas fired Super Bowl V winner Don McCafferty five games into the 1972 season because he refused to bench 39-year-old Unitas. John Sandusky finished the season and was followed by me. Thomas took his turn as head coach and then hired Ted Marchibroda before getting canned unfairly.

I sat out the rest of the 1974 season. It made for a leisurely autumn, a rare thing in a 60-year football career. I got in shape. I became a distance runner and a weight lifter. I regularly walked around the reservoir near my home in Maryland. It was a healthy respite, but it wasn't pleasant. The sabbatical ended when Don Shula called and said, "I need you, Howard." I would return to the Dolphins gladly and stay another four years before hearing the head coaching siren again, this time coming from the college ranks.

CHAPTER 7

BUILDING SWAGGER AT THE U

"It is one of the highlights of my career to have covered the University of Miami's first national football championship in 1983-84. I had a front-row seat for one of the great stories in college sports history: how Coach Howard Schnellenberger devised and led the stunning transformation of the Hurricanes into a national powerhouse for years to come. Schnellenberger led Miami to greatness with his football genius and remarkable moxie. But this was not just a triumph of sports; it also was a victory of marketing, public relations and civic pride. What he accomplished at the University of Miami was nothing short of a sports miracle."

— **Christine Brennan,** *USA Today national sports columnist; ABC News, CNN, PBS and NPR commentator; best-selling author; 1983 Miami Herald college football writer*

If you know the story of my time at the University of Miami, it might remind you of the Broadway show and subsequent movie *The Music Man.* When I reflect on those five magical years, Professor Harold Hill always comes to mind. You might recall him as the confidence man from the 1957 Tony Award winner. Hopefully I had a little more legitimacy than Hill, but I was just as desperate to prove myself to the local citizenry and sold them my own revolutionary ideas in the same fast-talking and frantic way. I started out telling them "Ya Got Trouble," and I ended up leading my own parade of "76 Trombones" down Main Street when the kids delivered on my big promises.

When I left the Dolphins for a second time, it looked like another suicide mission to some. Established coaches weren't interested in the Hurricanes job. UM alumnus Don James at Washington had already turned it down. George McIntyre, another alum, chose to stay at Vanderbilt. Lou Holtz, who was making a name at Arkansas, was talked up as a candidate but he expressed no interest. Don Shula assured me there would be a better opportunity down the road. He said I would be "nuts" if I took the position.

The program was perceived as a graveyard for coaches. They had suffered eight losing seasons in the previous 10 years. They were looking for their seventh head coach in that short timeframe. The football team was draining hundreds of thousands of dollars a year from the university budget. The Athletic Director's job was also a revolving door.

I balked at first, but then I went home and talked to Beverlee about the opening and we began to examine the positive side of the ledger.

On the personal front, we wouldn't have to leave our home in Miami Lakes. After moving six times since we got married, that was a plus for the whole family.

On the football side, the Hurricanes played in the Orange Bowl. Some saw the 76,114-seat stadium as an albatross, but it was a grand old lady with a few years of life left in it. I could sell high school athletes on the idea of playing in an NFL stadium, home to the second oldest college bowl game in the country. It could serve us well while we generated some community excitement and pushed for an on-campus stadium.

The local territory was rich in high school talent that had never been harnessed and kept at home.

The school was an independent and that allowed them to play a very attractive schedule featuring Notre Dame, Penn State, Florida and Florida State.

Finally, it is a private institution. There were no athletic policy committees. Nobody wanted to get their hands dirty, so it might allow a strong personality free reign. The leadership vacuum at the school meant I would at least have an opportunity to fill it.

So I took the job of head coach at a salary of $50,000 with another $30,000 a year in benefits, and I set out to become a football czar. Anything less and I knew I would suffer from Irsay flashbacks.

Deep inside I always had an ambition to be a college head coach.

In the pros you are a master technician in the game of football. In college you're all things to the kids: coach, father, academic advisor, chaplain and doctor. When one of your players undergoes surgery, you have to call his mother. In the pros that doesn't happen.

A college coach is just like the life coach that Tony Robbins makes his living preaching about at seminars all over the country. Robbins talks about helping people uncover what they truly want from their lives and giving them strategies to work toward their goals. Fostering success, bringing out the potential in each individual and helping them reach a new level of performance is every coach's responsibility.

Now I had my first chance as a head coach at the university level and I wanted to put my stamp on everything.

I was in the office before seven and rarely home before 9 p.m. because there was so much to do. The college football coach's job is to bring all the components of the program together. That means working with alumni, creating interest and bringing the fans back. Until I took the Miami job, I was a caveman like most people coaching football. Now I had to learn the art of promotion, and there was a lot of heavy lifting to do in the first three years on the job.

I relished my new role, but I quickly learned there was, indeed, trouble in River City. The administration had not been forthcoming about its plans, and the NCAA would be coming to investigate the football program.

The Board of Trustees was not confident about the viability of the football program. They had briefly considered dropping the program altogether and were now secretly contemplating a move down to Division 1-AA. I was not happy at all with that idea and immediately brought it up. The board went back into session and voted to table any consideration of that notion for five years, the length of my contract.

There were some early rumblings, but the NCAA investigation of practices under my predecessor didn't formally surface until 1980. It would set us back a year, but would not destroy our dreams.

I had to do something to reverse the doomsday attitude that existed around the program. So I called a press conference and announced my vision for where we were going.

I knew I'd better send a clear message that we had great confidence we could bring this team to national prominence in a short period of time. To the surprise of all, I said we were going to win a national championship in five years, knowing and recognizing that if we made a run at it, I'd get another contract. If we didn't do well, I'd get my ass fired anyway and they'd go to Division 1-AA.

That bold declaration of championship aspirations set the stage for everything that unfolded over the years.

Once we got that message out at the press conference, we couldn't leave it there. We had to sing it from the roofs of buildings, from the steeples of churches and from the mountain tops. I told every prospective assistant coach and every recruit our goal was to win the national championship and I believed we could do it. If I could attract coaches who believed in themselves, if they believed in the principles I laid out, and if they hooked their careers to that goal, it was possible. If they would go out and pass the same feeling to the players, it would be contagious and it could all happen.

I unveiled plans for a $4.8 million, 42,000-seat stadium on campus. The dream was as old as a drawing in the 1934 yearbook envisioning students walking to a football stadium. We spent $150,000 on feasibility studies and 18 months of energy trying to sell the idea before getting knocked down on the priority list for a couple of years by President Edward Thaddeus "Tad" Foote. Instead of seeing the excitement we could generate, he feared a campaign to build a stadium would negatively impact other university fundraising. He didn't revisit the idea until we had put up four winning seasons.

TAKING INVENTORY AND BUILDING ON SABAN'S FOUNDATION

I was coming in after Lou Saban. He was a heck of a pro and college coach who went on to Army. He really began the Miami turnaround. It would not have been possible to deliver on my promises in five years if he had not accomplished as much as he did in his two years.

Lou Saban did a wrecking job and a construction job in Miami. He'd broken every NCAA rule and left me a giant NCAA headache that resulted in the only sanctions ever against one of my teams. But he attracted some highly talented people. Jim Burt, the best defensive player ever on one of my teams, was already there when I arrived. I thank God that a couple of future professionals, Fred Marion and Lester Williams, were also on board to form a solid defensive nucleus.

Jim Kelly was there to build an offense around, and he had already been red-shirted by Saban. Boy was Kelly good. Like Namath and Gabriel and Bert Jones. That good.

Saban also left me the core of a quality coaching staff. Building a staff is always a challenge for a new head coach, and it has to be done in a hurry. Your first thought is to get rid of everyone and build your own team, but as I looked at Saban's staff, there was no need to clean house. They were 6-5 the year before, and they had recruited a lot of good players. Their defense was awesome, so I decided to keep pretty much the entire defensive staff.

I made Rick Lantz my defensive coordinator. He had been the Hurricanes linebacker coach for two years but had previously served as a coordinator and helped improve the defenses at Navy and the University of Buffalo. He eventually left us to join the Patriots and then became a head coach for an NFL Europe team.

Harold Allen had been with the Canes for 15 years and coached the defensive line. He went to high school in Florida, played at Miami and had produced NFL talent as a college coach.

Len Fontes would stay on for a third year and manage the defensive backs for me. He played that position for Ohio State's 1957 national championship team and had success coaching at the University of Dayton and at Navy.

Former Hurricane defensive back Mike Archer also came on board for his first full-time coaching position and started out helping in the backfield. He tells the tale that he was at a coaching conference in San Francisco when I was hired. He says I told him if he wanted a job to get his ass back to Miami fast. He took the red-eye and had his first job on the way to becoming a head coach at LSU.

Arnie Romero, a native Floridian who played at the University of Tampa, agreed to stay on and coach the defensive ends for a fifth straight year.

Bill Trout, who was a standout defensive lineman at Miami a decade earlier, was entering his fourth season teaching his position.

I was coming in after serving as offensive coordinator for the Dolphins, so I wouldn't have any trouble with anyone second guessing what I wanted to do on that side of the ball. I was planning to put in a pro-style offense, but it would take a mostly new offensive staff and two years to complete the conversion.

I got lucky when they made a head coaching change at the University of Florida. The transition from Doug Dickey to Charley Pell left a former Gator captain, Kim Helton, out of work. I needed an offensive line coach and Helton was a good one who was crushed when Pell let him go. I not only got a pissed off Gator to help in our annual matchups with the Gainesville gang but I landed a loyal coach and I found my offensive coordinator. The offensive line is a good place to be situated and run the offense, although it can be difficult for the quarterback coach to accept.

There was no need to clean house when I took over at the University of Miami because Lou Saban had a quality staff. In this staff photo I am kneeling in the center with Rick Lantz to my right and Kim Helton. Standing from left to right are: Earl Morrall, Hubbard Alexander, Larry Seiple, Lenny Fontes, Arnie Romero, Bill Trout, Mike Archer, Joe Brodsky, Harold Allen, Ron Sbrissa

Of course, I served as coordinator from the line at Alabama and I knew it would work with Kim. Kim would go on to an NFL career and later become head coach at the University of Houston.

We turned the offensive backfield over to two long-time high school coaches from the area who gave us obvious recruiting advantages. Joe Brodsky was a native who coached at Miami Jackson and Hialeah-Miami Lakes. He was with Saban for one year and would later coach with the Dallas Cowboys. I offered Ron Sbrissa his first full-time coaching position with the offensive backs. He had been a Hurricane volunteer coach for two years and head coach at Miami Central High School.

I brought in Hubbard "Axe" Alexander from Vanderbilt to coach my tight ends. He later moved into pro ball.

Two more future NFL coaches, Gary Stevens and Tom Olivadotti, would join us in a year and play keys roles in our success.

I also cashed in right away on two Dolphin connections to complete my new coaching team.

I gave Larry Seiple his first coaching job. He handled all the punting in 11 seasons with the Dolphins and caught 41 passes as a receiver one year. I put him in charge of my punters and wide receivers.

And in my coup de grace, I talked Earl Morrall into serving as a part-time quarterback coach. That was obviously a key step in developing Jim Kelly and the strong quarterback tradition at the U. A tradition that would stretch through my recruits, Bernie Kosar and Vinny Testaverde, and beyond to include Steve Walsh, Craig Erickson, Gino Torretta and Ken Dorsey.

It takes time to fully develop a quarterback. My offense was similar to what the pro teams use. We ask our quarterbacks to learn the whole package, from getting us into the right blocking schemes, to reading defenses and coverages, to calling audibles, running the no-huddle offense, as well as making the pinpoint, precision passes that are required to really make this system work.

In the NFL it normally took three to five years to fully develop a quarterback. In college football it takes two to three years to school a quarterback to the point where he can control and manage a game. It's easier if all you want your quarterback to do is hand the ball off 27 different ways and you have a prescribed receiver on pass plays. In our system, quarterbacks need to know how to do much more. They have to make decisions constantly, get us out of bad plays and into better ones, think on the run and then throw it precisely to the right man. That's hard to do with years of experience, let alone with only a few weeks of training.

I had a different idea of how a quarterback coach's job should be done. I wanted someone to be more of a personal coach for the leader of the offense. This coach didn't need to spend time worrying about game strategy or recruiting. I wanted him to be more like a golf coach, focused on technique and the quarterback's judgment.

I wanted him to be in the huddle during practice. To see how the play is called; to be evaluating the quarterback's communication. Is he enunciating? Who is he looking at? Can he chew someone out in there? How does he break the huddle? Does he speak loud enough? Does he do it with enthusiasm? How does he approach the line of scrimmage? When he gets to the line, what is the first thing he looks at? Does he look at the same thing every time? Who does he key? Does he receive the ball correctly or is there trouble getting the snap? If we're in the shotgun, does he look at the ball? Once he has the ball in his hands, where are his eyes? Is he picking out his first receiver? Is he back the proper distance?

If the quarterback is standing 7 yards behind center on the play, I want my quarterback coach 3 yards behind him. You know what the play is, you know what his first option is, his second choice and his third choice. You turn the same as he does. He has a stripe on the back of his helmet. You can see the stripe and you can see the arm. When he turns, you are looking over his shoulder and you see everything he sees. You want to know if he is making the right decisions. Is he coming off the first receiver too quickly? If the read is the first receiver is open, does he pop it? If that man is covered, does he move to the second receiver? If he's covered, does the quarterback move on to the third option?

I had coached Earl Morrall for three years with the Dolphins and he did the little things right. We had a general meeting and he seemed to know exactly what I wanted. He did all of the above, and after practice he would meet with the quarterbacks and build their confidence.

We were going to run a pro offense and prepare talented people to go on to the NFL. I was already known for the quarterbacks I had worked with during my career. With Morrall on board, Quarterback U was open for business and the signal callers were in great hands.

It would take most of the 1979 season, though, before the first valedictorian of the new academy would take his place at the head of the class.

In the spring I announced that for disciplinary reasons I was not renewing the scholarship of quarterback Kenny McMillian, who was at the top of the depth chart. That set up a healthy competition between two sophomores, Mike Rodrigue and Mark Richt, and red-shirt freshman Jim Kelly. Richt had thrown a touchdown pass in each of his first two games but missed the rest of his freshman season with an injury. Rodrigue started three games late in the same year.

We opened the season with an offense I called the pro veer. It was really just the option-oriented veer that Saban had used with a few more passing opportunities mixed in. I wanted to use schemes and terminology that were familiar to the players to ease the transition.

Rodrigue, at 6 feet and 180 pounds out of Tallahassee, was the most comfortable of the three running the option, and we decided to start the season with him at quarterback. Kelly, at 6'3" and 205 pounds, won the backup role, and Richt ended up taking a red-shirt year.

We won three games at home and lost the same number on the road to begin the season. Rodrigue was completing less than half his passes and had only two touchdowns through the air.

Kelly was showing me plenty in scrimmages and more when we started to ease him into games. It was my practice to give the backup two sets of downs behind center in the second quarter of games. I'll never understand why that is not a widespread practice. I'm not talking about creating quarterback controversies or rotations. This is about having someone else ready to go in with the first team when needed.

In week seven, Kelly showed us he might be ready to step up. He led us downfield in the fourth quarter and threw a 39-yard scoring pass to Pat Walker in a 25-15 loss at Syracuse.

We were about to play a ranked Joe Paterno team at Penn State's newly expanded Beaver Stadium. I had an inspired idea to throw a coming out party for Kelly in Happy Valley.

Kelly grew up in the same western Pennsylvania region that produced Unitas, Namath and Joe Montana. Jim was another legend from quarterback country. He threw for 44 touchdowns and almost 4,000 yards in high school and his East Brady team was undefeated in his last two seasons. Kelly wanted to attend Penn State, but when Joe Paterno talked to him about becoming a linebacker, he decided to play for Miami.

Our offense had been struggling, and we needed to give Penn State a new look. Kelly needed an opportunity to show Paterno he had misjudged a natural quarterback.

We came into the televised game as 19-point underdogs. We brought an 82-man squad that featured 53 freshmen and sophomores. We had yet to win on the road, and we still hadn't captured the attention of South Florida football fans.

I didn't tell anybody about the switch to Kelly until four hours before kickoff when we were at the pregame meal. I thought that way Kelly wouldn't be nervous about it. Well, after we ate, Kelly walked to the bathroom and threw up. When I was told about that, I wondered what I had done. I didn't learn until later that he had done the same thing in high school before games. It was like a pregame ritual that stayed with him even in the NFL.

Photo courtesy of the University of Miami

November 3, 1979. That's the day that should go down in history as when we turned the Miami program around in front of 77,532 crestfallen folks all clad in blue and white.

We had Kelly drop back and throw on almost every down. He had us out front 10-0 before Penn State could run a play. Kelly led us down field on the opening drive throwing mostly three-step passes, whether it was an out, a slant or a curl. He got us into the end zone with an 8-yard pass to Jim Joyner. We stayed on offense when

Jim Kelly helped me turn around the University of Miami. He was a talented and confident young quarterback who led us to an upset of Penn State in his first start in 1979 and took us to our first bowl game in 1980.

a pooch kick bounced back to us and we recovered it. We converted that into a quick field goal.

We led 13-10 at the half and then shut them out the rest of the way to win 26-10. Linebacker Scott Nicolas had 26 tackles and defensive end Tim Flanagan added 25 more to lead the defensive effort.

Kelly gave us the offensive energy we had been lacking. He was the most important player in what turned out to be the pivotal game in Miami history. He completed 18 of 30 passes for 280 yards and three touchdowns. Joyner would catch six of those passes for 177 yards and two of the touchdowns.

Our hometown fans, watching on television, saw a flicker of the Miami football future, but we wouldn't be able to repeat the magic right away.

We had the defending national champion Alabama team in the wings and then Notre Dame waiting. We were going to have to face both of them without our new air attack because bruised ribs would keep Kelly from contributing much for a couple of weeks.

We would go into Tuscaloosa and play Bryant while he was on his way to another undefeated season and a sixth national championship.

Coming off our win before that big crowd in Happy Valley, I was actually disappointed we were playing in the smaller Tuscaloosa stadium instead of what was then Alabama's larger venue, Legion Field in Birmingham. They still managed to pack in more than 50,000 fans.

I had been with Coach Bryant for his first three championships at Alabama, but I never wanted to be seen as simply the reincarnation of Bear Bryant. I understood his depth and his graciousness. Now, as I faced him across the field for the first and only time, I was committed to the more formal dress that he favored.

I found that sideline style, something I am always asked about, during Kelly's coming out party. That was a miserably cold day. We borrowed some capes from the Dolphins because we didn't have any foul weather gear of our own. I knew I was going to freeze, and I decided to wear a leather car coat that stretched to my knees. It had a sheepskin lining and it was very distinctive. Once we won the game, the outfit was almost a good luck charm. I wore suits from that day forward.

I realized my clothing made a statement. In a golf shirt and coach's pants you blend into the crowd. You look like one of the troops instead of the commander in chief. Dressed as I was that day, I commanded more respect. The referees could see me better. The team captains could spot me.

I wanted to look good, and I have never been fond of logo clothes. Until recent times, a coach wore a suit, a tie and a fedora. They didn't do much coaching during the game; they were more like academic supervisors. I decided I would be honoring the greats like Bryant and General Robert Neyland if I dressed up. Stick a pipe in my mouth and I could be General Douglas MacArthur.

We went in at halftime trailing 10-0, and I thought we had Alabama right where we wanted them. We were in the contest most of the day, but we couldn't muster any offense. We finished with 84 yards rushing and 47 more through the air. The Tide had 444 yards total offense using the triple option attack that had helped Bryant reinvent himself near the end of his career. They used two fourth quarter scores to humble us 30-0.

Kelly would return to help us beat Florida 30-24 in the final game of the season. Kelly was 10 of 17 for 165 yards against the Gators. He ran for one touchdown and passed for another as we finished undefeated in the Orange Bowl.

We had enjoyed only four contests at home all year. We played seven road games and traveled 28,000 miles, further than any college team in history. Even with a 5-6 record we had shown enough spunk with a very young squad that was learning fast. All but two starters would return.

With Kelly at the helm, passing records and winning seasons would follow immediately. I was confident enough that I quickly announced a bowl was the goal for the 1980 season.

WINNING THE RECRUITING WARS IN THE STATE OF MIAMI

With our first season in the books, I went back to work on campus, in the community and on the recruiting trail.

Recruiting is where I had the most help because the coaching staff lived that life with me. We really had just six weeks to recruit when I arrived the previous winter. We didn't have much of a chance to change direction, so we scattered to Ohio and Pennsylvania and New Jersey. The best we could do was try to close the deals we had been working.

We were sitting in the middle of a fertile football recruiting ground. We would always have to compete hard with Florida and Florida State for South Florida athletes, but carpetbag coaches were making annual treks to South Florida as well. They loved to come down in the winter, spend a week, visit a few schools and take home a few athletes to justify the trip. Every school seemed to come down and take one or two of our top athletes back north.

I knew we could blanket the area, build relationships and attract the best local players if we gave them a chance to play big-time football here at home in front of their friends and family. We would still recruit out-of-state athletes who wanted to play in the Sunshine State, but we would have a foundation of local talent to build on.

It worked out just the way I wanted my second time around. We signed 15 local players, including a defensive stalwart, linebacker Jack Fernandez out of Miami Springs. The group also featured two future starters on the offensive line, David Heffernan of Columbus High School and Juan Comendeiro from South Miami High.

Before we changed the recruiting dynamic, people said Florida got the blue chips, Florida State got the gold chips and Miami got the cow chips. No more. Now we would get the best players from I-4 south. I started to call that area the State of Miami.

We also landed two prep All-America running backs that would increase our offensive firepower. One locally and one from Ohio.

Robert "Speedy" Neal out of Key West was one of the early commitments from the home territory. He led all South Florida runners with 1,606 rushing yards his senior season in high school and shredded the local record books in numerous categories. At 6'3" and 240 pounds he was a Csonka-like runner with serious power.

Keith Griffin had an equally stellar high school career in Columbus, Ohio. He was the brother of the two-time Heisman Trophy winner Archie Griffin. Neal had the nickname, but Griffin came to us with 4.4 speed over 40 yards. Both would contribute immediately and help us for four years.

This was an impressive start, but the pace of signing local talent would accelerate with each successive year. For the 1982 season we brought in a total of 22 local scholarship athletes, including wide receiver Stanley Shakespeare from Lake Worth, defensive back Kenny Calhoun out of

Titusville and linebacker Ken Sisk from Miami Southwest High School. We also signed two big defensive linemen, Willie Lee Broughton, 6'5", 235, from Fort Pierce and 6'4", 220-pound Joe Kohlbrand out of Merritt Island.

Our roster for the Orange Bowl at the end of the 1983 season would include 86 players, 64 from Florida.

The first two years at Miami we had budgetary restraints that were unreal. A memo would come down in March or April that our budget was exhausted and spending was frozen. We couldn't make a long-distance phone call or buy a pen.

That wasn't the inspiration for my State of Miami recruiting plan, but the local emphasis did save some money. My coaches could visit most of our targeted high school players and drive home in one day.

Most coaches focus only on the football side. They worry about the team's performance on the field instead of the whole product. With five years to right this ship, I felt I needed to do more to market the program.

We had a long way to go to get where I wanted us to be. We needed to draw some attention to ourselves, so when the networks approached me, I allowed them to take their cameras into our locker room before games and at halftime. This was long before that became commonplace. I also agreed to wear a microphone on the sideline to give viewers more insight.

The broadcasters loved it and they kept coming back. The team had been on network television only once in the previous five seasons. They would carry 14 of our games over my five years and we would win 12 of them. Five times we would be carried nationwide in primetime and we would win all five games. In one of those nationally televised games we played Notre Dame, and we staged a spectacular halftime show after the network agreed to televise several minutes of it to give the university and the city some much-needed positive exposure.

I also managed to get a young businessman, Roy Hamlin, to do promotions work on a commission basis. I actually sold him the right to promote us. He paid us $2,500 upfront, and he had to cover his own expenses. We agreed he would keep the first $27,500 he brought in and then we would split anything up to $100,000 on an equal basis. After $100,000 he could keep 30 percent and the school would get 70 percent.

Our little experiment with the free enterprise system proved a great success. An independent television station was carrying our games without payment to the school. Hamlin started selling our media rights and collecting as much as $50,000 a game.

An agency had already come up with the colorful new U logo. Too many teams had a UM brand so they wanted to use just the U. They split the U—that's what sets it of—and they made it striking with the school colors. Nobody seemed to like it at first. I was inundated with people wanting to get rid of it. They wanted me to take the bullet and say I didn't like the U.

I told people we should keep it because there was not a lot of tradition at the school anyway. I told the old Miammah crowd we would make the logo known and instantly recognizable.

Today the U is everywhere and fans proudly flash the symbol with their thumbs and forefingers. The Texas Longhorns have the only thing that comes close. But being known as the U in the world of higher education is like being a big enough star to use just your first name on a marquee.

Hamlin put the colorful U on shirts and every other kind of merchandise. Before he started pushing the brand, you needed Lewis and Clark to help you find Hurricane items around town. The bookstore deep on campus was practically the only place with our gear. They had a few things tucked away back near the men's room.

Within five years, sales of Miami-branded items would climb from the bottom tier to second best in the country.

The administration was never involved, other than to accept the ever-increasing royalty checks. And they never said thank you.

They stood by and we established new ticket prices. We changed our game times. Hamlin generated a promotional film, *The Road to the National Championship*, long before that goal was accomplished.

As Miami fragmented into a city of subcultures, the university became more insulated. Few residents—particularly those transplanted from the Northeast or from Cuba—identified with or cared about the school. We were going to have to get out in the community to change that.

These were not good times in the city of Miami. We were reeling from race riots that took place in May 1980 in the black neighborhoods of Overtown and Liberty City. The trouble surfaced after four white police officers were acquitted on manslaughter charges in the death of a black man they tried to arrest after a high-speed chase. The medical examiner described the victim's injuries as some of the worst he had ever seen.

The verdict lit the fuse, but the problems had been simmering for a while. Liberty City had been the cultural center of the minority community for decades, but it was in decline and further impoverished when I-95 was built through the heart of it. Today Liberty City is known among young people as the location of Grand Theft Auto, a violent video game featuring robberies and murders. But it is a real place and it was a troubled place in the national spotlight after the riots.

TIME magazine suggested that the picture postcards of a perfect aquamarine city were now relics of a paradise lost. The magazine highlighted an epidemic of violent crime, a plague of illicit drugs and a tidal wave of refugees from Cuba and Haiti that threatened the area with the destructive power of a hurricane.

The city and the university had the same last name. What was good for the U would be good for the community, and what was good for the community would be good for the U. So we got more involved.

The city needed as much help as the university. The football program was capable of giving both of them a lift.

To get where we planned to go as a program, we needed more fannies in the seats and more financial support from the community. They weren't coming to us so we had to go to them.

Even before I had coached a single game I had accepted more than 200 local speaking engagements the first year. Now Hamlin had me before groups all across the southern half of the state. And it was clear we needed everybody to be involved in our efforts.

Our players and coaches ran 231 miles handing off a football all the way from Cape Canaveral to Miami. No one ever dropped the ball. We were sent off by a team of astronauts and arrived to live television coverage at the Fontainebleau hotel. We generated publicity and excitement for the team but also raised $44,000 for the Dade County Easter Seals campaign.

With heavy involvement from the players, we started a program to encourage academic excellence. We worked with Gov. Bob Graham on a program called "Hit the Books and Make the Grades." Players told their stories and highlighted the importance of staying in school and studying. We reached nearly every kid in Dade County. If they took our challenge and passed enough classes, we gave them tickets to a game in the Orange Bowl.

We reached out to the Spanish-speaking community with a radio broadcast and billboards. We attracted a small core of players from the Cuban community and then established a regular presence there.

I agreed to co-chair the Partners for Youth. We met with key community leaders every week to try to bring the fractured community together. We managed to raise more than $1 million to help low-income kids become involved in the arts and athletics. We gave direct assistance to more than 150,000 kids via summer jobs, as well as year-round cultural and recreational programs. We would eventually bring 5,000 Partners for Youth children to every Miami home game.

The first time we invited our young guests to the Orange Bowl, we put them in the upper deck. After the patrons below were bombarded with everything possible, we moved the group to the lower level.

We formed a "Cheer-ring" with local high school cheerleaders and bands to fill more empty sections of the Orange Bowl.

After playing at Southern Miss and enduring the "cowbells" that disrupted our play-calling, we provided our fans with our own noise-making "crickets."

We added a coach's radio program and a Hurricanes kick-off television show hosted by Chris Myers before he moved to ESPN.

The game day atmosphere improved steadily. The hard work in the community helped. Winning sealed the deal.

Paid attendance climbed. Gone forever were the days where players could look up into the stands and find their mother and father and uncle. We were starting to get a crowd, even if the visiting team didn't have a large alumni following in South Florida.

Paid attendance rose from an average of 26,066 in 1979 to 39,851 in 1981 and 44,555 a game by 1983. That was enough to revive serious talk of building a stadium on campus.

PRACTICING LIKE PROFESSIONALS

On the practice field we preached mental toughness. Practice perfect was the message. We had to have a well-trained army. That meant drilling the soldiers over and over again, long after they thought they had mastered a technique, until it was so natural to them they didn't have to think about it anymore.

We planned out each practice. Each exercise had a purpose. They were designed to produce either a physical or mental edge. We introduced more scrimmages and fewer equipment drills. Football players don't block a sled in a game, and it didn't make much sense to block one in practice.

We were teaching pro techniques and strategy. We were in competition with the Dolphins for the sports dollar but we worked together, too. My coaches would talk to the Dolphins staff about their approach and go to their camp in the off season to study. My players would go over and watch the Dolphins practice.

The college game was evolving into a junior version of professional football, and I didn't have any problem with that on the field. The basic mission of any team is to become the absolute best team that it can be. If we can do that, the victories will come. Following the same path as the professionals gave the team confidence.

This team was going to succeed because they practiced as hard as they could and kept going when I asked for 20 percent more. They knew why we had grueling workouts and pushed them past human exhaustion. They understood why we did our drills and why we did things over as many times as it took until we got it right. They developed the mental toughness we wanted and dug in when I insisted we wouldn't stop practicing until we ran 10 perfect plays at the close.

They mastered the techniques we were teaching. They paid attention when we talked about getting in the right position and pushing off on the correct foot, making sure the first step was six inches and not 12 so they could make the necessary adjustments as plays developed.

The team worked like hell in every practice, during every period of every practice, on every play of every period. If you are not improving, you are standing still or falling back. We had every player working on one or two things they needed to do to improve at their position. They needed to get a little better on every play. I told them if they did that on 65 snaps every practice every week, they would be ready when we played for a championship.

We practiced in all conditions. We drilled in the heat. Scrimmaged in the mud. Even practiced at midnight. We put them in every situation they could face in a game. If they were in a long drive late in the game, they were ready for that. They had already done it in practice.

If the sun was shining but the forecast for Saturday called for rain, we did wet ball drills. My crew would haul trash cans to the field, fill them with water and let us bob for wet practice balls. Every snap, every handoff, every ball thrown and every pass caught needed to be experienced with a wet ball.

Everyone needed to pay attention to detail. We had a plan and they had to follow it. Not everyone liked our 11 p.m. curfew but we needed discipline. If one of our players broke a team rule away from the field, we invited them to a 5 a.m. workout we called the breakfast club. Your position coach had to attend with you, and no one wanted to share that punishment with their coach.

We got everyone ready to play. We had a scrimmage each week that we called the "toilet bowl." We billed it as a bowl game to give it a little prestige. We kept score to show it was important. We named a player of the game. We demanded game day concentration and execution. Everyone got experience. During the season, the backups got most of the repetitions. If starters got hurt, their replacements had some experience.

We had the high calling to bring the University of Miami to national prominence. If I had anything to say about it, we were going to be ready. We were going to be the team in the best physical shape, the squad with the best technique and the greatest discipline on the field every Saturday of the season.

We were setting our goals very high and asking people to commit to them. My equipment supervisor, Rocky Rumenik, helped me crystalize the message. He gave me a picture of an oak tree with the words "To believe is to be strong" stamped on it.

I framed the picture, hung it on the wall and adopted those words as one of my motivating catch phrases. I repeated it until people internalized it. Eventually we would print those words on shirts and make it our team mantra.

A bowl was the announced goal in 1980, and Kelly believed enough in what we were doing to lead us there. Along the way he helped us win the state championship by beating both Florida and Florida State for the first time since 1962. That prompted me to create a flag declaring us state champions. That banner was huge in the recruiting world as I was redefining it.

Florida State came south boasting a 19-game regular season winning streak. They were ranked ninth in the country. Both of us were 3-0. The

Orange Bowl was buzzing with a crowd of over 55,000. The showdown would mark the first time we outdrew the Dolphins when both of us played at home the same weekend.

The game played out in electrifying fashion. It showcased our defensive captain and noseguard, Jim Burt. He forever defined excellence at that position with his play that day. Burt harassed the FSU centers enough to force 10 botched snaps. FSU fumbled away the ball on five of those plays. Burt had nine tackles in the game and saved his best moment for last.

We managed to get on top 10-3 after Kelly ran it in from 1 yard out in the second quarter. FSU pulled to within 10-9 with 39 seconds left. Bobby Bowden decided to go for the win. Facing Burt and a defense that had given up just 25 yards rushing all day, Seminoles quarterback Rick Stockstill dropped back to throw again. Burt shoved a lineman aside, leaped over a blocking back and batted away the pass.

Unsaddling the Seminoles gave us our best start since 1954 and vaulted us to 13th in the AP poll.

Florida State coach Bobby Bowden and I always put on a show in the press conference before our annual matches. We competed ferociously but we were friends and allies with a shared adversary in the University of Florida.

We weren't quite ready for our turn in the spotlight. We responded by losing three straight to high level competition. We lost on the road to highly ranked Notre Dame and Penn State teams. We were in both games until giving up late touchdowns. We fell 34-31 at home against a Mississippi State team that left town 5-2 for the season.

We had a week off and a chance to regroup. I met with my team captains, Jim Burt and Art Kehoe, at 6:30 a.m. on the Sunday of the off week. I needed to check the pulse of the team and understand what the players were thinking. They assured me the team's spirit was not broken by the losses. Everyone still had a positive mindset.

The regular season played out in three acts. After a 4-0 start and then three losses we would close out the year with another 4-0 stretch. The big third act set us up to accomplish our announced goal, but because of the mid-season slump, we had to work extra hard for it.

When bowl invitations started to go out, we were 6-3 with two more games to play. A 5-4 Houston team that we had already beaten managed to get invited to play Oklahoma in the Sun Bowl. We were a better team, and we posted our record against a schedule ranked second toughest in the nation.

I called a strategy session in my office. The Peach Bowl in Atlanta still needed an opponent for Virginia Tech so I called organizers to make my pitch directly. I told them it would be a mistake to overlook us because we were one of the best teams in the country. They eventually said we were on the list of possible teams along with Stanford, Indiana, Louisiana State and Kansas. I asked Coach Bryant and Namath to make calls to urge them to give us the spot.

We sent a delegation that included Athletic Director Harry Mallios and my administrative assistant, Billy Proulx, to Atlanta. They pointed out that we played a tougher schedule and had a better record than the competition. To allay any fears that we couldn't deliver a fan base, we pledged to sell 10,000 tickets to the game

A bowl was the goal and now we were close. We were not going to wait quietly for an answer. It really was too important to building momentum for the program. Too important to proving that the goals we were setting were achievable and were within our control. Too important to our dream of a national championship down the line.

We asked for a show of fan support. Businesses donated $5,000 for tickets to be donated to youth groups to pump up attendance at our final home game. One alumnus sent a $5,000 check to the Peach Bowl for tickets if Miami was in the game. Another supporter rented a plane to fly around Atlanta towing a sign urging the bowl committee to choose Miami. We had people bring canned peaches to the Orange Bowl. We gave the produce to the Lions Club to distribute to the poor. When Peach Bowl officials came to town they were greeted by a huge welcome sign and the message that we wanted the Peach Bowl bid. I asked for help impressing the committee and alumni made sure visiting bowl officials flew first class and stayed in hotel suites. We prepared Miami jerseys with their names across the back.

All of that certainly helped, but the question was really settled on the football field. Stanford, Indiana and Kansas all lost. Our club did its part with a 26-8 win over North Texas State. After the game, the head of the selection committee made the announcement to the team in our locker room. The players chanted "Peach, Peach, Peach" in response. Music to my ears.

There was still a little business to be done, though, on the way to our New Year's weekend in Atlanta.

There would be a stop in Gainesville along the way. With the early win against Florida State in the bank, we needed to knock off the Gators to claim the state championship. We did just that, dominating them all day.

They scored on their opening drive but nevermore. We answered immediately as Kelly threw for 61 yards in our first trip down the field. Wide out Jim Joiner hauled in a 15-yard pass to even the score. Linebacker Scott Nicholas, who broke the Miami career tackle record that year, intercepted Wayne Peace on the next Florida drive and the rout was on.

We were leading 28-7 late and the locals were none too happy with the new kings of the hill. They retaliated by pelting us with citrus, including tangerines, apparently brought to the stadium in celebration of their upcoming trip to a lesser bowl by that name. We learned later that students cored the fruit, filled it with liquor and froze it before taking it to the game. Once they drained their refreshment, they had cannonball-size refuse that they used like artillery as the game wound down. One of my assistants, Christ Vagotis, was struck in the head and knocked out.

We were not going to accept abuse like that from the crowd. If they wanted to act that way, we could show them how we felt about it on the field. Rather than let the final seconds run off the clock, I sent Danny Miller out to kick a 25-yard field goal on the final play. Tacking on three more points made it 31-7 and gave us our most lopsided victory in the history of the series. And a little bit of swagger.

We made enough noise about the unruly behavior that the president of the University of Florida moved his students out of the sections behind the visiting bench and into the end zone.

We were back in the Associated Press Top 20 and headed to a bowl game for the first time since 1967 and for only the fifth time in school history. We had piled up more yards on offense and scored more points than any team in school history. The records wouldn't last long. They were a new baseline.

As we stepped onto the national stage in the Peach Bowl, Kelly repeated what he did for us so often; he staked us to an early lead. He drove us 68 yards on his first opportunity and connected for 15 yards to a frequent target, Larry Brodsky, for the first score. Brodsky, who had 33 receptions on the year, caught four passes in the game for 80 yards. The clincher, though, was a 99-yard drive that ate up clock and moved us into the second quarter. It ended with a 12-yard draw play to fullback Chris Hobbs that put us ahead 14-0. Safety Fred Marion deflated Virginia Tech and set up that long drive with his seventh interception of the season, this one at the 1-yard line as the Hokies tried to answer Kelly. They would close to 14-10 in the second half, but Dan Miller booted field goals of 31 and 37 yards to give us the final 20-10 margin of victory.

With the benefit of a nationally televised victory, our check for a much-needed $330,000 and the Peach Bowl trophy in my grasp, I made it clear to all what the season and the game meant to the U.

"This is as good a place as any to stop and rest on our journey to the national championship," I said. "What we have to figure out now is whether we have a chance right away—next year—or whether we will need, well, intermediate steps."

We were running well ahead of my five-year vision. But we would have to suffer another refrain of "Ya Got Trouble" first.

NEARLY PERFECT BUT BOWL INELIGIBLE

The NCAA troubles manifested during our turnaround season. The NCAA announced by letter that they were starting an investigation. They had good reason to do so. The school hired counsel and I started making plans to deal with it.

When I first heard about the allegations, I got on the phone and called Doug Dickey. He had been head coach at Florida and was then the Athletic Director at the University of Tennessee. Dickey said, "You're damn right, we reported you." I told him if he ever found me or any of my guys doing something wrong, he should call me directly and I would do him the same favor. He said yes to that, but made it clear he wasn't going to withdraw charges against us for what happened under Saban.

With the NCAA letter in hand, I met with the team and informed them of the allegations dating back to 1976. It amounted to a lack of institutional control. The players deserved to know what was going on, but I asked them not to tell anyone, not their mothers, their dads or their girlfriends. We still had a signing period to get through and even with a reduced number of scholarships in the future we were going to continue to move forward. We decided to fortify the roster with as many walk-on players as we could convince to join us and who could get into school.

The sanctions were announced after the first game of the 1981 season. We were ruled ineligible for a bowl game that year, even though we fielded what may have been the best team I had in my time at Miami.

We played the toughest schedule in the country. We faced eight bowl teams from the previous season: Florida, Florida State, Houston, Texas, Mississippi State, Penn State, Virginia Tech and Notre Dame.

We finished 9-2 and ranked eighth in the nation. We were two touchdowns shy of being perfect.

We opened at home against Florida and came from behind in the fourth quarter to win 20-18. Danny Miller booted a 55-yard field goal with 40 seconds left. The kick caromed off the left upright and went through. A rainbow appeared on the horizon like a sign from the heavens. All was well.

Kelly didn't miss any serious time, and he was back at the helm when Penn State came into town undefeated and ranked No. 1 in the country in late October. With three Miller field goals and an 80-yard completion from Kelly to Larry Brodsky in the first half, we raced out to a 17-0 lead and held on at 17-14.

Without a chance to play in a bowl, we had to settle for another state championship. We completed this one with a 27-19 win over Florida State at their place.

We also got to relive our Peach Bowl matchup when Virginia Tech came to town in November. Kelly still had their number, going 20-27 for 209 yards and two touchdowns.

Kelly was spectacular all season, amassing 2,403 passing yards while completing 168 of 285 passes. Brodsky was his leading receiver again, catching 37 passes for 631 yards. Kelly would set the career record for passing yards at Miami. Brodsky would graduate with the career record for yardage as a receiver.

The only stumbles for the team were near misses on the road against Texas and Mississippi State.

Now we had everyone's attention. Back-to-back seasons with nine wins and a national ranking established our football chops. Our involvement in the community and the intensive efforts to recruit local athletes was helping to build the fan base.

Photo courtesy of University of Miami Athletics

Marc Trestman replaced Earl Morrall as my quarterback guru in 1982. He tutored Bernie Kosar and Vinny Testaverde and helped me establish Miami as Quarterback U. He became head coach of the Chicago Bears in 2013.

Kelly had one more year of eligibility, but Quarterback U was headed into transition. We were going to add important new faculty and students.

The staff help came our way when my defensive back coach, Mike Archer, met a Miami law student by the pool in their apartment complex and struck up a conversation. That was in the fall of 1981. Marc Trestman was a former Minnesota Gopher, who had been a backup to Tony Dungy at quarterback and then played briefly in the NFL as a defensive back.

At the time we were allowed to have eight full-time coaches, four part-time assistants and one volunteer coach. Archer told Trestman about our opening for a volunteer assistant coach and Marc was intrigued enough to come in to speak with me about the job.

Realizing he was a law student, the first thing I asked him was if his real goal was to develop relationships with the players and then use that to become a sports agent after law school. He convinced me that was not the case but that he just loved football and wanted to be around it.

Trestman started with us in the spring of 1982. He would graduate from law school a year later, just as the NCAA allowed teams to add a ninth full-time coach and the volunteer position was eliminated. Morrall wanted to remain part time. Trestman had an opportunity to join a major South Florida law firm, but he told me football was his career choice, so I brought him on board full time. As Kim Helton left for a job with the Tampa Bay Buccaneers, Trestman became an important partner to my new offensive coordinator Gary Stevens.

Trestman, of course, is the same guy who became head coach of the Chicago Bears in 2013. He put himself on that path by working with two new star pupils at Quarterback U: Bernie Kosar and Vinny Testaverde.

We didn't come by them by accident.

We had already recruited a top-rated local quarterback in Kyle Vanderwende. He was a three-sport star at 6'3" and 210 pounds. He had a strong arm and threw for over 1,600 yards and 11 touchdowns his senior season at Palm Beach Gardens High School.

When Kim Helton and I drove just up the road for a visit, we were happy to get Vanderwende to stay home. He was set to go to Indiana and would probably have started for Coach Lee Corso, but said he was turned off by the weather on a winter visit.

The Orange Bowl game that led to our national championship in 1983 was a bit of a family affair for me. My son Stuart played in the game. My son Stephen helped on the sidelines.

Beverlee bronzed the Italian half boots I wore on the sidelines for 12 seasons. Tucked into one of the shoes is a yellowing piece of paper on which my son, Stephen, chronicled my success in that period.

Paul Hornung, Paulie Miller and I have had many reunions over the years. Paul went to Flaget High School with me and then won the Heisman Trophy at Notre Dame. He gained further fame with the Green Bay Packers and as a television broadcaster. Coach Miller was our high school football and basketball coach. He was later elected Clerk of Courts. The three of us have remained friends through all these years.

ALABAMA CRIMSON TIDE
1961 NATIONAL CHAMPIONS
11-0

The 1961 Alabama team gave me my first taste of perfection. The squads were a little smaller and many players still played both offense and defense.

Photo courtesy of the Miami Dolphins

Our undefeated 1972 Dolphins team was invited to the White House by President Obama in 2013. The significance of our perfect season has grown over the years as it continues to stand unmatched. There is a tradition of inviting championship teams to the White House, but we never got an invitation during the Watergate turmoil. Coach Shula is seated on the right.

My three sons, Tim (next to me), Stuart and Stephen (sitting left to right) taken in the 1990s.

My son Tim at his 40th birthday party. Tim traveled the world as a model for Calvin Klein Obsession and then became a professional photographer.

My son Stephen in the prime of his life. We lost him at age 48 from a rare cancer of the endocrine glands, which required numerous surgeries over the years.

My son Stuart met his wife Suzie when my Miami Hurricanes participated in a fundraising campaign for Easter Seals. After my players and coaches ran a football from Cape Canaveral to Miami, Stuart sat down next to Suzie at a live telethon. The team raised $44,000 for the Dade County campaign and Stuart found a lifetime partner.

With our grandkids, Joey, Teather and Marcus

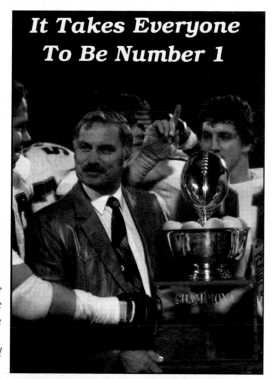

It Takes Everyone To Be Number 1

One of the mantras I used to inspire our national championship team at the University of Miami was the idea that it takes everyone to be No. 1. When we won it all, we memorialized the thought on posters.

Photo courtesy of University of Miami Athletics

Joe Namath addressed the Hurricanes squad in the locker room before the Orange Bowl game against Nebraska in 1983. I named Joe my special assistant in charge of upset and he delivered again.

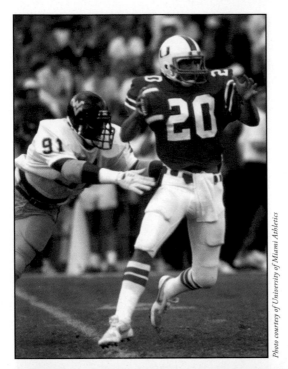

Photo courtesy of University of Miami Athletics

Bernie Kosar was one of the most cerebral players I ever coached. He led the Hurricanes to a national championship in his freshman year, was a first round pick of the Cleveland Browns and played 12 seasons in the NFL.

Photo courtesy of University of Miami Athletics

Jim Kelly (#12) and Albert Bentley (#16) were two very talented Hurricanes. Jim led us to the Peach Bowl in 1980 and then took the Buffalo Bills to four Super Bowls. Albert was still with us during our championship season and went on as a running back for the Colts and Steelers for eight years.

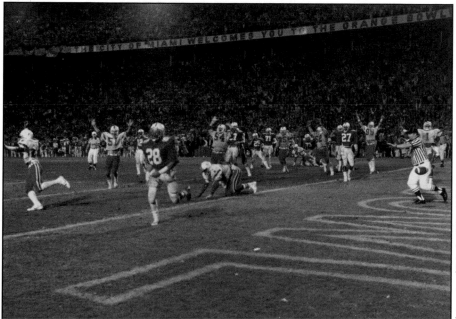

Photo courtesy of University of Miami Athletics

This was the pivotal two-point play at the end of the Orange Bowl game against Nebraska. Safety Kenny Calhoun dove and got one hand on the pass and the score stayed 31-30. A song called Hurricane Warning thundered from the stadium speakers and the celebration in Miami began.

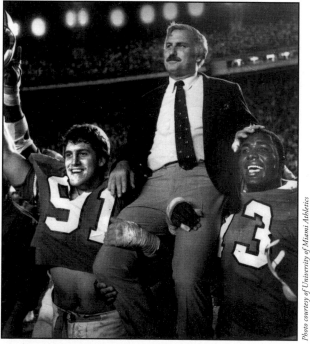

Photo courtesy of University of Miami Athletics

When we beat Notre Dame 37-15 in Miami in 1981, it was our first win over the Irish since 1960. That resulted in a celebratory ride off the field from Bob Nelson (#91) and Lester Williams (#73).

Photo courtesy of University of Miami Athletics

After I accepted the Orange Bowl trophy for our win over Nebraska, we had to wait almost 24 hours before learning the Associated Press rewarded us by naming the Hurricanes national champions.

Photo courtesy of University of Miami Athletics

After a ticker tape parade to celebrate our national championship, the Hurricanes were honored with a government proclamation and the presentation of keys to the city.

Boxing champion Muhammad Ali is a Louisville native, and he was a guest on the sidelines at many Cardinals games. We honored him and other Louisville legends, including Johnny Unitas, Pee Wee Reese and Mary T. Meagher at one of our games.

I got to hoist the Liberty Bowl trophy for the University of Louisville after we beat Michigan State 18-7 in freezing rain to cap a 9-3 season in 1993. Jeff Brohm played quarterback with two steel pins in the index finger of his throwing hand but was outstanding in the game.

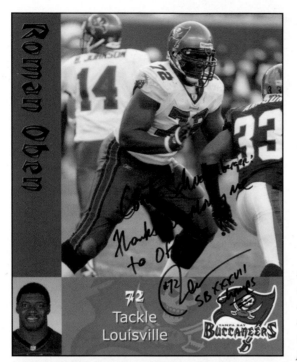

I converted Roman Oben to the offensive line at Louisville because I wanted linemen who could pull and get downfield and block. He excelled at that and went on to play 10 seasons in the NFL.

The University of Louisville named their football complex after me in 1998. They unveiled my name on the wall while I was in town with my Florida Atlantic team. I like to think I brought major college football to town, but this was an unexpected honor for a visiting coach.

After a cross-continent courtship, I married the love of my life on May 2, 1959. Beverlee supported me throughout my career, but after our children were grown, she was able to be a full-time ambassador at Oklahoma. She was popular on my Boomer-Sooner Blitz as we toured the state promising a revival of the football program.

My assistant head coach and wife Beverlee at the office.

A $4 million gift from Tom Oxley allowed us to build new athletic training facilities at Florida Atlantic University. Oxley, who owned Royal Palm Polo, was an early graduate of the school and embraced our football dream.

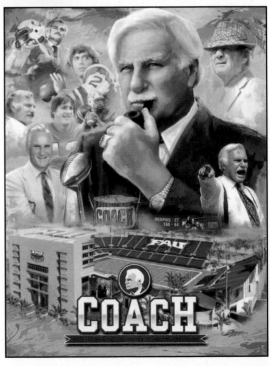

This poster that I give out at speaking engagements captures many of the highlights of my career. It has Paul Bryant and Don Shula behind me and an image of the new Florida Atlantic stadium in the foreground.

Photo courtesy of Todd Dawes and Guy Harvey Inc.

The bronze statue of me that stands guard inside the main entrance of the FAU stadium is 10 feet tall and weighs 575 pounds. Two of our football founders, Pete and Kerry Lobello, commissioned the bronze likeness of me. The artist for the image was Susan Cochran.

Photo courtesy of FAU Athletics, JC Ridley

Photo courtesy of FAU Athletics, JC Ridley

Don Shula helped me raise the profile of an annual rivalry game between Florida Atlantic and nearby Florida International University. He let us brand the contest the Shula Bowl and presented a trophy to the winner each year.

Photo courtesy of FAU Athletics, JC Ridley

In order to start the football program at Florida Atlantic, we had to raise $5 million in start-up money. We created a fund and solicited 70,000 alumni by mail, but we recruited by every means imaginable.

I called time out after a 29-year career as a head coach and retired from the sidelines at the end of the 2011 season. I still work for Florida Atlantic University as an Ambassador At Large.

Photo courtesy of FAU Athletics, JC Ridley

President George H.W. Bush visited during one of my Louisville Cardinal practices.

When President George H. W. Bush was still vice president, he sent me an editorial cartoon that elevated me at his expense. It was a kind gesture and the signed copy is very special to me.

My four-year career as a player at the University of Kentucky earned me a place in the ring of honor at their stadium. I was also named an All-American end in 1955 after playing under coaches Bear Bryant and Blanton Collier. I would later serve as an assistant to each of them.

University of Miami President Donna Shalala presented us with a crystal ball commemorating the 1983 national championship at a 30th anniversary reunion in 2013.

We knew we needed more than one young passer behind Kelly and Junior Mark Richt. I challenged my staff to identify the 10 best high school quarterbacks east of the Mississippi. We managed to bring in the No. 1 and No. 3 players on our board. Keeping everyone happy would be the next great challenge.

Testaverde came to us from Elmont, N.Y. He was 6'4" and 205 pounds but didn't start at quarterback until his senior year. He was All-State and honorable mention All-American. He went to a military academy in Virginia for a year to improve his grades before coming to Miami.

We found Kosar in Boardman, Ohio. He was a 6'4", 200-pound All-American in football and a standout pitcher on their baseball team. He completed 55 percent of his passes in high school. He racked up 2,222 yards and 19 touchdown passes his senior year.

Trestman brought me a written proposal to work with the young quarterbacks two nights a week in a classroom setting while the team was in other meetings. He developed a complete syllabus. Call it Quarterbacking 101. He started with my playbook but added transparencies, used the chalkboard and plenty of video. He talked theory and broke everything down. He actually gave them take-home tests so they could assess their own development.

With the future secure in the classroom, the sanctions behind us and Kelly still at the helm, we were poised for another bowl season. Kosar and Testaverde could redshirt behind Kelly, Richt and Vanderwende. It was a good plan, but it didn't last long.

Instead, in one of the most maddening seasons I have ever experienced, we would drop four games and miss our bowl opportunity with a 7-4 record that included losses of one, two and three points.

Kelly would miss most of the season after suffering a shoulder separation at Virginia Tech in our third game. Richt took over, but I had to suspend him for violating team rules. I ended up pressing Testaverde into service as a backup for two games and, of course, that cost him a year of eligibility.

Vanderwende started the final three games and won two of them. His one November loss, 18-17 to Maryland at College Park, probably kept us out of a bowl game.

I have always been able to accept a loss when I felt like the clock just stopped at an inopportune time. Those are games you lose, but your team is not beaten, and they would likely come back if there was just a little more time.

That wasn't the case when Florida State beat up on us in our house on October 30. The Seminoles came to town 5-1. We were 5-2. Both of us were ranked and in the national discussion. They thumped us 24-7. Richt threw for 273 yards but also had 4 interceptions. They converted a fourth-and-4 play late when their tight end Orson Mobley shook off three tacklers. Then they scored again in the last minute when we seemed to lose faith.

I called practice for 5:30 in the morning and everyone showed up except Richt. I assumed he overslept, and I sent an assistant over to roust him out of bed. It was a violation of team rules, and even with our season on the line, I immediately suspended him. Mark is now the highly regarded coach of the Georgia Bulldogs and he's forgiven me. When he won a coach of the year award, I spoke at the award presentation.

The head football coach is responsible for the growth and development of his team. It is important that he be respected, maybe even slightly feared, yet that he be known as a friend to his team. Certainly the friendship is one of father to son and not brother to brother. It is important that the head coach set the parameters, draw the lines, and then enforce the rules.

I have found over the years that young men look for this kind of discipline and this kind of guidance on what is expected of them.

Here's how one of my players, middle guard Darin McMurray, remembers that moment in time:

"There was no quitting on a Coach Schnellenberger team. I remember the time he believed we quit. We were playing FSU in 1982. We did not play well. Coach Schnellenberger felt we gave up. After the game the discussion was not good. Coach Schnellenberger said there would be an 11 p.m. curfew and a practice at 6:30 Sunday morning. The practice was the toughest practice I was ever involved in. It was long, it was intense and it was tough. That night our starting quarterback, Mark Richt, violated a team rule. Mark would be suspended from our team. Two lessons: You don't quit on the playing field, and it doesn't matter who you are, you break the rules, you don't play. He taught us to take the game seriously and to play by his rules."

If it wasn't a 5:30 practice, it should have been. But the point was made on anyone who had quit. Nobody on that team ever quit on me or on their teammates again, and that is what made us champions.

DELIVERING ON MY PROMISE

As we turned to my fifth season, it was clear how far we had come. The best evidence of that was that a 7-4 season could be viewed as a disappointment. The Canes were 14-29 in the four seasons before I took the job. They were now 30-15 over my first four seasons. We had changed the culture. We were now a source of pride in the community.

I had already signed a new five-year deal after my third season so there wasn't any contract pressure, but I still had a big promise to keep. It weighed on me as this memory of *Miami Herald* sports writer Christine Brennan illustrates:

"I'll never forget what Coach Schnellenberger said to me as we were standing in the rain during the University of Miami spring game in April 1983. It was raining so hard that water was running down Coach's face and falling off his nose. My notebook was soaked. Coach Schnellenberger looked out over the field and said, 'I've sold these young men on a dream. I've told them that we can win a national championship, and I've brought them here with that promise. I just hope I'm right'."

I would be trying to deliver with a roster that included 51 first-year or red-shirt freshmen, well over half our team. The national press thought it would be a rebuilding year, and they overlooked us in every preseason poll.

That may have been understandable with our quarterback question still unresolved. I had three young men who thought they should get the call. From a confidence standpoint, that seemed like a good thing. It made for a great competition, and I tried not to show any favor in the spring or the fall practices.

Vanderwende had the early advantage of having started three games after I suspended Richt at the end of the 1982 season.

Testaverde had the physical attributes. He was the best athlete, the best thrower, the best runner.

Kosar was the most cerebral. He was rock hard analytically. He could comprehend and remember. He had a mind like a mad scientist.

Stevens, Trestman and I were the only ones who gave the edge to Kosar. A few people thought we were screaming idiots, but we thought he was the one who could lead us the furthest. I told the media that it came down to who could beat Florida in our opening game. It seemed like a good way to explain it at the time.

We met with the three players in my office after we got off the practice field on August 25. Florida loomed just nine days ahead.

"I'm not going to beat around the bush," I said. "It's Bernie."

Kosar really won the job. He had the best scrimmages. He was the most comfortable reading the defenses and calling an audible. He had an intangible leadership quality, too, at a young age. It was a bit of swagger that was picked up on by the other players. They responded to him.

It was Kosar, too, who was best suited to work through the progressions of the all-purpose play that I had drawn up and Kelly had executed so well.

All the way back in grade school I would design football plays. Someone gave me a desk that had a chalkboard under the lid, and I could scratch out plays and make changes easier than on paper. The most important play of my career was one I developed at Miami once we started to drop back and pass more. This was really a wide open college play. It calls for one receiver to run a post and another to square in. It utilized the tight end and the backs to create all kinds of trouble for the defense. The quarterback could turn to any one of five receivers or we could run off of it. We used it 10 times a game and it was 50-50 whether it was going to be a draw or a draw fake and pass. I named it Rosalyn Right 106 Texas X Square In. The players called it the Texas play for short. That's the play I would call if we didn't know what else to call. We'd call it on first down. We'd call it on third and three.

It's the best thing I ever created. Eventually Bobby Bowden flattered me by picking it up for his FSU teams. It was such an important part of my offense that I had a glazier etch it on a big mirror that I placed in the trophy room in my house.

Kelly had used it to great advantage and I knew Kosar could master it for me. I gave him the job and he did not disappoint me.

My best coaching job ever had to be convincing Testaverde not to transfer and to accept a redshirt behind Kosar in 1983. That gave us the best one-two punch in the world over the next four years. I did it by convincing Vinny he was good enough to be an All-American, good enough to win the Heisman, good enough to be a first-round draft choice if he would wait his turn. I told him the wait might be two years. It might be only one year. It could be only one play.

To his credit, when Kosar came out of the Florida State game late in the season with an apparent injury, Vinny came over and said he was prepared to go in. That would have cost him another season of eligibility, but he was ready to make the sacrifice. Bernie was able to recover in time to go back in the game and we didn't have to make another tough decision. We ended up winning and we kept Testaverde for an extra year.

As it turned out, Kosar started in 1983 and 1984. Bernie would get his degree with a double major in finance and economics in just three years and leave for NFL stardom with two years of college eligibility remaining. Kosar would break Kelly's record for career yards passing in just two seasons. Testaverde would take over in 1985 and 1986. Testaverde would shatter Kosar's career record. Testaverde would win his Heisman, become a first round draft choice and play 19 seasons in the NFL.

We were committing to a rookie quarterback, but he would have three seniors in his backfield. Speedy Neal and Keith Griffin, two members of my original recruiting class were still with us. They were joined by Albert Bentley, who played high school ball in Immokalee. The only scholarship offer he received was from a small Midwestern college. Instead of taking it, he rode his bike more than 100 miles to our campus and walked onto the team. It took him two years to earn a scholarship.

At 5'8" and 208 pounds, he was quiet but intense. He fought for a chance to contribute, and in 1982 he was fourth on the team in rushing. This year he would bull his way to more than five yards a carry and over 700 yards rushing. He would join Neal and Griffin in the career 1,000-yard club.

All three senior backs were good pass blockers, but they were going to need help up front to protect Kosar.

We had to replace four graduating linemen. I had only Alvin Ward back as a starter. He was joined by another senior with some game experience, Michael Moore, but Moore would be lost for the season in our second game. That injury would push a red-shirt freshman from Miami, Paul Bertucelli, into the lineup at left tackle.

By recruiting at home we weren't getting our share of those big corn-fed Midwestern kids that populate most offensive lines. We were happy to transplant some smaller, more athletic, more mobile folks if they could be convinced the change was an opportunity to play.

I had been doing that for some time with great success. Realizing you are part of a team was what was important. Winning requires everyone to do their best for the team and do whatever is needed by the team.

One of the biggest sacrifices a player can make is to change positions for the good of the team. Over the course of my career I have asked a lot of people to do that. Getting people to accept a move from a glamor position to the often unappreciated role of an offensive lineman is tough though.

During his junior season at Miami, I moved tight end Mark Cooper, a very good blocker, to tackle. This is how he recalls it:

"I was a good blocking tight end, and Coach Schnellenberger was using ends more like flankers and I didn't really fit the profile. Two guys went down with injuries at tackle and he didn't have a lot of guys left. He said, 'Coop I need you to move to the tackle spot for me.' I'm thinking tackle, that's awful. I'm thinking I've got speed, how about defensive line? He looked at me and said, 'I need you at the tackle spot.' I wanted to debate it with him but there was no debate. 'I think you'll have an opportunity to play there and play sooner.' Then he told me about many others he had moved and who had success in the past. So I decided to give it a shot. When I thought about it, I realized this is Howard Schnellenberger telling me this and I need to do it. This was a man with a giant resume. So I went to practice and suited up as a 245-pound tackle. It was like getting into a fight every play. And I liked that. A week later down goes the next player and by the end of my junior year I was starting at tackle and working out and adding weight. That meeting changed my life. Coach Schnellenberger had a knack for seeing how guys move their hands and their feet and knowing what positions they could play."

Cooper graduated at the end of the 1982 season and spent the next seven years playing as an offensive lineman in the NFL.

Before he left I had already moved two defensive linemen from the 1980 recruiting class, David Heffernan and Juan Comendeiro, over to the offensive line. They would now start as juniors.

To complete an offensive line that we affectionately referred to as our retreads, I called on another junior, tight end Ian Sinclair, to move to center.

My son, Stuart, converted to the line from tight end as well. He could bench press more than anyone on my line, but he wasn't any faster than I was as a player. I needed receivers who could get down field and create separation between the corner and the safety. Tight ends needed to run at least a 4.7 40. He was around 4.8. Say hello to a fine interior lineman. He made long snaps from center, worked at tackle and played as a jumbo tight end in short yardage situations.

Stuart joined us after a nice high school career at Miami Pace and two years at Duke. He says he caught Hurricane fever in Atlanta while watching us win the Peach Bowl as a college sophomore. I told him we could use him, but I also explained we didn't give scholarships to transfers until they earned their spot on the team. It wouldn't be fair to make an exception. I told him he'd have to pay his own way the first year. He came on board, but Beverlee paid the bills until he earned a scholarship. That wasn't exactly what I had in mind, but you can imagine what it means to me that he played on this team.

The 1983 squad would boast a bigger than normal collection of players moving to and contributing at new positions.

Stanley Shakespeare came to us as a defensive back out of Lake Worth before we decided he was more valuable in the receiving corps.

Two more that stand out were freshmen from Miami.

Alonzo Highsmith, a future first round draft pick for the Houston Oilers, switched from linebacker to fullback.

Eddie Brown, who became a first round draft pick and rookie of the year for the Cincinnati Bengals, moved from corner to wide receiver when I needed some more outside speed on offense.

I also moved Reggie Sutton to wide receiver during the spring but a rash of injuries forced me to return him to the defensive backfield where he started as a freshman. He excelled there and forged an NFL career.

Before the injuries, I thought the defense could spare a few people. We had five seniors returning in the front seven and three starters back from a secondary that allowed only four touchdown passes in 1982. Seven of my eleven defensive starters would go on to play in the NFL.

THE OPENING LOSS

We had a very young offense as we traveled to Gainesville to start our 1983 season. Eight players from our 1982 roster had been drafted by professional teams. Six of them came from our offense, three from the line. We had talented replacements, but we were asking a lot of people to step up at the same time. It proved to be too many in a first game against a quality University of Florida team.

We matched up well against them, but we turned the ball over an incredible seven times. Freshmen were responsible for six of those mistakes. Usually deep in our own end. Speedy Neal lost the ball on the first series of the game after catching a screen pass at our 13-yard line. Eddie Brown fumbled a punt return. Alonzo Highsmith coughed it up on a kickoff return. Freshman halfback Darryl Oliver committed our fourth fumble and Florida led 28-0.

Kosar showed us a lot against a good Gator defense led by All-American Wilber Marshall. It would turn out to be the only game all season that Kosar would not register a touchdown pass. He was 25-45 for 243 yards. He threw three interceptions, but he never stopped competing. He was picked off twice in the fourth quarter after moving the ball down into scoring territory.

We averted the shutout with a 41-yard kick by Jeff Davis. He kicked it with just three seconds left in the game. We needed it to prove we could score and to establish the fact that we would never quit. We played them to a 3-3 tie in the fourth quarter.

This loss was different than the collapse against Florida State the year before. We had 298 yards of offense against a very good defense. They managed 311 against us but scored most of their points when we gave them the ball on the doorstep of our end zone.

In the locker room, I told the team we would have won if we made only half those turnovers or only gave the ball up at midfield. I didn't treat the coaches or players like they had lost. I have never taken losing lightly, but there are different kinds of losses. There are games you lose, and if the match had continued on, you would have gotten beaten even worse. This was not one of those games.

I believed we played well enough to win, and I was happy with how hard the squad competed against a Florida team that was one of the best clubs money could buy. The Gators would lose only once during the season but face the NCAA's wrath the next year. They were found to have committed 59 violations, including illegal recruiting, cash payments, phony jobs for players, even spying on opponents' practices. The school offered to forfeit six wins and Charlie Pell was forced out as coach.

Our national championship was won in Gainesville after that first game. I told the team this was just one game. We could win the next 12 and still win the national championship. I told the team, if they didn't believe this, don't come to practice Monday.

We had done that exact thing at Alabama in 1965 when we ran the table after an opening loss and claimed the title by beating Nebraska in the Orange Bowl.

After we got back to Miami and had a chance to watch the tape, I asked my quarterback guru, Trestman, what he thought. He said we chose the right quarterback and he would get better. I told him if that was true, everyone was going to think we were geniuses.

Everyone came to practice on Monday. The coaches acted like we had won the game. We just needed the veterans on our defense to give the youngsters on the other side of the ball a little time to gel.

The defense did exactly that with three near perfect performances. We would win five straight games without ever being behind on the scoreboard. We would give up one touchdown against Houston in the Astrodome and then shut out Purdue and Notre Dame at home. We played 44 quarters during the regular season. Opponents posted a goose egg in 28 of those periods. My defensive coordinator Tom Olivadotti had us in a basic 5-2 defense that just smothered opponents all season.

At the end of the regular season we were fourth in the country in yards allowed per game (259) and third in scoring defense, giving up under 10 points a game.

But here are two of my favorite defensive statistics for the season. Maybe ever.

The longest play from scrimmage that we allowed an opponent all year was 28 yards. That is the proof that the defense bought into our expectations on pursuit, our demands that no one take a play off, and our desire for an orange gang to be around the ball carrier at the end of every play.

And how about this stat? We allowed teams to score just 10 points in the fourth quarter all season. Those three points by Florida in the opener and then one touchdown by Cincinnati with 22 seconds left and the game safely tucked away.

This team had the right to hold four fingers high and claim the final quarter as their own every time we played. It wasn't wishful thinking; it was the product of their hard work. It was the ultimate expression of their personalities.

We had good team defense all year long, but different defenders stepped into the spotlight almost every week.

The captain of our defense was Jay Brophy, who had dedicated himself to football after quitting for a season. He felt he needed to step away from the academic rigors and the demands of major college football. He told me he had doubts about what he wanted to do with his life. I told him everyone experiences those doubts, but he should do whatever he needs, and I would have a scholarship for him if he changed his mind. Brophy went to work in a factory, and I know part of the pressure was to earn money for his family. He missed the 1980 season, but then called me after the Peach Bowl and asked to come back. He placed the call collect and I'm glad I took it. His talent was always there, but the heart and guts he showed when he came back proved contagious. Brophy was willing to do the hard work and he had the confidence that came from it. He believed in our dream and that helped others to believe in it, too.

Our game against Notre Dame was nationally televised in primetime. The defense sparkled, but Kosar was named player of the game after completing 22 of 33 aerials for 215 yards and a touchdown. That was his introduction to much of the college football world. The win was only our third against the Irish since 1955. We were now 3-1, and we made our first appearance in the polls at No. 15 and started our steady climb.

In our next three games we saw what it looked like if everyone on both sides of the ball played well.

We set a record with 613 yards of total offense in our 56-17 win over Duke in Durham, N.C. The following week we posted our fifth straight win, this one at home against Louisville.

Going into Starkville is never easy, but our defense shut down their option. With the 31-7 win, we were 6-1. We were now ranked No. 8 with a bullet.

Heavy rains made for miserable conditions and a physical game against Cincinnati at Riverfront Stadium. We managed to win 17-7.

Only their touchdown with 22 seconds left on the clock ruined our bid for a third shutout.

We hadn't trailed in a game since week two against Houston, but we would have to come from behind the next three outings to keep this magic alive. Each week we would dig ourselves out of a deeper hole, and that may be how we convinced our fans we were a team of destiny.

A scary injury to Tony Fitzpatrick ruined my day when we beat West Virginia at home. Tony was one of the emotional leaders of the defense at middle guard. He was a senior out of Saint Petersburg when I saw him dominate a high school All-Star game in Gainesville. At 6'0" and 210 pounds he was told he was too small to play major college ball, but what I saw was a lot of heart.

He tried to move a Mountaineer blocker out of his way and a tendon was jerked off the bone in his left shoulder. Tony looked down to see his biceps puddled near his elbow. Fortunately for the team, he never got the message that he would not be able to play again that season. He started rehabbing immediately and miraculously made it back for our bowl game.

Speedy Neal also separated his shoulder in the game and wouldn't play for the rest of the regular season.

Kosar threw two touchdown passes, five yards to Keith Griffin and 19 yards to Glenn Dennison. Dennison caught seven passes for 72 yards and broke the record for catches in a single season with miles to go before he was done. He would also set the career standard.

We were 8-1 and fifth in the AP poll. We were in line for a big bowl bid if we could finish the string against East Carolina and FSU.

We started to live dangerously, increasing our own degree of difficulty in each game. Against East Carolina we were behind 7-0 at the half and 7-6 in the final two minutes of the game. We had 6 because Jeff Davis' point after attempt in the third quarter was blocked. That snapped his consecutive streak at 54. Things got scarier still as the Pirates moved to our three-yard line with five minutes remaining. They came up short when they ran into our line on third and two and were snuffed by a Hurricane defensive huddle on top of running back Tony Baker.

East Carolina missed the field goal, but it would not have mattered. Bernie Kosar was set to march 80 yards when he got the ball. After a quick first down moved us out to the 35, Kosar looked to the sideline for some inspiration. He didn't usually ask and I didn't usually offer, but this was a good time for him to check in. I called for a deep pattern. Kosar dropped back and hit Eddie Brown over his shoulder at the Pirate 20. Brown was eventually shoved out of bounds at the 13-yard line. The play covered 52 yards and set up a one-yard dive by Kosar for a 12-7 victory.

We were 9-1, and all our dreams were still possible as we headed to Tallahassee.

The Seminoles led 9-7 at the half. In the locker room I wrote on the board what I had been saying all year: "It takes everyone to be No. 1." That was what was at stake now. I told the team I was proud of what they were doing on defense against a Seminole attack that was ranked second in the nation. I said I didn't see enough fire on offense, but I knew we could put 21 points on the board and that would be enough to win this game.

FSU rolled up 202 rushing yards for the night and another touchdown on the ground for a 16-7 advantage by the middle of the third quarter.

Bernie Kosar was determined to help despite being hit hard and nearly put out of the game. We were still trailing by nine, and Kosar was asking for smelling salts during a timeout. Vanderwende and the red-shirted Testaverde were warming up. Kosar could have left the game and still been a hero to me after all he had done. Instead, he told me that he could see every color of the rainbow but he knew where he was and he was going back in. That was just before he threw deep to Eddie Brown for a touchdown.

Kosar would complete 21 of 35 passes for 243 yards before he was done. Brown was his main target collecting eight balls for 150 yards. The biggest catch came off of our Texas play. It was a 37-yard reception for a score late in the third quarter. With it we cut the FSU lead to 16-14.

That was still the score when the Seminoles punted to us with 2:12 left to play. We moved the ball to the 2. As the final seconds ticked off, some people were probably wondering if Kosar knew what time it was, but he had already told officials to let the clock run down to three seconds.

We were happy to put the season on the foot of Jeff Davis. Jeff stood 5'6", and we affectionately called him the flea. Davis had missed two field goal tries already in the game but each was from outside the 40. Before he ran on the field Davis turned to me and said, "This one is for you." He says that was payback for a little bit of coaching I did the year before in a late season loss to Maryland.

Davis had missed a potential game-winning kick with 12 seconds to play in that game. He believed he got caught up in the emotion of the crowd and choked as he pushed the ball wide right. He left the field dejected, with his head down.

I went over to him, smiled and tried to comfort him. I told him to hold his head up. I promised him there would be another opportunity and said I knew he would make that one.

This was that opportunity.

Davis had been with me my entire five years at Miami and I had total faith in him. I visited him at his home in Clearwater just after taking the Miami job and closed the deal for my staff. He was a sidewinding kicker and had been an honorable mention All-American in high school. Even then he was nearly perfect on extra points, and he had a career best 48-yard field goal in high school ball.

We used him mostly on kickoffs until Dan Miller graduated following the 1981 season.

During the 1983 season, Davis had set a record for consecutive points after touchdown and was a perfect 10 for 10 from inside 40 yards. This one was from the 19-yard line and he drove it through just like one of those extra points that he was so special on.

He stood more like 6 feet tall when he walked off the field in Tallahassee. With his kick, Miami had won 10 straight games for the first time. It was the school's first 10-win season.

Fans knew what the kick and the game meant. One thousand Hurricane fanatics greeted the team as we taxied up to our hangar at the northeast corner of Miami International Airport at 1 a.m.

Seven thousand would show up a week later for a rally at our baseball stadium to see the U receive an Orange Bowl invitation. That brought us an unbelievable opportunity to play the No. 1 ranked team in the country. It also meant a $1.8 million payday for each team. Nebraska would have to split its bonus with the rest of the Big Eight Conference. As an independent, we could pump the whole sum into our athletic department budget.

We had reached a new plateau. We had built something of permanence and beauty and strength. We were finally climbing onto the perpetual motion machine that comes with regular bowl appearances. You get a big payday from the game and that alleviates the financial pressure. Your team gets several weeks of extra practice and that improves your play the next season. Your recruiting gets easier because of all the publicity surrounding the bowl. That means you attract better players, draw bigger crowds, earn better national rankings and head back to another bowl game.

THE COLLEGE GAME OF THE CENTURY

The run up to this Orange Bowl game would last seven weeks and be a celebration of all that we had already accomplished.

We would face Nebraska, a team that had finished in the Top 10 in the nation for 10 straight years. They had won 22 straight games and were being discussed in *Sports Illustrated* as possibly the greatest ever. They boasted stats that read like football science fiction. They were rushing for 404 yards a game. Averaging 7.3 yards a play. They set an NCAA record with 624 points. They were scoring nearly a point a minute. They had posted 84, 72, 69, 67 and 63 point totals.

Nebraska had an offensive line like no other: 6'7", 290; 6'3", 260; 6'6" 260; 6'3", 270; 6'3", 280. That massive crew led the way on what SI called their 545-yards-and-a-crowd-of-busted-bodies offense.

The Cornhuskers had the Heisman Trophy winner, Mike Rozier, who had carried for over 2,148 yards on the season. They had a wingback, Irving Fryar, averaging 13 yards a rush and 20 yards per catch. The quarterback, Turner Gill, was completing more than half his passes, throwing for 152 yards a game and rushed for 476 yards himself.

We loved the hype. It just made for a greater accomplishment if we beat them. My defensive coordinator, Tom Olivadotti, announced that we would not forfeit—we would show up. I expressed some surprise that their second team wasn't ranked nationally.

When the Las Vegas line on the game was announced at 11 points, I told reporters I doubted that Nebraska knew what a bunch of alley cats they were about to run into.

They were not to be trifled with, but we had 50 days to get ready for a January 2 bowl game and we intended to make good use of it.

It would be enough time for one of our defensive sparkplugs, Tony Fitzpatrick, to make it back. He would watch film of all 11 Nebraska games to prepare for his matchup with their imposing, 6'6", 260-pound center, Mark Traynowicz. Fitzpatrick would prove to be a football martial artist, using his opponent's weight to his advantage. He could read stances and get rid of his blocker with technique. Tony was quicker. He would use his legs and hips. He could also drop down and get up. Fitzpatrick would match Traynowicz in strength, plug that hole and even draw double teams.

The practice schedule gave us enough time to reset the backfield, too. Speedy Neal, who missed the final games of the season with a separated shoulder, would not be able to play. The long preparation period allowed us to give Alonzo Highsmith extra work behind Keith Griffin and Albert Bentley.

Highsmith was one of the few true freshmen we let play that season. He hurt his shoulder against Florida in the first game of the year and missed some action. He carried the ball just 19 times for 74 yards during the season, but now we were able to give him the equivalent of a spring practice and he showed us plenty.

My offense requires the running backs to be able to release and catch a swing pass. Bentley had caught 32 for 294 yards and Griffin 19 for 127 yards. Highsmith could run and catch the ball out of the backfield, too. He would give us one more dual threat.

Kosar had seven receivers who caught more than 10 passes on the season. Bentley was one of four players to catch 30 or more, joining the three primary receivers in that stratosphere.

Our tight end, Glenn Dennison, had large, sure hands and 54 catches on the season. He was a big enough threat that Nebraska would run a risk if they tried to double our wide receivers, Eddie Brown and Stanley Shakespeare. All three went on to play in the NFL.

We watched the Nebraska film and then the coaching staff met to come up with a game plan, just as we always did.

The Big Eight was a run-oriented league. We had seen a lot of different offenses, but Nebraska had not. If their opponents passed, it was in a desperate effort to come back from an early deficit. Our passing game was not our Plan B.

I was confident we would be able to score. We had already set a school record by posting 282 points, topping the total in our Peach Bowl season. We were going to see how much ground they could cover. The field is 100 yards long and 53.3 yards wide and we intended to make them defend it all. We wanted to try to stretch them into one-on-one coverage where we could.

We knew we couldn't give them the ball in our end of the field.

Olivadotti had an analytical mind. He could dissect an opponent's offense and see what made it tick, then program his defense to deal with it.

He believed it would be foolish to think we could stop the big red machine so he set out to slow it down.

We had to prevent the long runs Nebraska relied on and make them put the ball in play 10 or more times in a drive. When Gill ran the option, our ends and linebackers had to be able to shut off the outside and force him to the middle of the field.

We needed to make at least three big defensive plays.

I told Olivadotti that if he could hold them to 17 points or less in each half, we would win the game.

Once we had that plan, we just needed to convince the team it was a winning strategy. Our film sessions were designed to help our players understand the game plan and see what we had seen.

We flooded the players with positive thoughts, not just bold predictions of winning, but specific thoughts on how we would prevail.

We pointed to the lessons of our matchups against the three biggest and most physical teams on our schedule: Notre Dame, Purdue and West Virginia. All three were bigger; we were faster. We held Notre Dame to 102 yards rushing on 38 tries. That was 209 yards below their average. After an opening drive into our territory, we shut down Purdue completely. The first 10 times West Virginia rushed the ball they netted nothing. The result had been three easy victories. Two shutouts and a game where we allowed one field goal.

Nebraska could be the perfect foil, but we needed to have good pursuit and group tackling. We weren't going to bring down Rozier one on one.

We would rely on Eddie Williams to quarterback the defense. The 6'0", 192-pound senior from the Orlando area called the defensive signals and made all the check offs on the field. Olivadotti estimated that Williams made no more than five mental mistakes in two years in that role.

We got another defensive scare two weeks before the game when Jay Brophy broke a bone in his right hand and dislocated a thumb in the final scrimmage before we took a holiday break. Surgeons put a pin into the bone and gave him a fiberglass cast over the hand and thumb. Somehow he managed to play anyway.

As we approached the game, we tried to keep things familiar and consistent. We had specific goals, calm preparation and concentration in practice. The week of the game, we held one-a-day practices in the afternoon just like in other game weeks.

The night before the game we stepped away from all the bustle and spent the evening in our Miami Lakes hotel. It was time to rejuvenate and anticipate the game ahead.

I invited Joe Namath to speak to the team. I named him my special assistant in charge of upset. He talked to the players about winning the big one. It was his version of our "To Believe is to be Strong" theme song.

On game day he would join us on the sidelines along with Jim Kelly, who had brought us to the brink of all this.

Sleep wasn't that difficult for me. Some people get nervous before a big game, worrying about each and every detail. I usually sleep well before a game and then can't fall asleep the night after because I am replaying every move in my mind.

Newspaper polls indicated a Miami win and a Texas loss would be enough to give us the national championship. Before we kicked off, Georgia beat Texas 10-9. Nebraska was the last undefeated team standing.

The championship was there if we were up to our task in front of 72,549 fans. We were going to be playing in a stadium where we were 24-2 in my five years at the helm. It was the best home field record in the country over that period. Our only losses were to Mississippi State in 1980 and FSU in 1982. Nebraska lost three home contests in the same timeframe.

This game was going to be played in front of a huge hometown crowd, with just one corner of the stadium dressed out in red.

We were prepared. That was the special nature of this team. They approached the game in a very mature way. They had been through enough adversity to be wary, but they had seen enough success to know they could win this game.

Everyone knew what they needed to do. But preparation is only part of the head coach's job. Setting the tone for game day is also important.

The only thing that worried me was that the players might be too high. I had to walk like a zombie so they wouldn't get any higher.

My image is that I am as cool as a block of dry ice on the sideline. I attribute that to being in a lot of big games at Alabama, in Los Angeles and in Miami with the Dolphins and the Hurricanes. Calm was clearly what I needed to project in this atmosphere.

The game itself makes every list of the greatest matches in college football history and it deserves to be there. This one had everything. An upstart challenger. That would be us. A top-ranked team averaging 52 points a game, favored by 11 points and considered by some to be the best college football team ever assembled. We had violent swings of momentum. We had action lasting down to the last minute.

Although people recall the first quarter as all Hurricanes, it actually started ominously for us. They got the ball first and Turner Gill opened with a pass to Irving Fryar. Kenny Sisk, a senior linebacker and our leading tackler, brought Fryar down but injured his left knee on the play. He left the game and was not able to return.

Then they scared us with runs of 27 and 18 yards by their Heisman winner, Rozier. Three plays into the game they were living up to their billing.

The overall performance of our defense in this game was as gutty as any I've ever been around. We had so many injuries going into the game and then we lost another key player at the outset.

The knee injury to Sisk brought in Jack Fernandez. He was a senior from Miami, and he turned his chance into 15 tackles and a share of the MVP honors in the game.

All year I had preached that it takes everyone. Now one by one people stepped up.

Our defense held Nebraska to two yards on the next three plays and was able to stop the bleeding at our 28-yard line. Forcing them to go for a field goal felt like an early success. Then Kevin Fagan, a sophomore defensive tackle out of Lake Worth, blocked the kick and set our hysterical fans to furiously waving their Hurricane flags.

After the defense delivered, the offense came out inspired.

It would be our offensive line, not theirs, that dominated on this night. Our retreads proved their mettle. Sinclair, Comendeiro, Heffernan, Bertucelli and Ward would give Kosar enough time to survey the field and when pressed to get the ball to one of his backs. He would only need to find an outlet seven times. Nebraska would not record a single sack.

We wanted to stretch Nebraska both horizontally and vertically; we were able to do that right away and then come back and run the ball well.

Kosar hit Stanley Shakespeare cutting between defenders and picked up 23 yards. Keith Griffin ran one up the middle for 11 yards. Shakespeare hauled in another pass for a 22-yard gain. We were at the one in a hurry.

It would take three plays to get into the end zone. On third and goal Kosar faked to Albert Bentley and threw. Glenn Dennison delayed at the line and then slipped into the right corner. It took great hand-eye coordination to catch the ball after a deflection in tight space.

We were up 7-0 with 9:18 on the clock.

We got the ball back within two minutes and moved down the field again for a 45-yard field goal by Davis. It was his longest kick of the year. Alonzo Highsmith set up that score with an 18-yard power run on a draw play.

Ten minutes into the game we were on top 10-0.

Nebraska pushed back and moved to our side of the field. Cornerback Rodney Bellinger, who would make eight tackles on the day and bat down four passes, stopped Rozier three yards into the backfield to slow them down. When Gill was forced to pass, he tried to throw across the middle. Supersub Jack Fernandez batted the ball into the air with his right hand and then caught it when it came down. We had the ball again at our 35.

Four plays later, Dennison scored again on a 22-yard pass. They were trying to double cover our wide receivers so we changed Dennison's route

It was very special to me that my son, Stuart, played for my 1983 National Championship team at the University of Miami. Here he celebrates a touchdown in that game.

to send him down the middle. We took advantage of them trying to cover the 6'3" tight end, our all-time leading receiver, with one man.

We were up 17-0 at the end of the first period and felt we had established ourselves. We knew they could come from behind well, but not nearly as well as they go away from you if they get a lead.

We were ready to put them away for good early in the second quarter when Kosar was intercepted at the Nebraska 26 and they came back to life.

We had Rozier completely stopped in the backfield on one play, but he reversed field and picked up a big first down. Then I think they paid our defense a great compliment by going to a trick play that has become known as the fumblerooski.

Gill fumbled intentionally, leaving the ball on the ground while he followed the flow of backs and linemen to his right. One of their guards, Dean Steinkuhler, picked up the ball and ran 19 yards toward the flag at the left corner. Safety Willie Martinez and corner Reggie Sutton chased him down too late. That kind of gimmick either gets you a touchdown or a turnover. It's highly risky and there is no way to practice for it, no way to coach against it.

It was frustrating for us to give up the touchdown, but the call was a sure sign their line wasn't overpowering us.

We got a little out of sync on offense after that. Nebraska made some nice adjustments and Kosar struggled with the changes at the line. We were called for delay of game three times and had to punt for the first time.

Gill moved them 64 yards on 10 plays. The biggest chunk came on a 22-yard pass play from Gill to Irving Fryar on a third and six at our 47. They eventually scored on a keeper to get within 17-14.

I talked all week about how we would win by making Gill throw and I was impressed when he did. If I had known he was that good, I might not have said it. Still, the way they beat you is with their running game.

Our offense was struggling and our lead had mostly disappeared. Talking to the troops at halftime, I acknowledged the obvious: Nebraska had grabbed the momentum. But then I reminded them we had won the battle of the first half. We still had a three-point advantage and we just needed to get going again and win the second half.

My chalkboard message before we returned to the field was our theme: To Believe is to be Strong.

Our faith in ourselves was tested right away. On the first play from scrimmage, Keith Griffin lost the ball near our sideline. I helped him up and offered a little encouragement because there was a lot of football still to be played.

Our defense kept them from scoring a quick touchdown and taking the lead. We held them to a 34-yard field goal and the game was tied again 17-17.

Our offense came out smoking and put up two more touchdowns. Kosar completed a key pass to Eddie Brown, and then Highsmith finished off a 75-yard drive with a one-yard dive. Nebraska was forced to punt and we went another 73 yards with the ball. Kosar completed a sidearm pass to Keith Griffin and then an out to Eddie Brown inside the 10. Albert Bentley ran off tackle to the weak side and took the ball in from seven yards out.

Kosar was having another great day. He ended up completing 19 of 35 passes and set an Orange Bowl record with 300 yards passing. It is hard to say it was his greatest day, but given the importance of the game and the quality of the opponent, maybe it was.

We won the third quarter just as we had the first. We led 31-17, but we knew we weren't safe. We didn't want to let them get in the end zone fast. The defense did exactly what I asked them to do: They refused to give up big plays and made the Cornhuskers fight for every yard. We wanted to make them eat a lot of clock. They weren't completely cooperative. Nebraska scored with 6:55 left to make it 31-24.

We held the ball for five minutes and then lined up for a 42-yard field goal that Davis pulled to the left with 1:47 remaining.

They quickly moved to our 24, but we had them looking at a fourth down and eight play. That was where we should have ended it. Gill rolled right on an option and pitched to Jeff Smith at the last second. He rounded the corner and ran it all the way down the right sideline and into the end zone. It was 31-30 with 48 seconds on the clock.

Smith, of course, was their supersub, filling in after Rozier went out with an ankle injury in the third quarter. Smith averaged seven yards a carry during the season, and they didn't seem to miss much with him in there.

The Cornhuskers had never led in the game, but now they had a chance to win if they could convert a two-point try. On the other hand, a one-point kick would give them a tie and likely the title.

I was sure they would go for two. Tom Osborne wanted to win the game, not rely on a popularity contest to win a national championship. I'd have done the same thing.

We were going to decide this thing on the field.

The Cornhusker offense lined up on the left hash mark. Quarterback Turner Gill rolled to the right. He lofted a pass to Smith. Safety Kenny Calhoun dove in front of Smith and got one hand on the ball. Maybe just one finger. The ball hit Smith in the shoulder and dropped to the ground.

The score stayed 31-30.

A song called Hurricane Warning thundered from the stadium speakers.

It is almost impossible to tell you how proud I was of my assistant coaches, my football team and everybody connected with our program. We had accomplished in five years what a lot of people did not think could ever be done.

Out there in the stadium you could see what the game meant to the community. The love affair that had developed over those five years reached its fulfillment before a national audience.

After the Orange Bowl, I stayed up all night. We celebrated with the entire community. Everyone seemed to have a hand in it and everyone would get the benefit of it.

I appeared on *The Today Show* and then waited 12 more hours for the polls to make it official and confirm the dream had come true.

In a bit of serendipity, the Associated Press presented us with a newly named Paul (Bear) Bryant Trophy. Coach Bryant was no longer with us, but he would have liked it that I was the first one to hold it high.

CHAPTER 8

COWBOY WITHOUT A HORSE

"If Howard Schnellenberger stayed at Miami, they would have dominated all college football the way Alabama does now. They could have won 8 or 9 championships. Kids wanted to come there. If he stayed, we would have been the preeminent program in the country."

– Mike Archer, *assistant to Schnellenberger at the University of Miami, then head coach at LSU*

After we won the Orange Bowl and the national championship I was like a coaching comet streaking across the Miami sky. Emotionally, I was running around like Jim Valvano after his NCAA basketball championship that same year. He was looking for a hug anywhere on the court. I was looking for the next great thing.

My agent helped me negotiate a deal with the university that made me the highest paid college coach in the country. But it wasn't enough. I suppose I wanted what Don Shula had—a piece of the action. And opportunities to chase your fortune abounded. I looked around and saw the upstart United States Football League was throwing money and opportunities at players and coaches.

I danced a heady dance with multiple possible USFL partners before making a move that would explode in my face like a trick cigar.

I'm a student of political and military history, and when it was over, all I could do was take comfort in a quote attributed to Teddy Roosevelt, our rough-riding president:

"It is not the critic who counts; not the man who points out how the strong man stumbles or where the doer of deeds could have done them better. The credit belongs to the man who is actually in the arena, (...) who spends himself in a worthy cause; who, at the best, knows in the end the triumph of high achievement, and who at the worst, if he fails, at least fails while daring greatly (...)."

I did dare greatly, but perhaps not very wisely. Every time in my career that I made a decision to go somewhere on my own, I went bust. Every time I went someplace that God sent me, things went beautifully. This was another time that I indulged my arrogant side.

There are a lot of reasons I left Miami when I was seemingly on top of the world. Not all of them are well known. Not all of them were financial.

We tried to ignore the issues while my agent, Robert Fraley, negotiated a new long-term contract with the university. I would lose Fraley in a plane tragedy a few years later. He was with golfer Payne Stewart in a chartered Learjet when it gradually lost cabin pressure and everyone died from a lack of oxygen. But he set me up to become secure financially if I stayed at the University of Miami.

The biggest issue frustrating me was the stadium. I believed we needed to build one on campus. This was the moment to do it.

I already had renderings of a 42,000-seat facility. I had been displaying them prominently outside my office and in front of any group that would invite me. I think I showed the plans to half the people in town. I all but promised them that if we could win games and develop support, we would be able to build it.

I wanted us to use football to bring students and faculty and community together on the campus. The model is well known. It has been ever since Princeton went to the Rutgers campus to play the first intercollegiate football game on November 6, 1869.

You play on campus and you get everyone to come together to celebrate the university. You draw the alumni and the gentry from around the campus. You bring them in so they get to know and love the university.

I thought we had given the university leaders an opportunity they didn't have before to make the case to Coral Gables. This was the time for the community to help the university and make it a better place for everyone. We could do it without creating a traffic nightmare some local residents feared. We could avoid the worst of it because the new Tri-Rail system linking Miami to Palm Beach offered us the longest parking lot in history all along the railroad tracks. Everyone could ride to the railhead and then be deposited at the front door of our stadium. The security people said they could disseminate the crowd in a half hour. There was no longer any legitimate reason not to do it.

When the administration rejected the plan out of hand, I was stunned.

Then, as I set up my annual awards banquet, University President Tad Foote turned me down. He said he couldn't make it. He did eventually show up, but he was in a disheveled state. He was in work clothes and impaired. He insisted on taking the podium, and he gave a very unusual congratulations to the national championship team.

Though Foote's sad performance was recorded, the video was secured and has never been seen by the public to this date.

The final insult came when Foote questioned me about recruiting. He suggested we had made payments to get players. That never happened and I told him so. He questioned my veracity. He even asked that I take a lie detector test.

Our relationship was spoiled. Exit Howard Schnellenberger.

So I thought it would be a good time to take a real chance; much like Don Shula did when he left the Colts and came to the Dolphins. It was a chance I wouldn't have taken if I hadn't had the situation with Foote.

It had been a wonderful trip. I couldn't have had a better five years. If we had won it all the first year, it wouldn't have been nearly as wonderful. I don't regret leaving when I did, but it was unfortunate the way it all turned out. If I were in that situation without a crystal ball, I would do it again. It was a gamble, but at the time it was the right decision.

I say all that and freely admit leaving was the biggest mistake of my career. Fans like to speculate what might have been. So do I.

I have always credited Lou Saban for the work he did to set me up for success in Miami. He gave me Kelly; the cupboard was not bare. If he had left me nothing of value, we could not have accomplished what we did in just five years. We would have gotten there, but it may have taken seven or eight years.

The timing of a coaching change can cost a school an entire year. My departure came with the incoming class on board and the whole summer to prepare for the next season. A coaching change is always disruptive, but that's the best timing possible.

Jimmy Johnson would be the beneficiary of a lot of talent.

Quarterbacks Bernie Kosar and Vinny Testaverde, wide receiver Eddie Brown and fullback Alonzo Highsmith were all coming back. Johnson inherited linebackers Winston Moss and Randy Shannon on the other side of the ball. Everyone in that group would make their mark professionally. Shannon, of course, would return in 2007 as head coach of the Hurricanes.

And we had just recruited the best class any school had ever brought in. I left him 57 freshmen, including wide receiver Michael Irvin and seven others who would go on to be drafted into the NFL. Irvin, of course, would go to the Cowboys in the first round. Defensive tackle Jerome Brown went to the Eagles in the opening round. The Eagles also took defensive end Danny Stubbs. The Cowboys double dipped as well with tight end Alfredo Roberts. The Denver Broncos selected running back Melvin Bratton from that group. The Vikings grabbed defensive back Darrell Fullerton. The Saints drafted receiver Brett Perriman. Another receiver, Brian Blades, was chosen by the Seattle Seahawks.

That group kept my pipeline to the pros open for the next five years. They would stake Johnson to 52 wins over that period, including a 12-0 championship season in 1987.

Jimmy Johnson came in from Oklahoma State two weeks after I left. He had a lot of success at Miami, but he was a big disappointment to me on two fronts. He tarnished the image of the school, and he would turn out to be an ingrate.

He's the kind of guy who tears down a pyramid so no one can remember who preceded him. He trashed me and he did it to Tom Landry and Don Shula, too, when he took over the Cowboys and then the Dolphins.

At least in my case, Johnson didn't have anything to do with moving me out of the job. He just wanted the offices scrubbed of my image once he accepted the position. The staff I left behind was protective enough of my legacy that they took offense and they made sure to let me know.

The bigger sin was losing control of the program. Credit Johnson with securing the school's outlaw reputation. A string of arrests and news coverage of players having contact with agents hurt the school.

When one player was arrested for siphoning gas from a car, Johnson said he'd have done the same thing if he ran out of gas.

The bad boy reputation was cemented with on-field fights. Maryland and South Carolina vowed never to play Miami again.

Then Johnson got off the plane in Phoenix with his team dressed in battle fatigues. Arriving for the Fiesta Bowl that way wasn't as much a fashion faux pas as it was an example of Johnson's poor judgment. Talk about taking an image problem and shining a light on it.

Miami became the object of ridicule. *Sports Illustrated* writer Rick Reilly wrote a severe piece and went so far as to say the school was the only one in America that had its team picture taken from the front and from the side.

My old friend, Tad Foote, gave the team a 42-page code of conduct to follow. It included a dress code and the expectation that players follow all federal, state and local laws. I think Foote was missing me about that time, but I was well along on a new adventure.

SHADOW DANCING WITH THE USFL

I didn't pay much attention when the United States Football League announced its plans in May 1982. David Dixon, a New Orleans antiques dealer, was peddling the idea of a spring league with a strict salary cap and a handful of stars playing with local college graduates. It would be an off season diversion for pro football fans.

The USFL started playing in March 1983 with 12 franchises, nine of them in NFL cities. ABC and ESPN gave the upstarts visibility with television contracts. The league attracted more than 2 million fans and averaged 25,031 a game right away.

My old boss George Allen joined the league. He signed up to coach the Chicago Blitz once they offered him a share of team ownership. That caught my eye.

Showmen like Donald Trump, the owner of the New Jersey Generals, knew how to make a splash. Trump grabbed headlines by signing high-priced talent. He lured Heisman Trophy winner Herschel Walker out of school at the University of Georgia. That prompted a national debate about athletes leaving school early. It also showed the NFL the new league was playing hardball.

Trump would follow up by signing another Heisman Trophy winner, quarterback Doug Flutie. The salary cap was scrapped by the league.

As the war for players, fans and media attention became bitter, the USFL became harder for me to ignore.

And then Donald Trump came calling. The USFL was now on my radar big time. Trump wanted me to coach his team. I almost did. The night before we were to sign a contract, it became apparent to me that my boss was going to be Jason Seltzer, the team's president. Seltzer knew nothing about football. I was looking for control. I wanted to report directly to Trump and not to a hireling. I wasn't willing to repeat the mistake I made with the Baltimore Colts. And I wanted a piece of the action, something Trump wasn't offering. I ended up turning down that deal, but the USFL did not go away.

As it headed into its second year of play, the new league needed capital, and the easiest way for any league to raise money is through expansion fees. The Houston Gamblers, Jacksonville Bulls, Memphis Showboats, Oklahoma Outlaws, Pittsburgh Maulers, and San Antonio Gunslingers were added.

My University of Miami protégé, Jim Kelly, signed with the Houston Gamblers. The league continued to chase Heisman winners, eventually adding Mike Rozier of Nebraska to rob the senior league of three straight college players of the year. USFL teams would raid the NFL for stars like Reggie White and Steve Young.

Donald Trump wanted me to coach his New Jersey Generals in the USFL. I wanted more control than he was willing to give me and we couldn't come to an agreement on the terms.

There still seemed to be great opportunities in this league. Sherwood Woody Weiser, a hotel developer who controlled 9,000 rooms and had 17,000 employees, reached an agreement in May 1984 to buy the Washington Federals and move them to Miami. I knew him in his role as a trustee of the University of Miami. He offered me the deal I couldn't get from Trump. He was willing to give me a share of the ownership, make me coach and give me control of all personnel decisions.

I jumped at the chance. I wanted to join the same society as Don Shula and George Allen. I was to be a part owner of a professional team. The deal was announced and I went to work.

We had an office in Coconut Grove. We planned to rebrand the team as The Spirit of Miami, with a nod to Charles Lindbergh's bold trans-Atlantic flight and his plane that hangs in the Smithsonian. We were going to play in the Orange Bowl, which was still a perfectly good place to play. Kenny Herock left the Atlanta Falcons and joined our management team.

We started to put the pieces together. I did some marketing. I began to get interest from NFL players. I was talking to half the Tampa Bay Buccaneers and enjoying my role as a raider. I wrangled a commitment from their star defensive lineman, Lee Roy Selman.

Of course Selman never played for us. We never bought the team. In October 1984, Trump and Chicago's owner, Eddie Einhorn, made a power play in the hopes of forcing a merger with the NFL. They orchestrated a vote and got the owners to agree to switch to a fall schedule starting in 1986. That would mean head-to-head competition for interest in all our NFL cities. Our Pittsburgh franchise folded. Philadelphia and New Orleans had to relocate. Other teams merged.

Then the USFL sued the NFL for antitrust violations.

Sherwood "Woody" Weiser planned to buy the Washington Federals and move them to Miami. He offered me a share of the team and introduced me as his head coach at a USFL press conference. He later backed out.

My partner, Weiser, got cold feet and never signed the papers to buy the Washington team we were relocating to Miami. I was out of a job. Don Dizney would eventually buy the Federals and take the team to Orlando. I talked to him about joining that venture but nothing came of it.

The USFL would play a final lame-duck spring season in 1985 and pray for relief from the courts.

The suit against the NFL sought $1.69 billion. USFL attorney Harvey Myerson claimed to have a smoking gun that would show the NFL conspired to maintain their monopoly on professional football.

At trial, Myerson produced a memo from Jack Donlan, the executive director of the NFL Management Council, insisting that NFL teams should push USFL teams to increase the salaries of existing players. He also introduced a plan written by a Harvard Business School professor that was presented to NFL management and was designed to "conquer" the USFL.

Broadcaster Howard Cosell and Oakland Raiders owner Al Davis appeared on behalf of the USFL. Davis, always the maverick, testified in return for being excluded from the lawsuit. The NFL argued that the USFL was to blame for its own financial decisions and debt troubles.

In July 1986, a month before the USFL was to begin its first fall season, a jury found the NFL guilty of acting as a monopoly. The jury agreed, though, with the NFL's argument that the USFL had mismanaged itself. The jury awarded the USFL a symbolic $1. The USFL also collected more than $6 million in legal costs as the prevailing party, but the battle was badly lost. There would be no payday, no fall season and no merger.

I couldn't understand how the USFL owners screwed it up so bad. The move to the fall meant only a few teams could survive and at best they would be absorbed into the NFL. To win the suit and be awarded $1 was unbelievable to me.

Of course, I was well out of the picture by the time the league folded. My USFL adventure had left me worse off financially, but unbroken. Adam can't blame Eve for the temptation, and I have no one but myself to point to for this strange chapter in my life.

I had torn up my contract with Miami. I had left the USFL dance floor without a partner. I was now a cowboy without a horse.

CHAPTER 9

MY OLD KENTUCKY HOME

"I remember one afternoon kicking balls down the line in that old baseball stadium while others were practicing on the field. Coach asked me what I was using as a target. I told him I was shooting for the 420-foot sign on the wall. He asked me if I had ever been squirrel hunting. He said you don't shoot for the body, you aim for the eye. He told me to aim for the 0 in the 420 sign."

– David Akers, *Louisville placekicker and 17-year NFL veteran*

Fortunately my time out of the saddle was brief. Like Bear Bryant, I would eventually be called to come home. For me, that was to the Bluegrass State; more specifically, to the University of Louisville.

Here I was the dumbest SOB who ever lived because I left the Miami job for what turned out to be a mirage. It was an embarrassing position to be in. I had no income, and I was not getting a hell of a lot of calls from people wanting me to come coach for them. It was time to make a decision what to do with the rest of my life. Well, about that time I got a call from Bill Olsen, the athletic director at the University of Louisville.

Olsen said they were going to terminate their coach, and he wanted to work to develop a great program. He asked if I knew anyone I would like to recommend as his new coach. I said I didn't know for sure. I told him that's not what you have to do. You have to change the whole direction, the whole philosophy, the whole infrastructure if you decide you truly want to become one of the best football programs in America.

I told Olsen if he really wanted to make it happen, then maybe I could help find someone. They had to admit they needed outside help and believe they had the same vitality and the same potential as the University of Miami had in 1979 when they were getting ready to drop football.

I told him if he had the president and the Board of Trustees and the whole hierarchy ready to make a commitment to put their team in a position to play for the national championship, I could find someone who would be the leader of that movement.

We were talking in code, but he was asking me if I was interested. We were flirting with each other. I knew intuitively that he was feeling me out. When I told him I could find someone under certain conditions, he understood I was saying that was what it would take for me to be interested.

It was a courtship and it was a lengthy one. I was being coy after learning a few lessons while speed dating with representatives of three USFL teams and being jilted by the one I chose. This was all 16 years before George W. Bush asked Dick Cheney to direct the search for his vice presidential nominee. Like Cheney to follow, I searched and searched and I found myself.

It took nearly six months of negotiating with the governor and others before Olsen showed up again on my doorstep telling me of the work he had done. He had built the commitments to the program that were needed, and he asked me again who I could recommend. At that juncture, I told him I had found someone, but I didn't think there was anyone better suited for the position than me. I was coming off a national championship. I was brought up through the Catholic school system that is so important to the Louisville area. I had ties there through Paul Hornung and Paulie Miller and Bishop Flaget High School. I told them I would bring all that to the University of Louisville and use my relationship with coaches at high schools in Florida to improve the school's recruiting. With their resolute assurance they had the necessary support I would need to compete at the highest level, I was interested in the job myself.

This was a marriage that was destined to work. I had bargained and bargained and bargained. I had finally gotten everything I needed to make the job attractive. You can't allow a coach to feel stifled if you want him to succeed.

Now that I had the commitment from the administration, I knew I would be able to bring the larger community along. Turning around the team would be a harder slog than I had at Miami, but I knew it could be done.

Once we accomplished our goal and put the team into the national football picture, everyone wanted to know how we did it. I didn't have a script for it or any kind of plan on paper, but in many ways our journey mirrored the 12-step programs that have helped millions of people fight debilitating conditions related to alcohol or drug abuse.

It is folly to believe a coaching change is the only thing needed to right a struggling ship. Losing administrations have to do what Louisville did in 1984—take that long hard look at themselves.

They have to commit to getting well. It is not easy to admit that there are bigger institutional problems, but programs cannot be revived if they haven't come to grips with the real issues.

They have to get the right group of people leading the charge, develop the zeal to line up behind the recovery and climb to the top of the mountain. Everybody has to get behind the person in charge with an undisputed unison. Then they have to give the football club the resources to be great.

If the school is willing to do that and then hire a tough and tested coach that even the skeptics can believe in, it can succeed. You have to be willing to pay the coach well, perhaps more than the market says you should. If you hire the right person, someone with personal accomplishments and ties to the program or the area, he will be able to create a buzz, start the conversation, feed the optimism and build a storyline.

I was the right person for the University of Miami in 1979 and for the University of Louisville in 1984. I had the Dolphins experience that gave me credibility to lead a college team in South Florida. For my encore at program building, I was trading on my ability to recruit in Florida and my success there, but I was from Louisville and had been an All-American at Kentucky.

Ordinary programs become good programs and then great programs all the time. Look around. The program has to go through that painful period of cobalt radiation, but eventually you come out of it stronger, ready to succeed.

It won't be easy. It wasn't easy for us at Miami or at Louisville. You have to have an inner circle that stays strong and stands with you. At the first sign of trouble, some will become weak and no longer believe. You just have to know that not everyone that joins the bandwagon is fully converted.

That's why you need the commitment from the top before you begin. Then you need to do several things.

Announce your revelation. Tell it to everyone. Yell it from the rooftops. A dream is just a dream until you tell someone. Then it becomes a goal.

Prepare the field, plow the field, water and seed it. The field includes the student body, the alumni, the people who live around the university, and the people who believe their well-being depends on the university.

Continue to take inventory of your needs and your resources and acknowledge everyone who has participated in and helps you maintain your recovery.

From the time I arrived in Louisville in December 1984, I was consumed with gathering a coaching staff, recruiting, upgrading our schedule, generating media coverage and pursuing national relevance.

The first order of business was assembling a staff. You don't have to advertise for a staff when you get a head coaching job. You reach out to people you trust and you just answer the phone.

When I grabbed for and missed the brass ring of ownership in the USFL, most of my staff stayed at Miami. But with my new start in Louisville, 14 staff members and their families were willing to join the next crusade. My defensive line coach, Bob Maddox, and my offensive line coach, Christ Vagotis, came to join me along with strength coach Ray Ganong and trainer Mike O'Shea. Special Assistant Ron Steiner relocated as well. Their faith in me, their willingness to uproot their families and go with me was the highest form of compliment.

I brought in two players from my Miami team, too. Danny Brown, a defensive end, and Rocky Belk, a wide receiver, joined me to coach players at their old positions. I knew they could help me instill the work ethic we would need.

I kept Gary Nord from the previous Louisville staff. He was a Catholic from up that way. He played for the school and had been on the staff since 1981. I have always felt you should carry over at least one coach who knows the players from the pretenders. Nord was also expected to tell me where the skeletons and the mines were buried and provide some institutional memory.

Once I had my staff on board, the first thing we did was assess the players already on the roster. We had been blessed at Miami to inherit Jim Kelly, Jim Burt, Fred Marion and Lester Williams along with an array of local Division 1 talent.

When we looked into the Louisville cupboard, we were more than happy to find a quality linebacker in Matt Battaglia and a fleet receiver in Ernest Givens. The incumbent quarterback Ed Rubbert was somebody we could work with, even if he had thrown 18 interceptions for a nine-loss team in 1984. Rubbert would go on to play for the Washington Redskins in the NFL's scab year. Chris Thieneman, a defensive lineman, had enough ability to play in the Canadian league, but injuries limited him in his time with me.

I also inherited Bruce Armstrong, a junior who had played tight end for two seasons. He had 26 catches for 289 yards and 3 touchdowns as a sophomore. With his size, speed and footwork I thought he'd make a great tackle and I moved him there. Armstrong wasn't happy. He's still not talking to me because of it, but he was a natural and an impact player at tackle. Bruce would go to the New England Patriots in the draft and be named the NFL offensive rookie of the year. He played in three Pro Bowls as an offensive lineman.

Our assessment was that we had only five players that should have been recruited at this level. The balance should have been at regional schools like Murray State and Western Kentucky. We were seriously worse off than when we started in Miami.

My longtime assistant, Ron Steiner, says he never saw me as dejected as I was after the first day of spring practice. He says I looked old as I slumped in my chair. "I don't believe it," I told him. "Have you ever seen anything so bad?"

The next day I was back on my game. For anything to be possible, the coach has to believe.

None of what I saw could stop me from dreaming. Very few coaches have the opportunity to take Cinderella to the ball twice. It certainly seemed like a fairytale that I could win another title at Louisville, but now that I was in town, I was committed to it.

The local population thought I should be committed to the mental health facility at Our Lady of the Peace. I didn't care; I still wanted to tell the greatest story ever in college football. If we could do this a second time from scratch, there might be a special place in history for us.

Instead of seeing a championship in five years, I estimated it might take us 15 years. I gave myself a little wiggle room when I announced in unusually modest language: "We are on a collision course with greatness, the only variable is time."

We believed it could happen, but it would have to start with an upgrade in the recruits. While we began to build our network locally and throughout the Midwest, we leaned heavily on our old South Florida connections. We brought 18 players north from the Sunshine State as part of our first class.

The need to improve our facilities and eventually build an on-campus stadium was also heavy on my mind from Day One.

For starters, we would have to play at a minor league baseball field, circa 1957, with well-worn artificial turf. The press box was so rickety that we had a weight limit. Some members of the media had to sit in the stands.

The football offices were next to the baseball field in a one-story cement block building that backed up to the livestock barns for the Kentucky Fair. That left the offices with one defining feature—plenty of flies.

There was only one thing I could think to do about that annoying reality. I issued every member of my staff a fly swatter. To make sure they deployed our best weapon, I gave them a daily fly quota. People took the fly count seriously, but total relief came only with the onset of crisp, cold football weather each fall.

The livestock environment actually cost me a valuable coach, Marc Trestman. My Miami quarterback guru, who joined the Chicago Bears as head coach in 2013, hoped to join us but had allergies that couldn't coexist with the straw and the manure.

Our status as tenants on the fairgrounds property created obvious problems each August when the state fair was in town. We would flee to the university's Shelby campus for a training camp to avoid the worst of it and then try to co-exist with the animals and the visiting crowds when we came back. The rest of the year, when the sheds labeled for Jacks and Mules and other livestock were empty, we mingled with the Exhibition Hall clientele filing past our offices on their way to flea markets and gun-and-knife shows.

There were plenty of facilities needs and we managed to chip away at them over time. We put a new artificial surface in the baseball stadium and made a total of $2 million in renovations to our football complex. Two much-needed practice fields were constructed with proper irrigation and drainage. The size of the strength room was doubled. We got the school to dedicate an athletic dorm.

The fight to construct a first-class football stadium on campus would take years and we knew we wouldn't make major progress until we proved we could win and win against major conference opponents.

We did win our first home game in 1985, but it came against a familiar Division 1-AA opponent. We beat Western Kentucky 23-14 before 36,914 fans—the largest crowd ever to that time. It made for a rousing start to a new era, but we were going to have to improve our talent level and compete against nationally known programs to fill those seats regularly.

We would struggle early on at Louisville, but before my first class of recruits would graduate, we were on the board with a winning season.

We would play the Miami Hurricanes just once during my tenure at Louisville. Unfortunately, it had to be that first fall. I wish the game could have been played three or four years later. We would have been ready by then.

There was a lot of hype around my return to Miami with a Cardinals roster heavy on Florida talent. As it was, the pregame excitement exceeded what we could deliver. There was some polite booing on my arrival at the Orange Bowl stadium. I was fine with that. I appreciated the respectful treatment I got from my former players, who were not known for holding their tongues.

Vinny Testaverde seemed determined to remind me what talent I left behind down there. He threw for 295 yards. He had a 48-yard touchdown pass to tight end Willie Smith and a five-yard score to wide receiver Brian Blades. Testaverde, fifth in the Heisman voting that year and winner of the trophy the next year, also threw deep to future NFL great Michael Irvin. Irvin's touchdown reception covered 78 yards and gave him a school record with six straight games in the end zone.

The final score was 45-7. Our highlight was a 39-yard reverse run by wide receiver Ernest Givens, who was also on the way to a long NFL career.

The Hurricanes, who lost five games the year before under Jimmy Johnson, left this contest 6-1 on their way to the Sugar Bowl and a Top 10 finish. We limped out of Miami 1-7 on our way to a 2-9 season.

We would continue to flounder with 3-8 and 2-7-1 campaigns before we got the ship righted. Two of our seven wins in the three down years were against Western Kentucky. There were others against Murray State, Central Florida, Akron and Tulane.

That made for nine consecutive losing seasons against weak competition. It was enough bad football for everyone.

We didn't have too much to show in the win column for three years of hard work, but we were taking baby steps in the right direction.

We needed to show we could beat Division 1-A schools. On September 27, 1986, we beat Memphis State 34-8 to snap a 16-game losing streak against the top tier. That tie in 1987 was against a Big Ten opponent, Purdue.

We needed to show we could win on the road. On September 24, 1988, we upset North Carolina, 38-34, in Chapel Hill for only our second out-of-town victory since 1984, a string of 20 away games.

We had to prove we could win consistently and we finally started to do that in our fourth season. On November 12, 1988, we beat Western Kentucky, 35-17, for our sixth straight win, our longest streak since 1970.

Every year we improved our team and now we could ratchet up the level of competition. Upgrading the schedule was made easier by our independent status.

We stopped scheduling Western Kentucky, Marshall and Murray State and started featuring the likes of Boston College, Pittsburgh, Tennessee, Texas and Texas A&M. The improved schedule helped us garner more interest and the accompanying media attention, but we still needed to win some big games to raise our profile to one of national relevance.

Early on we struggled to get coverage in the spring when everyone in Louisville is focused on the Derby. We had to fight to keep a significant press presence once basketball season kicked off November 15. We competed with the basketball program for time and space even in August, September and October, but we never quit trying.

With the help of Steiner and my media guru, Roy Hamlin, we worked around the clock on marketing and advertising trying to reach uninitiated fans anywhere we could find them.

To draw more fans with my coach's television show, we brought in two different Pop Warner teams each week to run the play of the game. I would work with the youngsters. They would watch the play in the locker room and then I would walk them through it so they could see how the action unfolds. When I was done teaching, they would run the play and we would tape it for broadcast on the show. Then we took them to McDonald's for a burger. Kids and parents loved it. We had their grandmothers watching my show, too.

We took the show out on the road, producing it in all parts of Louisville and surrounding areas. We visited civic clubs and we set up in public libraries. We even went to my old schoolhouse at Flaget.

We went on a 10-day tour of the state. My crew would record people coming into our events and quickly add that footage at the front of the tape we were going to show them on the Cardinal football program. All of a sudden they saw themselves on the big screen as part of our team. They loved us out there in the nether regions.

We blanketed the Commonwealth, even got up to the Children's Home of Cincinnati. I invited the kids to a ball game and they joined us along with Cincinnati Bengal receiver Eddie Brown, the NFL rookie of the year and one of my former Miami players.

We decided to give Kentucky a taste of the Easter Seals Run that was so popular when I was at Miami. The first year the players began in Lexington at the Kentucky Children's Hospital and we ran our handoffs as far as Frankfort. We began the next day with the governor providing a breakfast sendoff and then continued running our plays down Route 60 all the way back to our campus. Sixty miles and immeasurable goodwill over two days.

Before we were finished, my publicity team put together a great "This is Louisville" night at one of our games. We brought in all the heroes from Louisville: Muhammad Ali, Pee Wee Reese, Johnny Unitas, the Olympic swimmer Mary T. Meagher and others. Each in their own car driving out into the stadium.

People thought I was a brazen hustler and maybe I was, but if we didn't go out and sell the gospel of college football, we wouldn't have had a chance to build the support we needed to have sustained success.

There was a lot going on to promote the program, but there was just as much effort going into improving the team.

My players had to climb every stair in the stadium as an exercise. We called it running the Matterhorn. We had a 2.5-mile route around the fairgrounds that made a good warm-up before double and triple workout sessions.

One night I had my field goal kicker practice in darkness except for a car's headlights. It seemed like it helped him concentrate.

I posted a sign over the exit in our locker room. It was a four-word statement of what I demanded in practice and games. "PRIDE. INTENSITY. ENTHUSIASM. ARROGANCE." As they went out the door, players slapped the placard to acknowledge their pledge to give me all of that on the field.

I looked up the A-word in a dictionary to make sure it wasn't a totally bad thing. Have you ever seen a great prize fighter who wasn't arrogant? Or a great military leader? It's just as rare to find a great football player who lacks it.

Arrogance proved to be the hardest thing to teach these kids. We're not talking bravado or false confidence. We're not abandoning good sportsmanship. We are talking about a conceit that comes from knowing you are fit, you can play longer and harder than the opponent.

My practices were always seen as tough, and some of my inspiration came from my military training that included time at nearby Fort Knox. Now I decided to let my athletes see what a real boot camp was like. It would show them our practices were not all that tough.

We made friends with the base leadership and brought the team up there.

I wanted my players to see a unit working harder than we were and see that they were doing it at 4 a.m. We watched the troops as they fell out. We ate breakfast with them and joined in their drills. We ran the obstacle course and crawled under barbed wire. At the end of our day, we had an Olympic-style sports competition with the soldiers. We held our own.

The general and I briefly went head to head. We competed to see who could throw a football the farthest and then throw a hand grenade with the best accuracy. I threw the football better than the general, but I made sure to lag behind him on the hand grenade toss. He rewarded my discretion by letting me drive one of his tanks.

Most of these kids had never been on a military base. It made a difference in their lives. It was a great day for morale building and contributed to the making of my football team.

Football is the last place outside the military where we have an opportunity to develop the proposition that the team is more important than the individual. They were starting to realize that.

We broke through in our fourth year, finally getting on the right side of the ledger. We finished 8-3, but couldn't snag a bowl bid. Of course we're talking about a time when there were only 15 bowl games and not every team with a winning record got to a post-season party. It was maddening to me, though, that we couldn't get an invitation. Bowl organizers didn't think we could bring a crowd. We hadn't shown them enough. Yet.

Maybe the most disappointing setback during that 8-3 year was a tough fight at Southern Mississippi. We had dropped the first two games of the 1988 season against Maryland and Wyoming. Then we caught fire. We beat North Carolina, Virginia and Virginia Tech. We would have swept the final nine games on our schedule and forced our way into a bowl except for a 30-23 loss to Southern Mississippi at Hattiesburg.

The 1988 campaign set us on a path to three straight winning seasons, including our 10-1-1 national coming-out party in 1990. But we lost to Southern Miss all three years.

They had a never-say-die kid at quarterback, who always found a way to frustrate us. That young man was the scourge of my Louisville teams. He beat us all four times he faced us in his career. As a freshman, in just the third game that he ever started, he gave me the worst whipping I ever suffered, a 65-6 drubbing. We put him on his way to Golden Eagle records he still holds for most plays, most total yards gained, most passing yards gained, most completions and most touchdowns scored.

Only now does all of that not hurt as much because I know where he went from there. He

To show my team a unit that worked even harder than we did in practice, I took them to Fort Knox where I had served in the Army. After competing with each other in throwing hand grenades and footballs, I managed to take control of a tank.

became the 6'2", 225-pound future Hall of Famer we all know as Brett Favre of the Green Bay Packers.

I had very good quarterbacks of my own when we were facing Favre. In 1987 and 1988 we had Jay Gruden. The following two years belonged to Browning Nagle, a 6'3", 225-pounder out of the Jim Kelly mold.

Nagle went in the NFL draft one pick behind Favre, but it nearly didn't happen for us. I had recruited Nagle hard out of Pinellas Park High School in Florida. He was a good fit for our program, and he was firmly in our camp until he decided to make one last official visit to West Virginia. I was sure he was going to join us and promised him I would hold a scholarship for him even if he made that extra trip. As it turned out, the Mountaineers matched him up with a beautiful young hostess and he became enamored with her that weekend. So my star pro-style passing recruit chose her and a spot behind Major Harris in the Mountaineers option offense. Neither relationship was satisfying for long, and Nagle came back to me like a prodigal son after one season.

All four seasons Gruden and Nagle were behind center, they threw for more than 2,000 yards and at least 16 touchdowns. Nagle started his NFL career with the Jets and Gruden played arena ball before going to the NFL as a coach. He became head coach of the Washington Redskins in 2014. Jon Gruden, the former head coach and television analyst, is his brother.

Winning solves a lot of your problems. Once Jay Gruden delivered that first winning season in 1988, things started to move at a rapid pace.

It certainly helped our recruiting. In February 1989 we scored a real coup, landing Louisville Trinity quarterback Jeff Brohm, who had captured national attention. He turned down Notre Dame and Southern Cal, among others, and chose his hometown school to get him ready for a professional career. He is now head coach at Western Kentucky.

Our pro-style offense was attractive to talented quarterbacks who wanted to play in the NFL. When we get that elite level of player and they have enough time to master the system, we are hard to beat. It is no accident that our three finest seasons at Louisville came behind Gruden, Nagle and Brohm when they were senior quarterbacks.

When we struggled, it was usually because I committed the unforgiveable sin of running out of top tier quarterbacks or we were developing a young one. A pro-style quarterback really has to be coached. He has to be groomed and he has to know exactly what he is doing.

Of course it's not all about quarterbacks. We produced some serious football talent at other positions, too, while I was at Louisville. Roman Oben was dedicated to opening holes when we were running and keen on protecting our quarterbacks when we were passing. Oben was another one I converted to the offensive line. I didn't believe in recruiting 300-pound linemen out of high school. These are 17- 18- and 19-year-old kids and they shouldn't be carrying that kind of weight. We also wanted linemen who could pull and get downfield and block. Oben could do it with the best.

On the defensive side, Ray Buchanan would chase down opponents anywhere on the field from his spot in our defensive backfield. He also intercepted eight passes in his best year. Defensive ends Mike Flores and Joe Johnson were wrecking balls that created enough havoc out of our 4-3 defense that we didn't have to blitz too often. Flores had a total of 27 sacks in his two best years. Johnson was right behind with 23 over two seasons. Ted Washington and Jim Hanna were rocks at defensive tackle. Mark Sander was a tackling machine at linebacker taking down more than 400 opposing players in a three-year span.

On any given week they were the guys we presented with our bone award, a femur that we hung from the locker of the player that delivered the most jarring tackle in the enclosed end of our stadium. We called that the crunch zone, and you knew the play of the day when you heard it.

All of the above went on to the NFL.

All of them stand out for me because they bought into our conditioning program.

They understood why we had a staff member, Paul Gering, living in the dorm with them. Why he checked on them in the classroom. Why we had a study hall and tutors available. Why we required a 2.5 grade point average when the NCAA demanded only 2.0.

They were smart enough to figure out that mandatory breakfast for the players wasn't as much about nutrition as it was about getting them up and ready to go to class.

They liked it that I wanted them to play like they were the first guys to hit the beach at Iwo Jima.

All of them were happy to sit down after the last game and hear what we expected of them in the off season. What kind of work we wanted them to do. What skills we wanted them to develop. What kind of times we wanted them running. What weight we wanted them at when they came back.

There are others who didn't go on to professional ball but who I won't ever forget.

Ronnie Bell joined us in the fall of 1987 as a transfer out of the Air Force Academy. He walked on as a kicker and by the third game of the season he had the job. He tried a 52-yard field goal and came up just short at the end of that game we tied with Purdue. To this day he insists that if the wind hadn't shifted against him at the last second up in their horseshoe stadium, he would have made it. But that's not why he stands out.

He was a tough little guy, who hated the small pads and the one-bar face mask that kickers wear. He said it felt like the cone of shame that dogs wear. Early in his first year he kicked off and saw a hole open up. Anticipating the kick return team would see the same thing, he headed there. Sure enough Bell met the ball carrier and he crashed into him. He hit the runner so hard his body buckled to the turf. The collision turned that sorry-ass one-bar mask to the side, and Ronnie was practically looking out the ear hole. His face was bloody when he came to the sideline. I grabbed his helmet, yanked that one-bar back to the front and yelled for my equipment manager to get him a real face mask. His cone of shame was gone for good.

Maybe he stands out because I caught him one time doing an impression of me in front of 60 players and boosters in the lounge area of the dorm. When I came up behind him it got deathly quiet, and he figured I was there without ever seeing me. I asked the crowd what Bell was doing. "Is he showing his approach to kicking extra points?" Then I mimed a kicking motion and announced "No good."

In 1989 Bell kicked 15 field goals and we posted another winning season, but the record was 6-5 and we probably underachieved with an increasingly talented team.

We beat Wyoming and then Kansas on the road to open strong. The 33-28 performance in Lawrence extended our winning streak to eight, the fifth longest in the country.

After a bye week, ninth ranked West Virginia came to town. To try to generate interest in the game and maybe help build a lasting rivalry, I designed a trophy that would stay with the winner. Both schools have a heritage in mining country and we called it the Coal Trophy. It would stay with the winner each year. The Mountaineers staked their claim to it in front of a record crowd of 39,142. We had a 21-10 lead early in the game but lost 30-21. The disappointing finish came after Nagle suffered a foot injury.

We went on to take our annual beating from Brett Favre, but this one was closer than most. We lost 16-10 at home and in particularly frustrating fashion. Favre beat us with a Hail Mary pass that hit a receiver in the helmet and ricocheted along the goal line. A trailing receiver made a miraculous reception and walked in for the touchdown.

We finished our season in December playing Syracuse in a nationally televised game that we dropped 24-13. The game was played in Tokyo to showcase college football. The exposure was good for us at the end of a season in which we logged 24,000 miles.

Our growing reputation and our willingness to go anywhere and play anyone would pay big dividends the following year.

With perhaps the best team in Louisville history, we started the 1990 season with a game on the West Coast. We managed just a 10-10 tie with San Jose State. It took real grit for our star defensive tackle, Ted Washington, to block two San Jose field goal attempts late in the contest. That left the score even and kept our dream of a special season alive.

After a couple of home wins, including one against Kansas, we hit the road again. We traveled to Morgantown and squeaked past West Virginia. Our defense and more specifically linebacker Mark Sander, our leading tackler for the third straight season and a future Miami Dolphin, shut them down after they went on top 7-0 in the second quarter. Klaus Wilmsmeyer, who would punt and kick his way into the NFL, gave us just enough offense. Wilmsmeyer connected from 41 yards before the half and then from 37 yards in the third quarter. He got one more chance from 42 yards with 3:47 left in the game and lifted us to a 9-7 victory.

In the locker room after the game I announced I wasn't leaving without the Coal Trophy we had given them the year before. We ended up camping our bus in front of their offices until the athletic director finally got it and gave it to us. That trophy meant something to us. Now we were winning against big-time programs and winning on the road. We were finally ready for primetime.

In October, we impressed a few bowl scouts with a big win at Pittsburgh. We jumped on top 27-6 and then held on to win despite giving up two late touchdowns. That helped us crack the AP poll at No. 25. The poll had been around since 1936. The only other time Louisville had made an appearance was during Lee Corso's stellar 1972 season when he won a Missouri Valley Conference championship.

We pushed our record to 9-1-1 and climbed to 20th in the AP poll when we went to Boston College and beat them in exciting fashion. Nagle got us into the end zone and on top 10-0 before being knocked out of the game on a hard sack. Linebacker Mark Sander returned an interception 27 yards for a touchdown and a 17-7 lead in the third period. Defensive back John Gainey preserved a final 17-10 margin for us with an interception of a Hail Mary try in the end zone as the clock expired.

This time there would be no denying us a place in a bowl. Our only loss had been to Brett Favre and Southern Mississippi, 25-13, in Hattiesburg. So how about a New Year's Day bowl? How about letting us play Alabama? Those were big dreams, but as fortune would have it, that's exactly the opportunity we got.

The Fiesta Bowl was in a bit of a spot. After voters rejected a paid M.L. King Jr. holiday for state workers, Arizona faced a tourism backlash. Plans for a protest at the game scared a few schools away.

We accepted the bid along with Alabama, and both teams wore commemorative uniform patches honoring King. The NAACP demonstration fizzled in a city, Tempe, that already gave workers the holiday and at a bowl that had a history of sensitivity on race and a black president in Dr. Morrison Warren.

We had the bright spotlight we were seeking and a chance to make a quantum leap forward. Alabama came in 7-4, slightly behind us in the AP poll, but they had allowed only 38 points in their previous seven games, and they were the clear favorite with the gambling crowd. Our home state rival, the University of Kentucky, hadn't beaten the Crimson Tide in 35 tries. If we could do it on this stage we would have a legitimate claim to being the leading football program in the state.

We felt like Rocky Balboa, or better yet, hometown hero Muhammad Ali. To quote him, we were ready to shock the world. As we were heading out of the locker room for the opening kick-off, Alabama players lined both sides of the small hallway leading to the field. They were smirking and talking trash. Maybe they thought they were going to intimidate us. They had no idea how hungry we were.

We came roaring out of our locker room and took complete control early. We worked from the shotgun formation and used a no-huddle offense to put pressure on their defense. Nagle threw for 223 yards in the first period, including an opening touchdown pass of 70 yards to Latrell Ware. Ralph Dawkins ran one in from five yards out. Anthony Cummings pulled in a 37-yard TD pass, the first of his two scoring catches on the day. Defensive back Ray Buchanan stuffed a punt and recovered it in the end zone to make it 25-0. We were perfect on everything except extra points. Nagle gave a superhuman performance, collecting a record 451 yards passing in the game. He was 20-33 throwing with three TD passes.

The final score was a stunning 34-7 in front of 69,098 fans and a national TV audience. It capped a 10-1-1 season and we climbed to the 14th spot in the final AP poll.

Now everything was different. We had changed the perception of Louisville football forever.

We could talk openly about a land swap to enlarge the campus and switch over from a commuter school to a residential campus. We could dream out loud about a 50,000-seat on-campus stadium.

The outpouring of pride in what we had already accomplished made believers where once there were only skeptics.

I told a reporter that everybody thinks I'm an arrogant, obstinate, blowhard. "No," the reporter replied. "That's what people thought when you were losing."

Karl Schmidt, one of my publicists, likes to describe me as a poker player. He says I have that mentality. I'm not sure if I agree, but I do often try to raise the stakes. Heck, I want to play for all the marbles. What's wrong with that?

It was time to move all my chips to the middle of the table.

We could finally shame Kentucky into facing us on the gridiron. The idea of Louisville playing Kentucky in football had been as dead as a dinosaur since 1924. The first few times I raised the possibility of renewing the competition, I was firmly rebuffed by Cliff Hagen, the basketball-oriented athletic director at my alma mater. After our 8-3 season in 1988, I began to sell it to our fans and the media as a legitimate idea. As soon as C.M. Newton took over as Kentucky athletic director in 1989 I floated the idea again. I told Newton we needed to play. I said it shouldn't take an act of the legislature the way it did in basketball. Newton agreed it was a good idea, but his bottom line was we would play once it was mutually beneficial.

When we beat Alabama, the Wildcats hadn't been to a bowl in six years. The needs of the schools were changing. After two more losing seasons for Kentucky, Newton was ready to deal.

It didn't happen until we forced them back to the table and they could see the value of it from a financial standpoint. I realize how much pressure they were under to avoid playing us, but the opposition came from a small fraction of their people. I hope that the ones that were not in favor of it are now happy the thing has happened. I think by and large they must be. It generates media interest for both programs and playing it as a season opener for both schools gets people talking football in the summer months.

The two schools signed a six-year contract in 1993 that restarted the series the following season. All the games had to be in Lexington, but right before we signed, I negotiated a proviso that if we ever built a stadium on campus, we would turn it into a home-and-home series.

It might be too much to say we suckered them with that last addition, but they didn't think it would ever happen, and the promise of bringing Kentucky to town helped rally our alumni and ensure we would build.

The series with Kentucky started in 1994. By 1998 the game was being played in Louisville.

We started the stadium drive by sending out questionnaires. We asked if there was support for an on-campus stadium

Browning Nagle mastered my pro-style offense and led the team to a 10-1-1 record in 1990. We ranked 14th in the final Associated Press poll that year.

and 80 percent said yes. We asked if they would buy tickets to support the construction. They said yes.

By October 1, 1993, we met our goal of raising $15 million in seat purchases and hoped to start construction within a year. The next step, getting the city and the state to approve a land swap with CSX Transportation, dragged things out a couple extra years. We had advanced the program far enough, though, that the stadium was a natural progression. The city's powerful business interests eventually pushed a $60 million stadium project across the goal line.

The state eventually deeded CSX about 100 acres of business property along Hurstborne Parkway, north of Shelbyville Road. We secured 90 acres just south of the campus.

They call the kind of land the university gained in the exchange a brownfield. It was an old scrap heap and repair yard for the railroad. It couldn't be sold because it was contaminated. There was battery acid and creosote in the ground. It can take years to clean something like that up. You need a front-end loader to peel the soil off and take it to an incinerator to be burned. They brought the incinerator to the site and they set it up and did the work in three months.

Winning the Fiesta Bowl revolutionized the program. It allowed us to enlarge that little landlocked campus and build what is now known as Papa John Cardinal stadium. I like to think it regenerated the city of Louisville.

After two down seasons, the football team rebooted and we went back to a bowl in 1993. This time it was with my next generation quarterback, Louisville native Jeff Brohm, at the controls.

Working out of a shotgun offense he helped us knock off No. 23 Arizona State at our place early in the year. He was 26-38 for 331 yards in a career performance. My all-purpose halfback Ralph Dawkins, who led the team in rushing three seasons and in pass receptions twice, pulled in a 25-yard touchdown pass. Our star defensive end, Joe Johnson, had four sacks in a 35-17 showpiece.

We backed that up with a 41-10 mauling of Texas—a score that surprised even me. At the post-game press conference a reporter asked me to analyze the team's performance. I told him I was in awe of my kids—until Monday. Then it's back to work. Football is definitely a what-have-you-done-for-me-lately business.

We opened 5-0 before losing 36-34 in Morgantown. We wasted a sensational performance by Brohm in this edition of the coal bowl. He was 22-39 for 270 yards and 4 touchdowns. We lost in large part because after three of those scores we gave up long kickoff returns. They booted a 36-yard field goal late for the win.

We beat Pittsburgh and Southern Mississippi, at last, for a 7-1 start.

We took a step back with tough losses at Tennessee and at Texas A&M, but finished the regular season 8-3, good enough for a spot in the Liberty Bowl and a matchup with Michigan State.

We deserved a significant bowl based on the difficulty of the schedule we were now playing. We were happy to face a Big Ten opponent. We were more than eager to prove we were not a one-trick pony when it came to bowl games.

This one was played on December 28 in Memphis, and conditions were less than ideal for our passing game. In 20-degree temperatures and freezing rain Brohm gave me a gutsy effort. He played with two steel pins in the index finger of his throwing hand but was 19 of 29, passing for 197 yards. They scored on the opening drive of the game and we were behind

The Fiesta Bowl win over Alabama catapulted us into an annual rivalry game with the University of Kentucky and opened the door to building a new stadium.

7-3 with 12:05 left in the contest when Brohm hit Reggie Ferguson for a touchdown from 25 yards out.

Joe Johnson and linebacker Tyrus McCloud pinned Michigan State running back Craig Thomas in the end zone for a late safety. Then we closed the scoring with one final touchdown drive for an 18-7 statement win.

We would open the 1994 season with the long anticipated match against Kentucky at Commonwealth Stadium in Lexington. We were rightly favored but they upset us before a rabid crowd of 59,162. We outplayed them but they outscored us. We beat them 23-13 in first downs and they beat us 20-14 in points. They broke a 14-14 tie with three minutes left to win the only game they would take all season.

Other than the massive buildup to that game the thing that stands out in my mind the most is how I rushed a young kicker named David Akers into the fray. I had recruited him out of the shadows of the Kentucky campus and then raced him out there against his hometown school. He struggled on that day and missed two short kicks. It could have been dispiriting, but he recovered nicely that season and had a remarkable college career. He would kick a 51 yarder against Texas A&M and a record 36 field goals for Louisville. He would go on to play in the NFL for 17 seasons and appear in six Pro Bowl games. Akers holds 10 NFL kicking records including the most field goals in a season. He deserves the record for the longest field goal ever kicked. Matt Prater topped him by a yard last year but did it in Denver, a mile above sea level. Prater dethroned him, but deserves an asterisk at least as much as Roger Maris did for topping Babe Ruth's homerun record in a longer season.

We would go on to beat Arizona State, Pittsburgh and North Carolina State and have a winning year, but we didn't do enough to get to another bowl game. We had given the city five winning seasons in seven years. We had won fourteen more than we lost over that period including our two bowl victories.

We were consistently playing before crowds of 35,000 in a minor league baseball park while waiting for a football stadium to be built. We were trading home games with Texas, Texas A&M, Arizona State, Tennessee, Pittsburg, Navy and Boston College. We had played Ohio State, Syracuse, Florida, Florida State, North Carolina, North Carolina State and Virginia Tech.

We had taken the program from basket-case status to respectability. We showed everyone that Louisville was football territory. I always believed that it was. I remembered the incredible support Flaget's football team received when I was there. The personality of the region and the way of life, I believed, was more akin to football than any other sport. The people in Kentucky, many of them, are underprivileged. They are tough. They have a hard work ethic. They are used to getting knocked down and having to get back up. I think they are a natural constituency for football.

When we gave them college football at the highest level, they responded to us, and I believe the excitement trickled down to high school programs all across the state.

I never got to lead the Cardinals onto the new field or work in the training facility and offices that got built at the north end of their new horseshoe stadium. I did come back for a visit when the complex opened in 1998 and later as a coach prowling the visiting sideline.

I can rest easy knowing I brought major college football to my hometown. And knowing we did it without a single NCAA infraction.

CHAPTER 10

OKLAHOMA INNUENDO

"Knowing the great coach and the honorable man he was, I went out there to see if I had misjudged him. I talked with athletes and people in the community and I determined the rumors were simply not true. I put my findings in my story in The New York Times. I was disappointed he was vilified. I guess he appeared to be an outsider to some but they made a mistake because he would have brought them to sanctified, glorified success."

– John Underwood, *award-winning writer for the Miami Herald and Sports Illustrated. Author of eight books, including Bear: The Hard Life & Good Times of Alabama's Coach Bryant*

People who know that gruff voice of mine might never be able to picture me singing the classic refrain from Richard Rodgers and Oscar Hammerstein II: *"Oh, what a beautiful mornin'. Oh, what a beautiful day. I got a beautiful feelin' Everything's goin' my way."*

Still, that was my mindset when I made the monumental personal decision to take my talents to Norman, Oklahoma in December 1994.

If you know the ending of this chapter before you read it, you probably expected me to introduce it with a funeral dirge. It is the most difficult period to discuss in my long football life.

We had been at Louisville twice as long as we had been at any other position we ever had. Beverlee and I had just built our dream house and moved into it the year before. It was 7,500 square feet just off the 18th fairway of an Arnold Palmer-designed golf course. We planned to live out our lives after football there.

I expected Louisville to be the last stop in my coaching career, even if I was miffed at the school for its decision to join a mid-level conference that would do nothing for the football program. The basketball coach, Denny Crum, was also opposed to the move, but the president, Donald Swain, moved against the advice of both of us.

I had advised against joining Conference USA because I didn't want to build our fall schedule around Cincinnati, Memphis, Tulane and Houston. I wanted to schedule and compete nationally. Now the Liberty Bowl was probably the best we could do.

On the heels of that new reality, Oklahoma Athletic Director Donnie Duncan asked if I'd be interested in moving west. Not to build a tradition, but to recapture one. He first spoke to me at a National Football Foundation dinner early in December.

I wasn't job hunting and I wasn't going to get into a beauty contest. I said I'd be interested if he knew I was the guy they wanted. I wasn't going to go through some type of elimination process when I already had my fondest dream in Louisville. I told him if I was their first and only choice or their last and only choice, I could be interested. In less than two weeks, he offered and I signed a five-year contract worth about $500,000 a year.

But it was never about money. I had just renewed my contract through 2000 at Louisville for almost $450,000 in total compensation each year. When I told them I was leaving, I was offered a $50,000-a-year increase if I would stay and a $1 million bonus to be paid at retirement. I didn't want to use Oklahoma to leverage more money from Louisville. That's done a lot today and I find it unseemly.

I was 61 years old and I thought I was striking a blow for every senior citizen in the country by taking on a new mission. Joe Paterno was 68. Bobby Bowden was 65. Neither was hinting at retirement, but they weren't accepting new challenges either. This revitalized me.

When they said I was the guy they wanted, I got really up for the opportunity. I am not ashamed to say I wanted the job because it gave me a better chance to win another championship. I wanted to do something no other college coach had ever done—win national titles at two different schools. Nick Saban has since turned that trick, winning a championship at LSU in 2003 before leading Alabama to the top of the mountain. I thought I would have a real chance to be the first to do it, but not necessarily in the first year.

I wasn't used to having all the raw materials on site when I got there. Here they had the young men, the facilities and all the things necessary to take this program back to its natural level, which was competing for national championships.

The vehicle was already assembled; I just needed to move it forward. At Miami and Louisville, we had to order in the parts, put it together, test drive it and do everything else before we had a vehicle that could allow us to compete. At Oklahoma, everything was already in place, and up until about 1988, they probably had the sleekest, fastest vehicle in the nation. They had won six national championships, three Heisman trophies, more Big Eight titles than anybody. It was only the last six years that the vehicle had started to sputter and not run so well. We needed to overhaul and fine tune it, and then maybe the old buggy would run full speed again.

Oklahoma Athletic Director Donnie Duncan asked me to come to Norman and clean up Barry Switzer's mess. The opportunity to chase another national championship with all the facilities and support any coach could want was attractive to me.

When I went out to Oklahoma, I didn't give it the deep thinking that I should have. This was a big-time program for many years and they had been right on the cutting edge. They were the best in the nation with Bud Wilkinson and Barry Switzer, and even when Switzer was forced out, they had just won a national championship. Theirs was a culture of winning; they had the recipe. I ran roughshod over what they had accomplished.

My mouth was on steroids. I guess I sold myself as some sort of savior. Less than two weeks into the job, on December 29, I watched a flat team led by a lame duck Gary Gibbs fizzle in the Copper Bowl. Afterward, I stupidly declared that everything before the Copper Bowl was B.C. and everything that happens afterward would be A.D. with all of the obvious implications of that.

I made another famously florid pronouncement that books would be written and movies would be made about my time at Oklahoma. The truth is that I was doing what I always did. I was selling with the same fervor that worked in Miami and Louisville. At each of my earlier stops I had to change a culture and convince people it was possible. This was a different animal.

When I told these people I was there to win a national championship, they simply believed me. Why shouldn't they? I had already done it and so had they. Oklahoma had dominated college football for decades. From 1947 to 1963 Bud Wilkinson posted a 145-29-4 record. He won three national championships. They slumped to a modest 64-33-2 over the next nine 9 years, but then Barry Switzer came on board in 1973. He was a remarkable 32-1-1 in his first three seasons and won back-to-back titles in 1974 and 1975. Switzer gave them memories that were positive to the tune of 157-29-4. He won another national title in 1985 before he was derailed by scandals and three years of NCAA probation in 1988.

Oklahoma teams had been in the wilderness for only a few years when I arrived, but it felt like a lifetime where football meant so much to so many.

I hadn't even settled into my grand new office that sits just up the ramp from the south end zone of Oklahoma Memorial Stadium in Norman when I made my unkind comments about the team's performance in the bowl game.

That game killed morale and set our recruiting back. I couldn't hire coaches until after the game was over, then to have it be a disgrace made our job harder.

After seeing all the blubber on the offensive linemen, I knew why they had lost. I was determined to be demanding about conditioning, but that was always my focus.

My all-too-public assessment was the team was out of shape, unorganized and unmotivated. I probably didn't need to add that they had disgraced the school in the bowl game. Those comments hurt me with some of the returning players and with Gibbs, who had done his best.

From my new office I looked out on 75,004 seats every day that were arranged in alternating crimson and cream blocks. These were the facilities I had only dreamed of having at Miami and Louisville. My job was to get the best out of these players and have their work be at that same peak level.

We certainly didn't need to be any bigger. I was known for fielding small and fast teams. I had never been faced with a team seriously overweight and in poor condition to my way of thinking.

One of the first things I did was institute a weight loss program. I flat out told some of the players they were too fat. I read one of them the equivalent of a Slim Fast riot act.

I had all my players scale the 72 east side steps of the stadium. I was surprised to hear they had never done that. I made it a requirement twice a day, two times a week, for four weeks. I made them haul themselves up 20-foot ropes hanging just outside my office. That's just for starters.

Not surprisingly, the team lost nearly 1,000 pounds. Offensive lineman Chris Campbell trimmed off almost 50 pounds, going from 335 to 286.

Then I simply went to work in my usual fashion. I put the team through tough and long practices in the heat of the day, hoping to improve their fitness. I drilled them hard in search of the core group that was willing to sacrifice for the team. Then I elevated those players, even if it was at the expense of players in their third or fourth year.

I benched Garrick McGee, a senior quarterback, in favor of a red-shirt freshman who gave me everything he had. I was making friends, but I was making some enemies, too.

A few players told the *Tulsa World* they had practiced longer than NCAA rules allowed, but they were asked to sign documents saying they were in compliance. The off-season practices were voluntary. Some felt they couldn't afford to miss them. If they weren't devoted to getting in shape on their own, it certainly wasn't going to help them to miss.

At one point when we came back to camp, a freshman player, Brian Ailey, was hospitalized with severe dehydration and heat stroke. There was a brief furor when he sued the university alleging that we willfully and intentionally ignored recognized safety precautions with respect to heat-related illnesses.

After I made comments to try to minimize the situation, there were suggestions that I was oblivious to the danger. That was ridiculous. At Flaget High School, long before University of Florida researchers developed what is now known as Gatorade, we benefited from a volunteer medical staff that fed us water I believe was laced with quinine. I was familiar with the heat prostration dangers from my own playing career that required me to take salt tablets and replace up to 15 pounds of water weight lost during games at Kentucky. I had grieved over Charlie Bradshaw's tragic experience with athletes losing their lives when he became a head coach. I had always given my players water breaks. My practices were no day at the beach. Yes, I wanted them right back out on the field, practicing even when fatigued. They are going to have to play in that condition late in a game, and the only way to be prepared is to practice when exhausted.

It gave me no satisfaction when friends sent me news clippings the next fall after six Oklahoma players were hospitalized for heat-related illnesses during a single practice under their next coach. The players returned to the field to find Popsicles offered at their water breaks.

In the end, the attention to Brian Ailey's plight resulted in a better relationship between the football program and Norman Regional Hospital. We also moved our morning practices up to 9:30 a.m. when it is a little cooler and took steps to ensure that we gave the full 5 minutes for the scheduled water breaks in our practices.

There was some grumbling by a handful of players about a reign of terror, but most people understood what we were about and were waiting to see the results.

Having 200 or 300 fans at every practice was new for me. Correspondents watching and calling in to radio talk shows to give updates on practice was different. Kickoff luncheons for 700 people came with the territory. Crowds of 4,500 at scrimmages and more than 10,000 for the spring game thrilled me.

Season ticket sales, which had dwindled to 45,000 the year before, rebounded by 5,000.

A media guide that was 392 pages and weighed over 3 pounds was impressive. Enough support to broadcast four coach's shows a week was unbelievable. I was on the air Monday, Tuesday, Thursday and Friday. Then I would make a guest appearance on a Dallas station early on Saturday mornings to reach our fan base down there.

My favorite show was done each Tuesday before a lunch crowd. I made a 30-minute trip from Norman to the Bricktown region of Oklahoma City to do a radio show from the Varsity Grill Sports Club. It was always well attended and a lively affair.

In general, I had a honeymoon in Oklahoma that lasted a full nine months. Perhaps it reached its crescendo with my barnstorming tour of the state's smaller communities after spring practice.

We had been welcomed like football royalty and now we set out to tour the kingdom. In a nine-day swing through the state we made more than 60 stops in 30 cities and towns. We called it a Boomer Sooner Blitz and traveled by car, bus, helicopter, plane and even in a horse-drawn schooner.

We traveled 2,290 miles. I thought the list of towns we hit was even more impressive than what Johnny Cash was rattling off in his hit song, "I've been everywhere."

We researched communities and selected ones that wanted us to be there. We were willing to go out into the hedgerows and byways and visit spots that were not normally frequented by Oklahoma coaches, but we didn't want to go without an invitation. We wanted the locals to set the agenda for what would happen in their community. That meant our program was different everywhere. Each town got custom treatment.

We opened in Pauls Valley and traveled through Woodward, Hugo and El Reno and on to Chickasha. We collected keys to the city in Seminole, Clinton, Weatherford and McAlester. We visited patrons at golf clubs and popular local restaurants. We spoke to civic clubs in places like Guyman and Altus and Broken Bow and Henryetta. We met workers at a meat processing plant in Yukon and a Wrangler jeans distribution center in Seminole. We addressed the Oklahoma Press Association at their annual meeting at Lake Texoma and talked to the faithful at the National Sand Bass Fishing Tournament and Festival in Madrill.

When the community responded in places like Muskogee and Lindsay, we turned downtown streets and convention centers into little football festivals. Community leaders presented us with gifts that we carried back to Norman and displayed in our football offices.

We were greeted by cheerleaders and noisy fans with banners and signs. We took questions, shook hands, posed for pictures and signed autographs until the last fan was satisfied.

I say we because Beverlee was with me every step of the way, welcomed like a First Lady of Football. She had been with me now at 10 stops over 36 years. We met while I was playing in the Canadian Football League. I was with the British Columbia team in Vancouver when I first saw the only love of my life. I wasn't much of a ladies' man. It was my teammate, Hornung, who turned heads and was nicknamed "Cuddles" at Flaget High. Hornung still teases me that I couldn't get a date in high school.

That didn't matter on this football trip in 1958. A Canadian teammate, Joe Poirier, was a graduate of McGill University in Montreal, and he worked it out so we could meet a few girls after our game there. One of them was Beverlee, a majorette for the Alouettes. We had a nice night together, but then I headed back to Vancouver and she stayed in Montreal. I played my first six games and then in the seventh week, who shows up on my doorstep but Beverlee. Her father had a friend with an ill wife 2,500 miles across the country. This friend needed someone to help with the children, so Beverlee's father sent her out there. It made for a nice façade and I wasn't complaining. We courted the rest of the season, but then I went back to Louisville and she returned to Montreal. We wrote to each other, and then she invited herself to Louisville to have Christmas with me and my family. We had a good Christmas and when New Year's came, she asked me to marry her. I declined, but after she went back to Montreal I recognized my mistake. It was still January when I said yes and we set the date for May 2 in Montreal. I didn't understand why nobody from Louisville wanted to come to the wedding. That turned out to be the first Saturday, always reserved for the Kentucky Derby, and even my family wasn't happy with our choice of dates. My parents came. My sister came, but my brother didn't. Attendance was so bad, I had to rent a best man in Poirier.

I took my first coaching job at Kentucky shortly after Beverlee and I were married. The first of our three sons, Stephen, was born in Lexington.

Our second boy, Stuart, arrived less than a year later. Some people call children born that close together Irish twins. They sure change your life. Our third son, Tim, was born when I was with the Rams.

While I coached through the decades, Beverlee did all the heavy lifting at home. In South Florida she was also very successful selling real estate. By the time I was a head coach, Beverlee had more time to be involved with football. She got to know my players by name and proudly cheered them from the sidelines during games. She hosted dinners for my staff and social events for the university. She was always a busy lady, but when we hit Oklahoma, our kids were all grown and living elsewhere.

Stephen was into a business career. Stuart was making his way in the construction industry in South Florida. Tim was traveling the world as a model for Calvin Klein Obsession.

Now Beverlee had the time and interest to be a full-time ambassador touring the rural parts of the state with me.

At one of our functions, the line to get Beverlee Schnellenberger's autograph was somewhat longer than the line to get mine. And my line was always serpentine. At our previous assignments, Beverlee hardly ever signed an autograph. Here she was warmly embraced and responded in kind, personalizing each signature. Instead of mindlessly scribbling her name, she would add a Bible verse or a brief message to a youngster urging them to behave or "Be sweet, always."

Her greater involvement in what was expected to be my last crusade made the brutal ending of the Oklahoma campaign all the more devastating. But let's not get too far ahead of ourselves.

Out there on the road with Beverlee, I talked about multiple championships to be won. I told my newly minted Sooner Nation we could win and we would win. I told them our goal was to win the national championship as quickly as humanly possible and to win it as often as possible.

If Lebron James were listening, he would have been proud of me. Not one, not two, not three.

Oklahoma fans loved hearing that they were going to be back on top. I said we were going to win right away. I believed it was possible to compete for a title in as little as three years. I never shared that timetable, but I did warn the faithful not to bet on their team, that it wasn't wise to risk their money on things of the heart. Five years would have been plenty of time to give them what we all wanted. They expected it all that first season, and they believed they heard me promise just that.

The mistake in a nutshell: I didn't make the necessary adjustment from trying to generate football interest to trying to manage it. I simply added to the mania.

We traveled with memorabilia, including the national championship footballs and the Heisman trophies. I didn't do enough to credit the architects of that success throughout the years. I simply promised more were on the way.

Maybe I would have done better by taking a page from my mentor, Bear Bryant, and poor-mouthing my first-year team. But that clearly has never been my style.

Instead, I just kept talking about returning to the glory days. A reporter from the Houston Chronicle asked me what would happen if it took a while to get there. What if the natives grow restless?

I made no allowances for that. "You can't be intimidated by somebody who wants the same things that you do," I said. "My disappointment will be greater than theirs. My elation will be greater than theirs. No one wants to win here any more than the coach."

I talked up my team to everyone, especially the national press. Though we were coming off a 6-6 season and I was handing the quarterback job to a freshman, we opened at No. 15 in the preseason polls.

It might have been better to explain all summer that installing new systems was yeoman's work. There would be a different defensive alignment. A new pro-style offense would replace the long-favored option. It would take a little while for a young quarterback, any quarterback to master my program.

While I was proclaiming a new Sooner era, behind the scenes there was a group loyal to and led by Barry Switzer that saw me as an outsider and wanted me gone from the moment I was hired. I was warned early on by the athletic director, Duncan, to be sensitive to the Switzer camp, but I paid it no mind.

At one point in the Boomer Sooner tour, I said the team I was putting together would make Sooner fans forget about Barry Switzer. Imagine my surprise when we feted him at halftime of an early season game.

The successful spring tour was itself a nod to tradition, but not Switzer. Bud Wilkinson had made a similar run across the state back in 1946.

The Switzer camp certainly wasn't happy with me. Each change that I announced was received like a poke in their collective eye.

A new formal team walk from Sooner House down Asp to the stadium on game day was met with skepticism. Why anyone would oppose a procession of players followed by the Sooner schooner, the cheerleaders and the Pride marching band was beyond me.

Modifications to the team's classic uniforms were greeted as blasphemy. The new uniforms featured numbers on the shoulders, stripes on the pants, and white shoes. We kept the details under wraps until the opening game, but hours of speculation filled the airwaves for weeks in anticipation.

The slam was that I was disrespecting tradition. Right or wrong, my thought was that tradition for an 18-year-old kid is about four years. Tradition is a good thing for the alumni, but it doesn't mean that much to today's players.

The biggest affront to the old guard, though, was that I wasn't interested in the alumni helping with recruiting. Boosters were proud that they had helped attract talented players in the past, but that opens the doors to improper gifts. If they knew of a good prospect, we were glad to hear about the player, but I needed them to leave the recruiting to my staff. Out of necessity, I put some limits on their access. Sorry, no more boosters in locker rooms and on the sidelines on game day.

Playing loose and fast in recruiting is what had brought Switzer and the football program down. When Duncan invited me on board, he told me the NCAA was not to blame, that it was the university's fault.

Switzer, you should know, still craved redemption after his unhappy demise. In 1987 Switzer had won the Big Eight Conference again as the NCAA investigated the school. In 1988 Oklahoma was put on three years of probation, banished from television for two seasons and barred from bowl appearances during that period. They also lost seven scholarships for each incoming class while on probation. Among the violations was that one recruit was paid to become a Sooner.

Switzer resigned in 1989, and despite 16 years of success, he left behind an outlaw program. He as much as confessed while making a final statement that he was totally disgusted working within a set of rigid rules that does not recognize the financial needs of many of our young athletes. "I am not making excuses," he said, "but simply giving an explanation when I say it was difficult to turn my back on these young men when they needed help."

He apparently knew better than the NCAA what was fair. Switzer wasn't willing to follow the rules and he said so. But it wasn't all about paying players. OU was becoming a troubled program. Charles Thompson had a high profile drug issue. Brian Bosworth talked openly of steroid use. There were charges of gang rape in the athletic dorms; players were making news with their guns. As more members of the team misbehaved the latest joke in the football world was: "What do you say to an Oklahoma football player dressed in a suit?" Answer: "Will the defendant please rise."

They were going to have to live with my changes in some of their traditions. They wouldn't have any choice if we could win football games. We managed to do just that the first three times out of the gate.

San Diego State gave us a chance to show we could handle a team that threw the football out of a no-huddle formation and show improvement over the Copper Bowl disaster when we had problems with BYU's explosive offense.

There were some magical moments. The fans were in a frenzy when the team sprinted onto the field and headed straight to the stands in the north end zone to slap hands with the friendlies. Our first play, a pass out of the shotgun, drew a roar from 71,119 fans.

We would amass 596 yards and win 38-22 in our debut. My 5'8", 225-pound junior running back, Jerald Moore, charged 159 yards and managed three touchdowns on 14 carries.

But there were hints of trouble ahead. Freshman quarterback Eric Moore struggled with seeing the field and completed just 11 of 22 for 143 yards with one interception. We gave up 22 fourth quarter points, including two touchdowns that followed long interception returns. We were assessed 15 penalties for 129 yards. We weren't showing the focus, the stamina or the discipline we needed to play at the highest levels. It would take time to correct course.

After the game, I told the assembled crew they were adapting and would get better for the next five years as they learned the system. It was clear to me it wasn't all going to happen at once.

We would win 24-10 over Southern Methodist University the following week, but it was nothing pretty.

As I walked to my car after the game, a youngster came up to me and said, "Good win, Coach." He got me to autograph a program. Then he asked me, "When is the offense going to start clicking?"

My thought was they train them young in Oklahoma.

We would actually climb into the top 10 after a 59-10 win over North Texas, but it was a bit of a mirage. We didn't score in our first six possessions and turned the ball over twice in that timeframe. It was 10-10 late in the first half. We did run for 346 yards, but Eric Moore completed just 5 of 13 passes with an interception.

We were 3-0 but still hadn't played a significant opponent. And things quickly went south once we did.

At that moment, I had five quarterbacks who had gone through my system and were playing in the NFL: Jim Kelly, Bernie Kosar, Vinny Testaverde, Browning Nagle and Jeff Brohm. Any one of them could attest that it takes time. The system works, but firm patience is required.

Across the Sooner Nation, there certainly wasn't any appreciation that it takes time to get a new offensive system working smoothly. I already

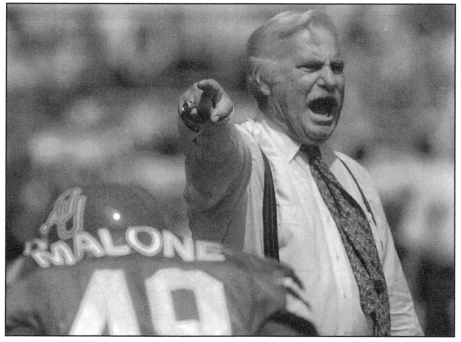

We got off to a 3-0 start and climbed into the Top 10 in the AP poll, but it was mostly downhill from there. I did manage to get my 100th win as a head coach when we beat Missouri later in the season.

said that was my fault. We always want things to happen overnight. The reality is it doesn't work that way.

In freshman quarterback Eric Moore, I had a kid with the arm strength to eventually make the plays. He was as quick as a jackrabbit running up a creek bank, and just as hard to catch. We decided to start him because it would pay off in the long run. He needed only time and experience. He still struggled with last-second adjustments and audibles. Our job was to get him ready. We didn't do it fast enough.

Next up was fourth-ranked Colorado in a rare night game in Norman. We had the first sellout crowd in eight seasons. ESPN came to town to broadcast it and some of our weaknesses were more fully exposed.

We jumped on top 10-0 with the help of a blocked punt and still led 17-14 at the break. We had nothing in the second half, managing just 28 yards of offense in the third quarter and not much more in the fourth. With Koy Detmer injured, Colorado backup John Hessler threw for a school record five TDs. He was 24-34 for 348 yards. We gave up TD passes of 42 and 71 yards. We held firm at 17 points. Colorado put up 38.

I came to regret a pregame statement that I hoped Detmer played because I didn't want an asterisk next to our win if he sat it out.

We came out of the Colorado game with our top three backs hurting. We did what anyone would have to do and turned to the next three on the depth chart. I gave thanks for our Toilet Bowl scrimmages. We were using the same full-speed, full-contact scrimmages each Monday for players who didn't get much action on Saturday.

The Monday bowls are not glamorous events, but they get the backup players in competitive shape under game-like conditions. Few teams do it, but I had held such a scrimmage every week during the season for years because I wanted to use every available moment to develop the players. If youngsters come into the program, watch the games, watch the starters scrimmage and never have contact like this under game conditions, they never get the edge they need before being called upon.

We ended up playing three substitute backs the week after the Colorado game and that made us vulnerable on the road for the first time that season. We managed to put down Iowa State 39-26 and keep hopes high for the Red River Shootout with Texas.

The rivalry with Texas provides one of the nation's greatest showcases of college football. The game is played each year in the Cotton Bowl in Dallas on the state fairgrounds. The stakes were enormous as they are in many rivalry games when both teams are nationally ranked.

During a speech to a ladies' club before the game, my offensive coordinator, Gary Nord, got a standing ovation. "I hope you girls will still love me if for some reason we get stuck on the 1-yard line against Texas," he said in parting. A little old lady stood up and replied, "Yeah, we'll still love you. And we'll miss you, too."

The season was on the line in this game. Writers asked me if it was the biggest game of my career and I had to say no. That caused a stir, but what else could I say. I had already won a national championship. I didn't believe I had anything to prove.

It is kind of sad to say that winning at Oklahoma is not a thrill; it is an expectation. Still, there's no true pressure on a football coach. Pressure is on the guy who's making $250 a week and has to feed his family.

To get in the spirit of things for this game, we decided to open our practice at the fairgrounds the night before the game. Anyone with an admission to the state fair could get into the stadium and watch our practice. Fair officials and fans embraced it, even if traditionalists brought up stories about Switzer and Royal spying on each other. There is nothing anyone was going to learn about my Sooners by watching us go through our warm-up drills that they couldn't have learned beforehand.

We started poorly. Eric Moore, playing in his hometown, fumbled on the third play from scrimmage. We gave up the ball at our own 39. Two minutes later we were down 7-0. The next time we got the ball we failed to make a first down and suffered a blocked punt. Texas fell on it in the end zone. They added a 69-yard home run to make it 21-0 in the first 9 minutes of the game. Texas was on the brink of another touchdown at our 6-yard line before a holding penalty, a diving deflection of a pass by cornerback Larry Bush and then a sack by Cedric Jones pushed them back out of field goal range and changed the flow of the game.

That allowed Nord and the offense to stick with our game plan of attacking the Texas defensive front. One more Texas score and we would have abandoned the run for the no-huddle catch up game.

If it wasn't panic, there was grave concern. Somehow we found our poise.

For the next two periods, we were clearly the better team. We switched to our senior quarterback, Garrick McGee, as we tried to collect ourselves. He led us on a 98-yard drive with Jerald Moore collecting 45 of them. Jerald Moore was the dominant player on the field, piling up 174 yards on the day. We trailed only 24-10 at halftime.

We came to within seven points on our first drive of the second half, moving 61 yards in six plays. Eric Moore returned under control, scrambled to his left and threw an 8-yard touchdown pass to P.J. Mills in the corner.

We got a good defensive play that knocked the ball loose as Texas attempted to return a punt. We took over the ball at the Texas 22 and Jerald Moore ran for another TD to tie the game.

The defense that had looked so porous in the opening quarter did a phenomenal job stopping the Texas ground game and star runner Ricky Williams. If you took away Shon Mitchell's long touchdown run, Texas managed just 28 yards on 25 carries. Our domination in that area was evident when they went for it on fourth and one at our 11-yard line with 9 minutes remaining in the game. They pitched out to Williams on an option, but linebacker Broderick Simpson stopped him.

Before every game I led my team in reciting The Lord's Prayer. We won as many as we lost in my one season at Oklahoma, but that wasn't a good enough start in a football-obsessed state.

We had our chance to win with 31 seconds left in the game. Field goal kicker Jeremy Alexander came into this game 11 for 11, but he was not able to perform flawlessly on this day. After making an early field goal, Alexander missed from 53 yards in the third quarter and then his 42-yard attempt was wide left at the end, spoiling what would have been an exhilarating come-from-behind victory.

The 50th consecutive sellout crowd for this rivalry game left with the scoreboard announcing a 24-24 tie.

The game was a microcosm of our season. We played well in spurts, but struggled for consistency. Almost. Close. Not good enough.

I'll never know for sure, but everything might have been different if that ball had gone through the uprights in the final seconds against Texas. What I do know is that the air went quickly out of our balloon.

It was the beginning of the end for our season. We were 4-1-1, but we would lose four of the next 5. When we lost to Kansas 38-17, someone suggested that I stood exposed like an impotent Wizard of Oz. The team certainly seemed not to believe any more than the dejected Sooner Nation.

We managed to beat Missouri, 13-9, which impressed no one even though it made us 5-2-1 for the season. It was my 100th win as a head coach against 74 losses and 3 ties. If that milestone win had come against Texas, it would have been very special. Coming here, as it did, there was no joy to be found, and it would turn out to be my last win at Oklahoma.

We shut down completely. We lost 49-10 to Kansas State, 12-0 to Oklahoma State and 37-0 to the No. 1 team in the nation, Nebraska.

We ended with a 5-5-1 record. It was better than my record at the end of my first year in Miami and better than my start in Louisville. But this was the wrong place to go 5-5-1, even if they were coming off a 6-6 season.

The year before the team had lost its bowl game in embarrassing fashion. We were not even eligible for a bowl.

We were 2-5 in the Big Eight and that was the worst anyone had done in 30 years.

The loss to Kansas State was the worst defeat in 50 years.

The back-to-back shutouts to end the season were the first in 53 years.

My predecessor, Gary Gibbs, was blamed for the fan apathy that I tried to reverse. His record had been 44-23-2 over six years, closing with that

6-6 session. His sin was seen as his 2-15-1 record against Texas, Nebraska and Colorado. I just closed out the year 0-2-1 against them.

My record proved to be an unmitigated disaster.

In a typical moment of preseason excess, I had named myself Supreme Commander of the Sooner Nation. Now I was made the Supreme Scapegoat.

I am a big boy. I have received many ovations and taken my bows through the years. I can take the hit, too. What I can never forget is how nasty it got. What I can never forgive is that they tried to crush Beverlee along with me.

When we were no longer winning, the reign of terror was to blame. And the reign of terror was blamed on a drinking problem.

One player, the senior quarterback I benched, reported smelling alcohol on my breath at a university function. Another said I always had a red nose and red ears at practice.

That would eventually lead to a radio caricature of me on KOKH by host Mike Steely. He offered up a character that was a mix of General Patton and Harry Caray. In a rumbling voice a little like mine, he would talk about valor and courage and the battle of the trenches. My military penchant is a fitting target. But the kicker was the voice of Howard would slur and hiccup and occasionally the character would pass out.

I had become a running joke at O'Connell's, the landmark watering hole just a block from the stadium. A place I never frequented. I have never been drunk in public. I don't believe I have ever been intoxicated in private. I did occasionally drink alcohol, though I vowed never to do so again after this smear.

Beverlee, who doesn't drink at all, was rumored to have a drinking problem, too. She was said to be out shoplifting merchandise. My glamorous wife was once criticized in Louisville for wearing a full-length fur coat to a November game, but this was the first time she had ever been exposed to anything like this nastiness.

At the end of our stay in Norman, she only left the house to get groceries or go to church. She would try to do that before dawn or at other odd hours when she wouldn't be seen.

The university's athletic compliance officer interviewed players and athletic department personnel about the allegations and my personal habits.

It was a climate meant to force me out. If the administration was not actively behind the rumors, and I suspected some dirty tricks, they did nothing to stop the nonsense. In fact, they fueled it with their supposed investigation.

I felt we were doing the right things to develop the program, but I wasn't getting support any longer from the administration. The inaccurate reports and hurtful rumors produced a no-win situation, and I did ultimately resign the week before Christmas, two days after the anniversary of being hired.

A few months after I left Oklahoma, *The New York Times* published what some saw as my football obituary. I took great solice in some of their findings and conclusions, even though the thought that my life in football was over would prove premature.

Under a banner headline saying "The Coach Takes a Beating" and this subhead: "Howard Schnellenberger Did Something Unforgiveable at Oklahoma: He Lost Football Games," there was nice photo of Beverlee with me and the following caption: "Innuendoes 7, Schnellenberger 0."

John Underwood, a veteran *Sport Illustrated* writer interviewed me for the piece. I'll give you just a few bits of it here. The lead said that my departure was a resignation only if you are willing to call a public hanging a suicide.

The article suggested the rumors and innuendoes say more about Oklahoma than about me. "Any rumors that I ever heard," university president David Boren told *The Times*, "were disproven. I mean totally."

University administrators denied Barry Switzer played any role. Surely he did, at least indirectly. The day I was hired Switzer commented that someone would have to tell me where Norman, Oklahoma was. He said I didn't fit. He was very vocal in wanting someone from his camp in charge. As I went out one door, he came in through the other. Shortly after I left, the school announced they were renaming the football complex in his honor.

To replace me, they quickly appointed Switzer protégée John Blake, who played for Switzer and later worked on his Dallas Cowboys staff. Blake had never been a head coach, but he was from the inside. I was, by contrast, the first person from the outside to coach there in 30 years. An outsider didn't have a cut dog's chance.

On Saturday afternoons in Norman, the faithful sing: "I'm a Sooner born and a Sooner bred. And when I die I'll be Sooner dead." I had no Sooner blood, no Switzer ties and now they rejected me like a body repelling a transplanted organ.

I have never talked to Switzer about my short tenure. I did run into him at a recent Kentucky Derby, the one won by Orb. He asked me to pose for a photo with him. Then he asked Beverlee to do the same. It was hard to pose with a smile, but we obliged.

In its search for answers, *The Times* quoted the chairman of the Board of Regents saying I raised expectations too high.

In summing up the situation that chased me out of town, Underwood quoted a former Sooner player who now heads a drug rehabilitation program and is very involved with the university. Jim Riley pointed out that it was Switzer, not Schnellenberger, who was arrested on a driving-while-impaired charge, and truly scandalized the school.

Riley said there was no reign of terror, only a bunch of players who needed to learn how to work.

"This is Oklahoma," Riley said. "It has nothing to do with drinking or heat prostration or anything else. It has to do with 5-5-1, and losing to Oklahoma State."

I plead guilty to that.

CHAPTER 11

MY LAST HURRAH

"Coach is the greatest magician that football has ever known. He can take 'nothing' and make it into 'something.' No tricks, just hard work and dedication. I've seen it done, I know."

— **Johnny Frost,** *University of Louisville linebacker and assistant coach at Florida Atlantic University*

The most thrilling thing I have ever done as a coach was lead the Florida Atlantic University football team onto the field for the first time. I felt like a proud father watching his son take his first steps. This team was mine in a way that no other team ever could have been. I was there at the conception and then the birth, the baptism and eventually the confirmation of this group.

I had been with the Dolphins for their undefeated season and we had won national championships at Alabama and at the University of Miami, but this was much more personal. Each of my earlier successes was a different animal and they are hard to compare, but this thrill cannot be surpassed.

It was simply more meaningful to me to create a football team where there was no program. Everywhere else I was a hired hand. Here I was the proud father. This was my family. These were all my kids.

Florida Atlantic was the third time I was given a full opportunity to build a football house, but it was the first time I got to meet with the architect. I got to lay the foundation myself and see the construction through to completion. I had been successfully rehabbing homes, now I was building my own.

To fully appreciate this, you have to understand there was no tradition, there were no uniforms, there wasn't a helmet or a shoulder pad on campus when I arrived. Hell, there wasn't even a nail where you could hang a jock strap.

At first I was not interested in getting back into football, but there was something exciting about being part of the birth of a program. It rejuvenates you. It infuses you with energy.

It would give me another unexpected decade as a head coach, send me to two more bowl games and let me deliver an on-campus stadium for my team before retiring from the ring.

My football encore was the brainchild of a former Rutgers football player by the name of Dr. Anthony Catanese. He was the president of a 22,000-student commuter school sprawled across seven campuses in three South Florida counties.

Football at FAU was Catanese's brainchild. He believed football would give FAU the last general credential it needed to enter into the senior level of universities. He thought it was the one and only thing that could bring all seven campuses together in common purpose.

Before becoming president of the university in 1990, Catanese was asked by the Florida Board of Regents what he thought would boost FAU's profile. He told them football. He said all the great universities play football, and you are compared academically with who you play in football. He believed it was important to the school's image and reputation and alumni and students that a school be in the big leagues both academically and athletically.

When the board hired Catanese to steer the development of the 1,000-acre main campus in Boca Raton and all of its satellites, he concentrated first on academics, student needs and fundraising. He kept the football idea alive when he ended his commencement ceremonies by announcing to great cheers the score of a future Orange Bowl: Florida Atlantic 21, University of Miami 10.

This was a man after my heart.

Catanese had the vision and the enthusiasm. In the spring of 1998 he tracked me down and brought me in to help make it a reality. I didn't sell the idea to him. He was the driving force behind it. He wanted me to lead his crusade.

He believed I could bring everyone together under the flagstaff of the Fighting Owls and I was intrigued, even though I had just started a new career.

After my falling out with the Oklahoma power structure and the bitter ending there, Beverlee and I retreated to South Florida where we had been so happy and enjoyed so much success. We spent a lot of time together like normal people do. I certainly would have preferred to continue coaching at that juncture, but it didn't happen. So we did as God intended us to do and made the most of it. We saw more of our sons and grandchildren. I began working as a stocks and bonds broker.

I had my degree from the University of Kentucky School of Commerce, but I had never even bought stocks or bonds. I didn't invest at all. My wife balanced our checkbook. Still, I went in search of a firm to sponsor me and found one where several former Dolphins players worked. So I had to get a license, had to pass a national exam known as the Series 7. I was living in Miami Lakes and driving up to Boca Raton for classes. You study and take practice exams for about three months. First school exam I got a 49 and you need 70 to pass. Took some more classes, then tried the state exam and came back with a 56. You have to wait a month to take it again, so I studied some more and tried it again. This time I got a 68. I was going to practice until I got it, but you can only take the test three times and then you have to wait a year. Beverlee and my three children were waiting to see if I could rise to the occasion. I took about 400 practice tests before giving it one more try. I knew full well people were starting to think of that old saying about what it means if you are doing something over and over and getting the same results. I got a 76 on my final attempt. Then I found out the average passing score is 72, so now I'm Phi Beta Kappa.

That was where I was, just settling in with a new career selling mostly municipal bonds for A.F. Best, when Florida Atlantic got in touch. The idea to recruit me was Catanese's, but the first sales pitch was made by Athletic Director Tom Cargill. We had a two-hour lunch at Shula's restaurant in Miami Lakes. He said FAU was ready to launch a football program and I was the first person they decided to call. I was flattered enough to want to meet with the president.

When I was speaking with Catanese to try to decide whether to take the job or not, he indicated that he had taken a major survey of the students, faculty and staff, and there was overwhelming support for the idea of a football team. He said he had commissioned a feasibility study that surveyed 550 people from the local business community. Numbers from his surveys rolled off his tongue like game statistics used to spill off mine at a Sunday night staff meeting.

More than 40 percent of the business people surveyed had a family member who had taken classes at FAU. Better than 75 percent had attended an athletic event at the university. Upwards of 60 percent regularly attended football games. Ninety percent wanted to see FAU start a football program. Fifty-eight percent said they would attend games with their families. Eighteen percent said they were very likely to purchase season tickets.

I took what he was telling me at its face and most of it proved to be accurate. The man had done his homework and I came away convinced this was a high priority for him. If it's a high priority for the president of a university, it has a good chance of success.

Catanese asked me what I thought and I told him "Football in Paradise" sounded like a good idea. He asked me if I thought the school could build a winning program and I told him they would need to build a stadium on campus. He said he would love to do it, but we would have to raise the money.

It didn't take long to fall in love with the notion, though I made my commitment in stages.

Catanese offered me a three-year contract for $90,000 a year and a state car. My plan was to help get things rolling and continue working in the financial industry. Fortunately, I had a lot of flexibility in my new position with A.F. Best.

My job at FAU was to hire a secretary, help raise $5 million in start-up money, get approval from the state Board of Regents, recruit a staff, plan an athletic facility and then hire the head coach.

When the agreement was announced in April 1998, Catanese told the Palm Beach Post I was the head of football operations and I was responsible for "everything."

That didn't sit well with me at first. I was happy to be the point man, but I knew I was going to need a lot of support from professionals at the school. I wasn't hired to be the coach either, though Catanese says he always knew I would be the first coach. He read me well.

He stamped my brand on his football program and let me run with it. He knew I would delight in showing people that reports of my football death were premature. I ran through four sets of tires and put 250,000 miles on the car. He got a full-time worker at a part-time salary.

We agreed we would start playing at the 1-AA level, the second highest in college ball. But the bowl championship level was our goal from the start.

Spoiler alert: No one saw it coming, but we made the Final Four in the 1-AA playoffs in our third year. We joined Miami, Florida and Florida State in the big boy league by our fourth year. We were playing in bowl games and winning them by the end of our sixth and seventh seasons. No one had ever done it that fast and no one will ever do it again.

Where did we start? They gave me a desk in the FAU Foundation office. They gave me a partner in the person of Susan Peirce. She knows the development game as well as anyone, and I was ready to meet the titans of business and work any room once we had a plan in place.

Over breakfast at a Boca restaurant we began to draw up a timeline for key events. We would eventually print that vision on a glossy brochure with a football field as a backdrop. The pace was going to be frantic, but things needed to happen in the right sequence. We wanted to recruit our first class of players for the fall of 2000 and play our first game in September 2001. It all culminated with a move to Division 1-A and construction of an on-campus stadium. We needed to jumpstart our fundraising program quickly, but not until we made a few preparations and laid the groundwork.

We put up a website.

I committed to a radio show three nights a week. We followed immediately with a weekly television show and a regular Sunday column on the front of the local sports section. We were the talk of the town. We were everywhere.

We started a speaker's bureau that accepted every invitation and always sent the same FAU representative—me.

I started to introduce myself as director of football operations and jack of all trades because I was responsible for marketing, advertising, fundraising, facilities planning and kissing babies.

We started beating the football drum before the movers and shakers. When I spoke to the FAU Foundation Board, it felt like I was in the locker room at the Orange Bowl. Next up was the Boca Raton Chamber of Commerce, the Sunrise Rotary Club, the Palm Beach County Chamber, the Palm Beach Kiwanis, the Broward Chamber and the Miami Touchdown Club. There was no end to the list of clubs and organizations that showed an interest. I gave presentations to 100 groups in the first five months.

The faculty senate gave me an opportunity to speak. The majority believed the time had come for the building of a football program on this campus. There were several hardcore professors that felt it was not the university's business to develop a football team, but of the 50 or so educators at the meeting, only two were of that persuasion. At the end of the session, I felt there was plenty of support. Today there really isn't anyone who believes it was a mistake. I think the way the administration handled it in the first few years let it happen without a great struggle on campus.

I spoke to 1,300 incoming freshmen and their parents at an orientation in August. To reach the rest of the student body I used a different approach. I ordered a foot-and-a-half-high stump sawn from cypress and took it to the main university cafeteria every Wednesday during the lunch hour. I'd climb up and preach about the future, about bringing football to their campus. I handed out bumper stickers celebrating our undefeated team. If they asked, I gave a history lesson on the origins of the political stump speech.

By now I believed this was the most important job I'd ever had. Football was going to allow high school students to become part of the FAU family before they made their decision to attend a college. It would affect the lives of hundreds of players. Football would impact the lives of every student that came through these doors, along with the alumni and the fans. Their quality of life could improve with football. It would give alumni a point of pride and a reason to return to campus.

With an all-out push, it didn't take long to sell faculty, students, alumni and community leaders on the idea of Football in Paradise. The final hurdle, though, was the Board of Regents. They would decide whether we would play football at FAU and their mindset was simple: "Show me the money."

We gave ourselves one year to raise enough money to impress the Board of Regents and win their backing for the program.

Susan Peirce did some preliminary interviews with community leaders. She told them where we were headed and asked them what questions they had about the plan. Then she devised a pamphlet that addressed the most frequently asked questions. We created a fund and solicited 70,000 alumni by mail.

We considered every small check we received a vote in favor of football. There were lots of votes. But we were going to need major donors as well to reach our targets.

Thanks to a donation of $530,000 by a supporter who wished to remain anonymous, we reached our first goal of $1 million in August, three months ahead of schedule.

We were busy knocking on the doors of corporate chiefs. We were working in a wealthy community populated with financial firms and internet companies. I would chum and she would fish. I would use my football history to lure them in, and she would close the deals and sign them up.

Fifty thousand was our asking price to be recognized as a founder of the football program. I arrived at the figure after seeing the ease with which some people were able to donate $10,000.

It is easy to support a team that is established and has won a championship; it takes a stronger belief and greater courage to stand behind something from the very start. We told people we were trying to do something important for the community, and it would take bold action on their part to help us accomplish it.

Howard Guggenheim, who was a senior vice president at Salomon Smith Barney and vice chair of the FAU Foundation board, became the first to step up. A dozen more followed quickly.

My new friends in the financial community were expecting me to bring ball players and football supporters into their offices, but instead I brought some of the financial people along to support FAU football. Funny how those things turn out. A.F. Best made a gift of $50,000 to the program and was another of our founding donors.

By the time we made our second presentation to the Board of Regents in March 1999, we had 21 founders enlisted and had raised $3 million in just 10 months. The board gave us unanimous approval to start the program.

Of course, there was a caveat. They required us to raise a total of $6 million for facilities and another $5 million to run the program. We would exceed it over a three-year period.

Everything was moving faster than anyone had dreamed. FAU football was going to happen. Reporters stopped asking me if I was smoking something funny in my pipe.

We unveiled the fledgling football program using a Gypsy Rose Lee striptease strategy, slowly revealing a little more but making sure to keep everyone's interest until we could play our first game.

The first hint of football ecstasy came with a helmet design. President Catanese brandished the helmet overhead when we returned from our successful meeting with the Board of Regents, and the newspapers displayed us in a triumphant pose. We promptly presented helmets to each of our founding donors.

We knew where we were going, and we were determined that getting there was going to be fun. It was time to celebrate with a pep rally and bonfire.

We called it the Hallelujah Football in Paradise Pep Rally and Bonfire. It started with a celebration in the gym. The dance team and our cheerleaders put on a show. We had a gospel singer perform Hallelujah backed by a church choir. We recognized all our big donors to that date and then moved outside to create a spectacle that attracted about 2,000 early fans.

Never mind that our rally competed for attention with our nationally ranked baseball team. They were across campus at the same hour winning their 31st game of the season. Even John McCormack, our baseball coach, said he could see football was generating a tide of interest that would lift all sports.

The Goodyear blimp flew over the football party with a lighted display that said: Hallelujah Finally Football in Paradise. A hearse backed through the crowd and two men dressed

Photo courtesy of FAU Athletics, JC Ridley

The Board of Regents gave us approval to start the Florida Atlantic football program in March 1999 and President Anthony Catanese and I returned to Boca Raton triumphant. We presented helmets to all of the major donors who helped me raise the $11 million we needed to launch the program.

as pallbearers removed a makeshift plywood coffin carrying a huge teddy bear that had to stand in for the mascot of our first opponent. A pallbearer took the bear from its coffin and drove him onto a spike at the top of the woodpile. President Catanese put a torch to the pile and the bear was consumed.

We captured even more attention on July 12, 1999, as we announced a $4 million donation and the signing of a head coach at the same time.

The gift was from Tom Oxley, an early graduate of Florida Atlantic, who was owner of Royal Palm Polo. He lived on campus in the school's infancy and embraced the possibility that football could transform our campus and student life.

His $4 million ante covered half of the eventual cost of the athletic training facility and practice fields we would build. The Oxley Athletic Center would lift us out of the catacombs of an ancient field house that couldn't compete with the facilities at my old high school. The replacement was even nicer than the Hecht Center at the University of Miami.

The facility would be 61,000 square feet. Everything in it was first class. The lockers for players, coaches and managers were all made of oak. It featured a 4,000-square-foot weight room with $175,000 worth of equipment. There was an academic center with more than 50 computers, an auditorium with 110 theater-style seats and an audio-visual room for instruction. There were five other classroom/meeting rooms, a reception area, an athlete's lounge, offices for coaches, a training room, a doctor's office and administrative offices. We also built a founder's room for the people who made it all possible.

We broke ground for the facility on September 29, 1999, and when the doors opened in January 2001, the founder's room showcased 102 plaques honoring leaders who each gave $50,000 or more as part of the $14 million raised to start the program.

We announced the Oxley gift to marching band music and had our cheerleaders on hand. We had students model our new uniforms as we tried to help people visualize this team that didn't yet exist. We changed the school colors from blue and silver to red, white and blue. We unveiled solid blue jerseys with white numbers trimmed in red and accented with red, white and blue striping.

I guess I would have preferred a name like Titans, but back in 1971 the FAU campus had been designated a burrowing owl sanctuary by the

Audubon Society and the bird became the university's mascot. The school dropped the burrowing part of the nickname a decade later.

Burt Reynolds, who played his college ball at FSU but owned a playhouse in nearby Jupiter, commissioned a sculpture of a menacing owl flashing its talons in flight. I embraced the ferocious image and stationed it outside my office. We would be known as the Fighting Owls and the Big Bad Burly Birds.

When I think about it, I enjoyed pretty good luck with birds over the years. The Ibis, the Cardinal and the Owl all served me well. Put all three on one scale and they probably wouldn't weigh five pounds. Not exactly a lion, a tiger, and a bear, but winners all.

AN OLD WARHORSE RISES FOR ONE LAST THRILL

The announcement that I would be the head coach was greeted as anti-climactic because Cargill had put it out there that I had a right of first refusal and I was already hiring a staff to begin recruiting. But my stepping into the role wasn't as certain as many believed.

I actively considered two other real possibilities before making my decision. The first was Mark Richt, my former Hurricane quarterback who was then the offensive coordinator of the Florida State team. He was named head coach at Georgia in 2001. The other attractive possibility was David Shula, the son of Don Shula and a former coach with the Dolphins, Cowboys and Bengals.

I was out there talking to high school coaches about recruits and they kept asking me who would be the coach. I would mention my top two prospects, but they would invariably ask me why I shouldn't do it. They said they would rather send their kids to someone proven.

It was the same with FAU's trustees. They kept reminding me I was a pretty accomplished college coach, one who was 100-77-3 in 16 years as the man in charge.

Truth is, I had some concerns about myself. I wanted to be sure the fire was burning strong enough and my health was what it needed to be for the job. If there were no birthdays or mirrors, I wouldn't have known how old I was. But I was 65 when we started this. At an age when most people were retired, I needed to be sure I was ready to go again.

I really did not think I would coach again, but the stars seemed aligned in the right configuration. Besides, Joe Paterno was still coaching at 72. I still felt like when he finally retires I'll have another seven years.

So this old warhorse rose again to undertake perhaps my most important battle ever. Everything in my life seemed like preparation for this assignment, and I signed a seven-year contract worth $150,000 annually plus television, radio, endorsement and camp revenues.

After I made my decision, Catanese, the scoundrel, says, "You know, I wanted you to be the coach all along." I reminded him that he never said as much, but assured him his support was very important to me. I had learned at least twice that things don't work well without the backing of the top man.

I knew I couldn't do the job alone, and I started naming a permanent staff within a month.

At Miami and Louisville I brought in coaches who liked the idea of saving a program from a slow death. At FAU I brought in a staff of thrill seekers. They were guys who totally believed that we could get it done.

Joining me were five assistants who combined for well over 100 years of coaching experience, plus three former pro players getting started on their coaching careers. I came to the task with 36 years of coaching experience and rings of my own. Together we had six Super Bowl rings and nine collegiate championship rings. Two had played for or coached with Paul Bryant, and three had played for or coached with Don Shula. Two were former head coaches.

My assistant head coach, Kurt VanValkenburgh, had 26 years at Union, Colgate, Virginia, Vanderbilt, Maryland, Louisville, Oklahoma and Purdue, leading defenses as coordinator at four of them. My offensive coordinator and quarterback coach, Larry Seiple, had 24 years coaching experience after playing with the Dolphins. Defensive Coordinator Kirk Hoza boasted 16 years of experience, including a head coaching stint at Whittier College.

Fred O'Connor had 16 years in the business and was a former offensive coordinator at Southern Miss and Villanova. He was also an interim head coach while in the NFL with the 49ers and had served as head coach at Catholic University.

Arnie Romero had been recruiting in South Florida for 30 years and had worked at Miami, Central Florida and Iowa State. Christ Vagotis also had 30 years in the game and was with me in Miami, Louisville and Oklahoma.

Complementing the long-time veterans were three younger assistants making the transition from their playing days. Alfredo Roberts was a former Hurricane and a two-time Super Bowl winner in Dallas. Mark Sander was a Louisville alum coming off three seasons with the Dolphins, and Mel Mills had played arena ball after leaving Louisville.

When I was in the business of fixing programs, I always said it would be easier to build one from scratch. On the other hand, there are a lot more things to do in building your own, such as creating uniforms, starting a booster program, buying field equipment and such. From that perspective, building a program is much more time-consuming. But a new program is a lot like a blank canvas. We were painting what we wanted.

The fundraising and program-building would continue, but football operations were beginning.

We had temporary football offices so bleak that there was no reason to hang around. So we branched out and observed high school practices and drills. We visited 325 high schools south of Orlando. We established a relationship with each of those high schools that no university in Florida has and that no cherry-picker from up north could dream of building.

We didn't really open our recruiting in competition with Miami, Florida and Florida State. We let the lions have their share, and whatever was left we went head to head with anybody else from Florida or from out of state. We did very well against the big name schools from up north, even before we had a football team.

I gave my coaches three marching orders when looking at athletes: first, make sure that the athlete has the desire to get their degree; second, make sure that the athlete is a solid citizen and that he is coachable; last, that the athlete has enough athletic ability to compete in the college environment.

We wanted to sign our first class in February 2000 and begin playing in September 2001 after bringing on a second core group in February of that year.

We recruited almost exclusively in South Florida. I wasn't blowing smoke when I tried to justify our football program by pointing to a real need to offer more scholarships in Florida.

When we announced our program, there were 607 colleges playing football. There were 112 at the 1-A level, 119 in Division 1-AA, 158 in Division II and 218 in Division III. Florida had just eight schools playing football: four in 1-A and four in 1-AA. Ohio had 33 schools playing football, Texas 29, California 24. Even Georgia and Connecticut each had 11 football schools.

The numbers said the state was ripe for another program. With a population of 15 million we were producing 300 Division 1 players each year and only 80 were staying in Florida on scholarships. That meant 220 were going out of state to play football. They had to leave their families and the great environment here just to stay in the sport. That didn't seem right to me.

As we focused on recruiting local talent, we had something powerful to attract them: the prospect of playing in front of their friends and family. That was a very important selling point we made, along with letting them know they would be part of building a winning tradition. We told them that if they wanted the kind of adulation that comes with bringing a program to life, then this might be the place for them. If they wanted their picture in the first press guide or they wanted to go into the record books as part of the first team or be the first to make a tackle or score a touchdown for Florida Atlantic University, they should come along for the adventure.

Early on we got a verbal commitment from a top local player. Olympic Heights running back Anthony Jackson, the Palm Beach Post player of the year, announced his plans in December. Jackson had been recruited by Florida, West Virginia and Ohio State. He quickly went from recruit to recruiter, talking up his choice of FAU at a high school All-Star game in January. He helped bring us several players. Each one said they were going to join Jackson because they wanted to play as freshmen and start for four years. Those pledges, though, were not binding until letters of intent could be inked on February 2.

I was in my office at 5 a.m. on signing day, checking the phones and the fax machine. I felt like I was at election central and the precincts were reporting in.

We were there with every other football-playing university in the state celebrating our incoming class. We were competing for the first time and we were not shut out.

The day generated great excitement. We held a signing day party and 100 people came by to see our results. We had some declared walk-ons model our home and away uniforms and run through some mock plays.

As we got each commitment, we would hang up a blue jersey with the name of the signee on the back. The first letter to arrive and the first jersey hung up on a lengthy clothes line belonged to Mauratae Johnson of Suncoast High School in West Palm Beach. He was 6'1" and 180 pounds and led his team in receptions and interceptions. He was a team captain and All-Conference.

Jackson, who made the early pledge that proved so helpful, came through, but only after a signing ceremony at his high school at 1 p.m.

We were anxious for some bodies to fill our jerseys; we were looking for the right personalities to wear our helmets. We hoped for 20 and enlisted 23 scholarship players on signing day. At last our football dream had some humanity.

We got the county's top two running backs: Jackson who had rushed for 1,644 yards and 20 touchdowns as a senior and tailback Doug Parker, who led Atlantic High School in Delray Beach with 24 rushing touchdowns.

Our first class also included the leading passer in the state, Garrett Jahn. He was set to walk on at Florida State when Mark Richt called me and recommended him for scholarship consideration. Jahn was a 6'3" All-State talent out of Tallahassee Leon High School. He threw for 2,553 yards and 23 touchdowns and was an honorable mention player on the USA Today All-Star team. Florida State already had Chris Weinke and was deep at the position.

We weren't very interested in assessing needs with the first class; we were looking for the best students and athletes we could find. We ended up with 10 players for the offense, 12 for the defense and one who could play both ways. We had 19 players from our home territory of Broward, Dade and Palm Beach counties. Four from other parts of the state. Each of these kids could have gone to a Division 1 school outside of Florida.

Within a week, I added another quarterback, our first out-of-state scholarship player, Jared Allen. He would go head to head in competition with Jahn until our first game. Allen was of equal stature at 6'3" and was a two-time All-State quarterback out of Oklahoma. He completed 171 of 282 passes for 1,973 yards and 18 touchdowns as a senior but didn't get an offer from the Sooners.

We would hold our first practice on August 28, 2000, using blocking sleds, tackling dummies and other equipment we purchased from the production crew that filmed *Any Given Sunday*—the Oliver Stone–Al

Pacino film about the fictional Miami Sharks. We gathered with 24 scholarship players and 141 other athletes who hoped to walk on and make our 2001 opening day roster. We started slowly and introduced a few new plays each day.

I committed us to a gradual pace, progressing as the ability of the players and their conditioning would allow. It would be the only time that we wouldn't have to be in a hurry. We weren't getting ready for a game. We didn't have to take them past the point of endurance. We concentrated on fundamentals. That was even more important because we didn't have any older players around to show the freshmen what to do. We had the option of repeating things a second or third time when needed. If we were moving too fast, we didn't hesitate to back up for a day or two. If the players were worn out, we could take a day off occasionally and let their bodies catch up. Still, we drilled hard enough to pare the group down from 165 to 125.

With no games to play for another year, we posted a schedule and held a series of scrimmages on the various FAU campuses. We opened in Boca Raton and then played in Jupiter and Davie and at the Royal Palm Polo Club. We billed the final contest as our first Homecoming event.

We paired our first scrimmage in Boca Raton with a celebrity golf tournament and a roast that was meant to provide a few laughs at my expense. All of it, of course, was in keeping with our not-forgotten theme, raising a little money.

Jim Kelly was there to tease me about his time at Miami. He cited what he called my failed disciplinary tactic of making my son, Stuart, his roommate in the football dorm. "We used to send Stuart out for the beer," Kelly said.

John Y. Brown, the former Kentucky governor, poked fun at my penchant for publicity. He said he didn't know anything he could say about me that I hadn't said already.

There was plenty of teasing about the merchandise we were peddling that celebrated our undefeated—even if untried—football team.

Outside, on our practice field, we set up temporary bleachers to seat 1,800 fans for the scrimmage. The crowd that rolled in from our first ever tailgate party was easily double that. We had a pep band on hand along with a dance team and cheerleaders. Kelly roamed the sidelines along with Earl Morrall and Roman Gabriel.

All through the fall of 2000, we were able to practice and draw inspiration from the Oxley Center that was rising beside the practice fields. The construction energized coaches and players alike. We built on that energy with the announcement of a deal to play our games at Pro Player Stadium, the home of the Miami Dolphins. We then scheduled our first spring game to be played there in April 2001.

Now we had two wow factors for recruits. They would get to train at the Oxley complex and they would be able to play at Pro Player stadium. It was a very expensive temporary home while we tried to finance a stadium on campus, but it impressed prospective players.

We went into our second recruiting season more conscious of our needs. We had a couple of good-looking quarterbacks, but we needed more help on the offensive line, at linebacker and in the defensive secondary. It was something like what happens in a schoolyard game. You pick your first 11 and then realize your center isn't big enough and you take the biggest remaining player. Our second class included 13 players 6'3" or taller and 250 or heavier.

We got commitments from 31 players, 28 from south of Orlando and 17 from our home three counties. Five of our newest players came ranked in the top 100 prospects in the state.

The program was allowed to offer 63 scholarships at the 1-AA level. We would start our first season with 54 players on scholarship and 36 walk-ons. Since everyone in the first class took a red-shirt season while we geared up and most of the second class would play right away, we were destined to have a major exodus and some rebuilding to do after our fourth season of play.

As the first season approached, we announced that our opening opponent would be Slippery Rock University on September 1, 2001. We commissioned inaugural game artwork for tickets, posters, media guides and game programs. All of it was specially created by a renowned sports artist, Todd Dawes, who did the same kind of thing for the Florida Marlins as they debuted at Pro Player stadium eight years earlier.

The drumroll continued as we released a full schedule and introduced our radio broadcast team and then celebrated a TV contract with the regional Sunshine Network.

Coca-Cola helped us fan the publicity flames when it celebrated our inaugural season by producing a special limited edition six-pack of 8-ounce contoured bottles—something usually saved for newly crowned national champions.

The team was also featured on the cover of Bell South phone books distributed to every home and business in Boca Raton, Delray Beach, Deerfield Beach, Pompano and Coral Springs.

Our latest reinforcements would have just 29 practices with the team before we played our first game. Our average age was 19.5 years. We would field 70 freshmen who had never played a college game and would go against varsity squads. There wouldn't be much pressure to win right away, but patience can be fleeting, and we knew we would have to turn some heads before we lost everyone's attention.

This was going to be something very few coaches ever experience. Before the first game, I promised only one sure thing: we will get better. Every day, every week, every game we would become a better team.

We endured very few setbacks as we built momentum toward our first game. One of our few disappointments was that we envisioned fielding a marching band, but when we couldn't come up with the $250,000 start-up money in time, we had to live with a much smaller pep band, and we turned to Palm Beach Lakes High School to provide pregame and halftime shows.

We saved our worst nightmare for the eve of the Slippery Rock game. We let a bureaucratic malfunction result in 13 players, including seven starters, being declared ineligible for the opening game.

We had only one person working to guarantee NCAA compliance and certify the squad's eligibility. Certifying every player was a monumental task and we fell short. It wasn't inevitable, but it happened because there were so many new student athletes and an incredible amount of paperwork to process all at once.

I got involved too late and boy was I pissed. I compounded my mistake by trusting that the problems would be worked out at the last minute with a late push by the administration. There were many more than 13 players still ineligible a month before the season started. We were paring down the number every day.

I said nothing about the problem to my coaches or the team. I let all the players practice as we prepared for the game. I even took the entire squad on the bus for the trip to Pro Player stadium. I guess I was hoping for divine intervention. I didn't get it. The athletic department eventually reported that their last contact with the NCAA was at 5 p.m. the night before the game. The answer was still no for the fateful 13.

At the stadium, with 25,632 fans about to cheer us as we took the field for our first game, I took those athletes aside and told them we had failed them and they wouldn't be able to play yet. My message was they needed to be there in uniform with their heads up and supporting their teammates on the sidelines. They did, but the team played like it had been hit in the collective solar plexus. My great staff scrambled, but we had handicapped ourselves. Obviously it was disturbing to the team. We were not able to put the full strength of our squad on the field at the outset. It was distracting at the worst possible moment and we were hammered as a result.

We were young and lacking depth before the snafu (look up the acronym and you will appreciate my state of mind at that moment). Our offensive and defensive lines were decimated. We were going up against a senior-laden club, and we had taken the chemistry out of our own mix.

I had gambled and lost, but there was still a game to be played.

The two-year quarterback competition between Garrett Jahn and Jared Allen would be decided in the course of the contest. The two of them were roommates and friends. They had been very evenly matched from the beginning. With no clear winner, I actually had them flip a coin to see who started the game and promised them the loser would play the second quarter and we would go with the hotter hand in the second half.

Jahn won the toss but it wasn't much of a prize on this day. He was a good pocket passer, but he needed a line in front of him. Doug Parker took the first handoff for us and was dropped for a loss of three yards. We were coping with disaster behind an overmatched offensive line. Jahn threw two interceptions under pressure.

In the second quarter, our fill-in center snapped the ball over Jared Allen's head. Allen dealt with that kind of adversity better than Jahn, and on this play he retrieved the ball and threw a 19-yard completion to Justin Thomas for a first down.

Maybe expectations in the stands were lower than mine, but our fans seemed to have a good day, and they continued to cheer us as we left the field down 33-0 at the half.

We scored our only touchdown when Todd Poitier blocked a punt and fell on it in the end zone. Parker ended up with 40 yards rushing on 16 carries. Allen won the starting job going forward by completing 9 of 18 passes for 52 yards while running from a posse on every play.

The final score of Slippery Rock 40 and Florida Atlantic 7 rightly sizes up the scope of our humiliation.

Our gracious opening day fans continued to show us unconditional love. They were still standing and chanting F-A-U as the clock ran out. They were apparently happy to have football at last and they were willing to wait a little longer to celebrate winning football.

If that game marked the birth of the program, the press deemed the FAU football baby premature and in intensive care in a sports incubator. The football coach was immediately placed in the stocks in the public square.

The media had been so supportive of me during the long build up. Now they administered what felt like a flogging with 50 lashes. They were attempting to retract all their previous kind words.

It could have hurt us badly. With defeat there is a gloom that hangs over you like a cloud. And it's all right to bleed a little before you rise up again, but you have to jolt yourself out of it the next morning. A coach has to be the ever-lasting optimist. All we needed was another football game to relieve the pain and regain our good name.

We traveled to Daytona Beach the following week to play Bethune-Cookman, a team ranked No. 22 in the country. The game was played before a rain-soaked crowd of 7,421. It proved to be a magnificent show of determination and effort by our still overmatched team. We got three more of our players certified, but we needed a halfback to play corner and a true freshman with 30 practices under his belt to start at linebacker.

We were up 24-21 entering the fourth quarter and they pushed for a go-ahead touchdown. We came back with a 71-yard touchdown pass from Jared Allen to wide receiver Larry Taylor. Taylor caught two passes on resurrection day and brought them both into the end zone. The other pass from Allen was a 41-yard completion. Allen also ran one in from 7 yards out. He was 11 for 24 for 210 yards and had no interceptions.

We had to withstand a last-minute 47-yard field goal attempt that fell short, but we survived. We won 31-28.

PUTTING OUR OPENING DAY JITTERS IN PERSPECTIVE

The events of September 11, 2001 put our little academic qualification tempest in proper perspective. Following the terrorist attacks, our scheduled game against James Madison was postponed and never made up.

In the aftermath of 9-11 and during the ramp up to war in the Middle East, the stock market and then the economy in general suffered. The downturn had an obvious impact on fundraising nationwide. It was even more pronounced in South Florida where the hijackers lived and trained. We were also reeling from an anthrax attack that killed photo editor Bob Stevens at the American Media offices about three miles away from our Boca Raton campus.

A lot of things could have derailed us if we would have let it.

With an off week, we managed to get the majority of our players declared eligible and the disqualification storyline began to change, then move to the back pages until it was finally put to bed. All but two of our displaced players would join the team over the next three weeks.

We came home to Pro Player stadium to face Marist in front of an announced crowd of 12,559. We would get our first home win, 31-9. Allen was 8-16 for 162 yards and two touchdown passes. Anthony Jackson ran eight times for 63 yards and Doug Parker added 63 yards on 12 carries.

We won three of our first five games but then lost four straight. A 27-9 victory over Albany let us end the season on an up beat and close the year with a 4-6 record.

It was a season of could-have-beens and should-have-beens, but in the end it was a respectable showing, and we went forward with the confidence we needed. We had some special players and we had something to build

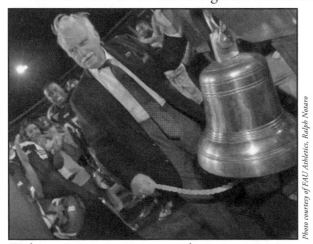

With a start-up program, you have to create some traditions. We started ringing the Taylor victory bell after all our winning games.

Photo courtesy of FAU Athletics, Ralph Notaro

on. Yes, we were outscored 245-177, but nobody in the stands was wearing a bag over their head.

Doug Parker rushed for 572 yards and caught 22 passes for 220 yards. He scored 9 touchdowns. Jared Allen was 77-173-7 for 1,185 yards and 6 touchdowns. Larry Taylor caught 22 passes for 398 yards. Anthony Jackson gave us 981 all-purpose yards: 191 rushing, 51 receiving and 739 on kickoff returns. I'm not sure I'm all that happy with the last number. When you give up a lot of points, you get to return a lot of kickoffs.

On defense, Mauratae Johnson, the first recruit we ever signed, collected 48 solo tackles and 30 assists. Ramon Rickards had 9 tackles for a loss. Taurian Osborne recovered three fumbles.

We were committed to building our team with freshmen and that shaped our early destiny. Freshman teams don't often beat varsity teams. It didn't matter how badly I wanted it to happen or others wanted it to happen, it was going to be a matter of time. It takes a whole lot of battle under fire—a tempering of the steel experience—and you can't rush it. We knew the offensive line would be a weak spot since linemen need more time to develop. We were under size and often injured. We were forced to start 12 different players on the offensive line while waiting for everyone to grow and add strength. We would have to endure one more difficult season, but our boys would be maturing by season three.

There was nothing we could do except bite our lips, give them experience and try to be better the next game and the next game. After each season was over, we worked to get them bigger and stronger. Then we gave them some more experience in spring and brought in the next class. Two more classes of reinforcements and we would be in a different situation.

We stepped up the competition in our second season and we had some more expected growing pains. We scheduled three 1-A teams and played five ranked 1-AA teams. We played Tony Romo's Eastern Illinois team, Connecticut, Utah, the University of South Florida and a playoff- bound Bethune-Cookman. The losses mounted, but we kept learning. To the uninitiated it looked foolhardy. It made for a 2-9 record, but the players understood it was part of our building process. It strengthened us.

In the end, it did just what I wanted. It showed our players they needed to work harder to get where we planned to go. The first year schedule didn't show them where they needed to be. Now players recognized how big and how strong they had to be to compete at a higher level. Now they demanded more of themselves in the strength room. The defensive line added some weight. The offensive line got stronger.

I was especially heartened to see the weight room full of players the day after our second season ended.

As we looked ahead to the start of the 2003 season, though, the critics were crowing. They were saying that the polish on my resume was starting to fade because we posted a 6-15 record in my first two seasons. I am not sure what they expected. I thought we were right on schedule and the work that off season left me confident.

Then in June 2003, the financial pinch began to show. The university announced it was dropping three football announcers. The interim athletic director, Dick Young, cited budget constraints and announced the school would not be able to retain radio announcers Dave LaMont, Jimmy Cefalo and former Miami quarterback Steve Walsh. Young said the budget situation was dire and would be for several more years.

The football program lost well over $1 million in year 2. The FAU Foundation made up the difference, but the university was determined to spend $500,000 less on our third season. The high-profile cut of announcers saved only $15,000. The school installed an assistant sports information director, John McMahon, as the sole voice on our flagship station, WLVJ-1040, for the 2003 season.

They should have waited. If they knew what we had in store for them, they might have figured out a way. We were moving up in class. For two years we had struggled to field a competitive team, and we didn't focus on our win-loss record. We had severe personnel shortages. Our goal was to improve every week and we did. Now we were mature, we had another cavalry coming in the form of 14 incoming freshmen. We were approaching the 63 scholarships that were allowed for Division 1-AA.

We were 4-6 and 2-9 with no experience and a severe lack of depth. Now we would have 90 veteran players on the first day of fall practice, including some transfers from Division 1-A schools. Players that move down to 1-AA don't have to sit out a year. We picked up a couple of key players on both sides of the ball that way.

Linebacker Todd Poitier had joined us earlier from the University of Florida and was a big help for two seasons before injuring his neck.

Quentin Swain, who won a state championship at Miami Northwestern, came to us after two seasons at the University of West Virginia, and he would become our leading tackler in our third season. He was one of only four seniors on this team and the only senior starter.

We picked up quarterback, Danny Embick, out of the University of West Virginia and a wide receiver, Roosevelt Bynes, out of the University of Pittsburgh.

Our offensive line was maturing as we hoped and expected. Right tackle Kenneth Campos anchored that group as a 6'5", 275-pound junior.

We got a boost with the return of running back Doug Parker after a season lost to academic troubles. Parker flamed out academically just as I had at Kentucky and I gave him a second chance. He admitted to me that he hardly ever went to class his freshman year. He wasn't making smart decisions even as he excelled on the field. Many players in that situation never make it back to play again. He did, but it took a full year to repair his grades. My running back coach, Fred O'Connor, stayed on top of him. Parker mowed lawns to support himself and went to Palm Beach Community College to make up 17 credits.

We also got a talented tight end, Anthony Crissinger-Hill, back from academic trouble and a broken collarbone. He was 6'3", 205 out of Jefferson High School in Tampa and sat out the 2002 season.

We had clear leaders now in Jared Allen and linebacker Chris Laskowski. Allen was the face of our offense and had learned a lot from adversity. He was getting rid of the ball quicker and making better decisions. Laskowski led the 2002 team with 84 tackles from his weak side position. He also had a team best 11 tackles for a loss.

Laskowski was a special category of player: a walk-on. He joined us in our inaugural season with no guarantee of a scholarship and forced his way into the lineup. Chris played in every game as a freshman and then became our defensive signal caller as a sophomore. Now he was on his way to being a two-time defensive MVP.

Allen and Laskowski bought into the "Team Above Self" sign posted above our locker room door. They each led a unit where the players grew up together and trusted each other. The school with the best teamwork wins football games.

At this critical juncture, I was certainly a little more positive. My message at the annual Florida Sports Writers Association conference was that for the first time our team could legitimately compete with the best teams on our schedule. We had a team comprised mostly of juniors, but they were juniors who had played—out of necessity—nearly every game for two years. We had a bunch of athletes who had started 21 games. We now measured up from a talent and experience standpoint.

The kids could feel it. The red-shirt juniors started talking about pushing for the 1-AA playoffs in just our third season.

I said a winning record would be nice. My pronouncement to the media was simple: "I think this is a very important year for us. Certainly a 6-5, 7-4, 8-3 type of season would be very helpful at this particular time."

I undersold it, if you can imagine that. Maybe I was getting old, or less bold. We were about to go 9-2 in the regular season and then deep into the national playoffs.

BREAKING THROUGH AT WORK AND HOLDING ON AT HOME

The season would be a bittersweet one for me. My oldest son, Stephen, suffered from a rare cancer of the endocrine glands, which required numerous surgeries over the years. The day after the Orange Bowl victory that gave my University of Miami team its national championship, Stephen began radiation therapy. Remarkably, he rebounded time and again to the point of being able to make 20-mile bike tours, lift weights, and play tennis and golf. Stephen graduated from the University of Miami with a degree in business. He worked in publishing, real estate, insurance and computer sales. He also organized numerous events to raise more than $130,000 for cancer patients. Although Stephen needed frequent medical care throughout his life, he lived normally until an operation early in 2003, after which he went into a three-month coma and suffered a severe brain injury.

Beverlee and I had been with him almost daily for six months. By August, Beverlee urged me to go back to the team. "It's time for you to take care of 90 kids," she told me. "I can take care of one." My heart stayed at the hospital in Miami, but my focus and my energy returned to the team.

Beverlee stayed to care for Stephen, and she wouldn't get home from the hospital until midnight each day. Stephen endured therapy and rehabilitation twice every day as he fought to regain his speech and motor skills.

Beverlee would tell Stephen to get better so they could go watch a game. She'd say, "You're in two-a-days Stephen. Remember what your father tells the players: 'Be strong'."

Stephen was tougher than any football player I ever had. He's tougher than I am. Beverlee, who is the other real hero in this story, constantly reminded Stephen that he was his parents' hero and that there were no football players as strong as Stephen Schnellenberger. He would recover enough to attend a game by the end of the season, and God let us have him for another five years. He lived to be 48 before passing away. After this recovery, he could often be seen in his wheelchair on the sidelines at FAU football games.

My challenge in this period was that the team was looking at me every moment and I couldn't show dejection, despair or depression. I had to dress up, whistle and lead them. I had to give my family the love and care they deserved and still give the other people I was responsible for what they needed from me.

With the great staff I had, it was possible.

We opened the 2003 season against a Division 1-A team, the University of Middle Tennessee, at their place in Murfreesboro. My team of true believers pulled off the unthinkable.

We earned a startling season-opening upset the hard way, with a 98-yard closing drive. We had no timeouts when we got the ball with 1:42 left. On fourth and nine from our 38-yard line, Jared Allen lofted a 62-yard pass to Roosevelt Bynes, the University of Pittsburgh transfer. Bynes cut across the field and caught a perfect spiral in stride at the left hash 30 yards downfield and went in untouched. The team chased after him down the sideline. The clock said 0:00 and the scoreboard showed us on top 20-19.

That drive was spectacular enough, but we scored two touchdowns in the final three minutes. We pulled to within five with a 75-yard drive that wrapped up with 2:53 remaining when Allen hit Bynes from seven yards out.

The win was huge. It was comparable to the Penn State game when Jim Kelly debuted and put Miami in the national conversation. We came out of the game ranked 24th and suddenly we were in the elite of Division 1-AA with Appalachian State, McNeese State, Georgia Southern, Montana, Western Illinois, Villanova, Furman, Bethune-Cookman, Penn and Delaware.

It was enough to bring *USA Today* to town to feature the team. It was our twenty-second game and our fourth outing against a school from the upper division. We were the youngest 1-AA team ever to knock off one of the big boys. We moved overnight from laughing stock to legitimacy.

It was no accident. It was a real harbinger of things to come, but we would stumble and lose badly to Valdosta State and then fall to another Division 1-A opponent, the University of Central Florida, before proving ourselves for good.

We gave Central Florida a big scare. Allen almost repeated the miracle of Murfreesboro. We had a 21-20 lead midway through the fourth quarter in front of 25,144 UCF fans in the Florida Citrus Bowl. They jumped back on top 33-21 with 2:26 left before Allen went to work again. He marched the team 81 yards, ending the drive on a five-yard touchdown pass to Anthony Crissinger-Hill with 39 seconds left. Allen completed a two-point pass play to Bynes to make it 33-29. We recovered an onside kick and drove inside the UCF 20 with several seconds remaining. Central Florida escaped when they broke up two passes near the goal line in the final seconds.

Allen finished 26-40 for 352 yards and three touchdown passes against a team we were going to have to learn to defeat, along with the University of South Florida before we were seen as a threat to Florida, Florida State and Miami. In time we will get there; it is not a sprint.

We rattled off four straight wins, including two in our new home stadium. After two years in a cavernous and very expensive Pro Player, we removed ourselves to Lockhart Stadium. Instead of being 35 miles from campus, we were now 15 miles away in Fort Lauderdale, where we planned to play from the start. A Major League Soccer franchise, the Fusion, had blocked us from that sensible option for two years. With no other choice we went with Plan B—Pro Player—while waiting to build a stadium on campus. Steep rent and sparse crowds at Pro Player created that budget shortfall we were enduring.

Now that the Fusion had folded, we were able to play in Lockhart at a cost of $60,000 a game, down from $100,000 we were paying the Dolphins. We went from a 70,000-seat facility to a cozier 20,000 seats with every fan closer to the playing field. It wasn't ideal, but it was near our downtown Fort Lauderdale campus and more centrally located for all of our faculty and students.

As we prepared for our eighth game of the 2003 season, we were 5-2 and ranked No. 23. The team was reaching a confidence level that it never had before, and I began to treat the squad a little differently. Day by day at our practices I demanded a little more. As we got ready to face a 5-1 University of Northern Colorado team, my offense didn't seem as focused as it should be during a midweek workout. So I kicked them off the field.

One of my top players, Doug Parker, thought I was joking. I wasn't. He thought I just wanted to get his attention. I did, but a bluff of ending practice wasn't going to do the job. I sent the entire offense to the showers.

"This is my field," I bellowed. "Get off the field." It's better not to let a team practice bad habits.

The players held a meeting. I was told Jared Allen did most of the talking. They came back the next day with better concentration. We practiced a little longer. And we left Lockhart Stadium on Saturday with our sixth victory, guaranteeing our first winning season.

The game came down to the final play. When we sent the defense onto the field for the last play, the unit had two instructions: no penalties and no touchdown. They delivered. Northern Colorado completed a desperation heave that got them to our 7-yard line as time expired. We kept them out of the end zone and won the game 21-19.

It took some grit to prevail. Allen sprained his knee in the third quarter with us leading 14-6. He was 11-15 and was playing up to his standard as the seventh best passer in 1-AA ball when he had to leave the game.

Allen's consecutive pass streak of 161 throws without an interception ended when a Northern Colorado player intercepted a ball that was deflected.

Backup Danny Embick, the University of West Virginia transfer, came in as Northern Colorado quickly made it 14-12. Embick, who had thrown only 11 passes in limited action to that point in the season, responded. He ended the game completing 8 of 9 for 132 yards and led us to a touchdown early in the fourth quarter to provide the winning margin.

Our fifth straight victory boosted us to No. 19 in the weekly poll. Now we really had a chance to make the 1-AA playoffs that some of my players suggested was their goal before the season. We knew we had a shot because a member of the selection committee told the press we were under consideration.

FITTING OURSELVES FOR
A GLASS SLIPPER

The 1-AA field consists of eight conference champions and eight at-large berths. We were an independent, so there was no chance for an automatic bid. We would have to impress the selection committee. They would look at our record, our strength of schedule and the poll rankings, but it is still a subjective call.

I couldn't stop the team from thinking about it, but I didn't want anyone to dwell on it. For maybe the first time in my career, the players were selling an ambitious idea and I was playing devil's advocate. That was my public posture, but privately, I was expecting us to go. While I downplayed the playoff talk as premature, I arranged for the school to submit bids to host the first three weeks of the playoffs if we were selected.

If we didn't make the playoffs, it wouldn't have meant everything went down the toilet, but we would have lost a great opportunity. These were important days to the program.

To make sure our break-through season really mattered, we had some unfinished business to accomplish.

Gardner-Webb came to our new house 6-2 and off a bye week. They had beaten us in our inaugural season, 35-19, gaining 561 yards of offense. They were easily the toughest of our final three opponents.

They had whipped up on a team full of freshmen playing their eighth game in 2001. Now all those players were juniors starting their 30th game.

My Owls were bigger and wiser now, but my captains were both banged up. Allen needed a brace on his knee. Laskowski was playing with a cast on a broken left hand.

We thought of the game with Gardner-Webb as a playoff contest, and the captains both played despite their injuries.

We were leading Gardner-Webb 28-17 in the third quarter. They were on our 4-yard line with a first and goal when we picked off their veteran quarterback. That was the way the day went: we gave up a lot of yardage but stopped them on key short-distance plays.

Allen shared time with Embick. Allen was 9 of 13 for 140 yards and Embick 6 for 8 and 56 yards. Each threw for a touchdown. It was enough for a 31-26 victory that moved the team up to 15th in the national poll.

We had a well-timed bye week at that point, and it allowed Allen,

Laskowski and a few others to heal. We were going to have to win two more regular-season games.

Next up was Siena at home. We had taken a few beatings in our start-up days (we lost 61-14 at UConn and 41-6 to Eastern Illinois), but now we enjoyed ourselves in a different role. We scored on our first seven possessions. Allen was sharp enough that I was able to sit him after his third touchdown pass at the beginning of the second quarter. Our first team defense refused to let Siena score and we led 44-0 at the break. The second team was nearly as stingy, allowing only a field goal in the second half. With the playoffs looming, I thought it was important to give the reserves some serious playing time and preparation. The final score was 51-3.

Our offense was performing extremely well. We were second nationally in passing, completing 65 percent of our throws for 250 yards a game. The Sienna romp was a prime example. Allen was 7 of 8 passing for 77 yards and three touchdowns, and Danny Embick was 5 for 5 for 62 yards. We had 17 touchdowns passing and only four interceptions. Our efficiency rating was off the charts at 165.23. Only San Diego was better at 169.53.

The minute the Siena game ended, we shifted our focus to Florida International. I loved it that our rivalry game would have national importance in just our third season. We had just five days to prepare to meet them on their field. We had played just once, the season before, and beat them, 31-21. We dubbed our clash the Shula Bowl to add spice to a game between two schools who were practically next door neighbors.

Both programs had strong ties to the Miami Dolphins. I had coached with Shula and Florida International's coach, Don Strock, had played for him. Shula had allowed us to crown the winner of the game in his name and even joined us to present a three-foot-tall custom-made trophy in the winning locker room.

The game proved to be a classic rivalry match. FIU jumped on top 17-0. They scored the first three times they got the ball. It seemed like a cruel way for us to go out. Instead, we mounted the biggest rally in our young history. We scored our first points when running back Daveon Barron threw the first pass of his college career to wide receiver Matt Prudenti. It was what we needed to get the blood flowing again. My offensive coordinator, Larry Seiple, called the play. We had only put it into our offense two weeks earlier. I told Barren to make sure it was there before throwing the ball. He took a toss from Allen and ran to his right. He saw Prudenti wide open and let it go for an 18-yard touchdown. We came right back with a 12-play, 78-yard drive with Doug Parker scoring from a yard out to make it 17-14. Allen put us on top with a pass to Crissinger-Hill just before the half.

Deep breath. Still alive, but nowhere near safe.

FIU kicked a pair of field goals to creep back in front, 23-21, going into the final period. They got the ball back with 10 minutes left at their 26. On first down they tried a reverse. Laskowski and lineman William Gray sandwiched their receiver during the transfer and set off a scramble that ended with linebacker Quentin Swain picking up the ball at the 3 and diving into the end zone. Allen, who ended the game 22 of 32 for 281 yards and one touchdown, threw to Larry Taylor for a two-point conversion and gave us a 29-23 lead. We added a field goal for the final margin of 32-23.

Walking off the field after an energetic celebration, I shook hands with hundreds of fans. I told anyone who would listen that there was no way the selection committee could keep us out of the playoffs now. I had finally caught up to my players in public confidence.

The next day, an overflow crowd of about 500 jammed into the Oxley Center to watch the playoff brackets revealed on ESPN. We held our breath until we got word we would, in fact, be in the playoffs. The network announcers celebrated us as the quickest startup to advance to the playoffs. Georgia Southern, a leading 1-AA program, made it in their fourth year.

The crowd chanted F-A-U as we were shown in the first bracket on the telecast. Our first playoff opponent would be Bethune-Cookman. We had played them each of our first two seasons. We got our first win ever on their field and they beat us on a return visit. We didn't have them on our schedule in our third season and were happy to see them matched against us in the playoffs. We were going to be traveling back to Daytona Beach.

My kids, who had the courage to come to a start-up football school knowing they might get manhandled by more mature teams in the first couple of years, were going to compete for a national championship in just their third season.

We had gone from 2-9 to 9-2 with more football to be played.

It meant something to be in these playoffs because only 16 schools got in. There were 121 Division 1-AA football schools at the time, so it wasn't like the NHL where everyone moves on. Four consecutive weekends of football would culminate in a championship game in Chattanooga, Tennessee.

In the first round, Allen faced a steady stream of blitzes from Bethune-Cookman. The effect of that was to turn our offense into a boom or bust operation. He completed just 9 of 22 passes, but they went for 204 yards and we came out on top, 32-24.

Round two took us to Flagstaff to play Northern Arizona in a dome at 7,000 feet elevation. There was a lot of talk about the effects of thin air and the supposed second half advantage to the home team.

The sign near the visitor's locker room amounted to psychological warfare: "Catch your breath: You are at 7,000 feet above sea level." I countered it by telling my team the truth: "You are the best conditioned team in 1-AA football and you are not to worry about altitude."

The only effect the high altitude had on us was that Mark Myers kicked a career-long 53-yard field goal at the end of the first half to stretch our lead to 24-3. With an early edge that ballooned to 41-3 at one point, we never really had to find out if there was anything to the thin air hype. We expected a high scoring affair; we didn't expect to be the only one scoring for most of the game.

We won 48-25, but I don't think it was the thin air taking a late toll. They made their comeback against our second string. Allen was 17-28 for 228 yards and three touchdowns. Tight end Anthony Crissinger-Hill had 6 catches for 129 yards to become the first 1,000-yard receiver at FAU.

It was our 10th straight win. We moved on to the national semi-final round and based on a bid I had submitted two months earlier, we were named a host team. We would play Colgate at Lockhart Stadium where we had won five straight since the home opener against Valdosta State.

We were still playing and we managed to bring the semi-finals to South Florida. But it was December 13 and school was out of session. A week earlier and we might have achieved our first sellout at our 20,000-seat home. We settled for a crowd of 12,857 mostly FAU fans. It was special. There was a great tailgate scene and college-style excitement.

Colgate jumped in front 9-0. We briefly got within two points after Parker ran it in from 1 yard out. They came right back on an 80-yard drive and then recovered a pooch kick and scored again for a 23-7 lead.

We were behind 30-10 in the third quarter when I decided to call a huddle with the team. We needed a miracle and I tried to inspire one with an impromptu speech. I asked each one of them to think about what they could do to help get us back in the game. I wanted them to know I wasn't quitting.

They gave me their best. We rallied for a touchdown that made it 30-17 and then scored late to finish down 36-24. Many of my players shed tears on the field after the loss. Getting to the title game would have been priceless, but it was not meant to be.

Allen finished 22 of 39 with a 1-yard touchdown pass to Parker. Allen gained 266 yards through the air but was picked off three times. Crissinger-Hill had six catches for 114 yards and Bynes grabbed three more for 33 yards. Parker ran eight times for 47 yards.

It just wasn't our day. We didn't match up well with a power running game. Colgate held onto the ball all day behind Jamaal Branch. He had 45 carries for 130 yards and scored his 29th touchdown of the year. He had 12 100-yard games that season and a record 2,271 yards total. Colgate improved to 15-0 and extended its win streak to 21 as they went on to play Delaware for the championship.

The lasting memory of the game, though, will be thousands of our fans standing, applauding and chanting F-A-U, F-A-U at the end of the day. *Miami Herald* writer Greg Cote said for once winning wasn't everything, or even close.

Before the game there had been a little buzz about whether I could become the second coach ever to win titles at the 1-A and 1-AA levels. Jim Tressel is the only one ever to do it, capturing his titles in the logical order, first at Youngstown State and then at Ohio State. It wasn't to be for me and I had no desire to make a second run at it. I had a different agenda: carpe diem—seize the day—and move to Division 1-A.

Making the 1-AA playoffs as an independent made us more attractive as we shopped for a 1-A conference to join. Conference affiliation was critical for us because it would guarantee the necessary five home games against 1-A opponents. We were talking with Conference USA, the Mid-American Conference and the Sun Belt Conference.

Our timing couldn't have been better because there were major changes unfolding across the country. This was early in the giant shuffle that resulted in a major reorganization of conferences nationally. Schools were realigning into 12-team leagues that could schedule a championship game between winners of two six-team divisions. When the Atlantic Coast Conference grabbed Miami and Virginia Tech from the Big East, a chain reaction followed. In what seemed like one giant scrum, the Big East took five teams from Conference USA; USA took teams from the Mid-American and Western Athletic conferences. The PAC 10 also raided the WAC and the WAC in turn poached New Mexico State and Utah State from the Sun Belt.

That brought the Sun Belt Conference calling at Florida Atlantic University.

We were a little ahead of schedule when the invitation to join the league came in December 2003, but we jumped on it. The subsequent addition of our rival down the block, Florida International, made the Sun Belt all the sweeter for us.

The move was ambitious, but it didn't come too soon. It would take us a year to transition into the league. There were some commitments to honor first, but we were ready to play in a conference with South Alabama, Middle Tennessee, Western Kentucky, North Texas, Arkansas State and New Mexico State. Teams at the highest level in college football could offer 85 scholarships instead of 63, so we would get deeper and better. The maximum number of scholarships that can be awarded in any one year is 25, so we would move up to our full complement gradually.

We would be returning all but one starter from our 11-3 season the year before. Because of that scrimmage-only autumn when we redshirted an entire class, we would bring 29 fifth-year players and a total of 41 seniors into the 2004 season. This squad would have been a favorite to win it all in a 1-AA playoff and might have qualified for a bowl in 1-A, but we were officially in transition and ineligible for post-season action at either level. We would have to make all our memories in the regular season.

We came out smoking hot. We opened in Hawaii against a Division 1 team coached by June Jones. They were 9-5 the year before and sported Timmy Chang, a quarterback being touted for the Heisman. It felt like a bowl game to us at the start of our 12-game schedule. Many of the players' families made the 4,856-mile trip with us to the Big Island. We visited Pearl Harbor and the Dole plantation.

Then we took the field as 22-point underdogs. Chang was chasing the NCAA career passing record and he threw for 302 yards and two touchdowns.

We stopped him twice, though, on fourth down plays in the fourth quarter and handed Hawaii its only home loss of the season, 35-28 in overtime.

We were down 28-22 when we started our final drive in regulation on our own 36. Allen moved the ball to the Hawaii 31. We called a timeout with fourth down, 11 yards to go and 30 seconds left. I called for "Deep Baby, Go," a play that sends three receivers on post patterns and Crissinger-Hill, our tight end with wide-out speed, ran straight ahead. He pulled in the prayer of a pass in the end zone for a tying touchdown. The extra point was blocked and we headed to overtime. Parker, who ran 19 times for 88 yards in the game, scored from seven yards out to win it. Allen finished 28 of 44 for 291 yards and two touchdowns. Crissinger-Hill had 15 receptions for a school record and 183 yards with two touchdown catches.

We took home a $175,000 payday, but the win was even bigger.

Next up was perennial Sun Belt power and defending champion North Texas at their house in Denton. The same cast of characters that carried us the week before and the year before led us past the Mean Green, 20-13. Parker scored the winning touchdown with 29 seconds left. He had 27 carries for 128 yards. Allen was 18 of 25 for 245 yards. Crissinger-Hill had four catches for 71 yards.

We continued to play at that high level on the road against Middle Tennessee, Texas State and Northern Colorado until we were 5-0 and one of only eight undefeated 1-A teams in the country. We finished the 2004 season with a 9-3 record and sent our first senior class off with a third straight Shula Bowl victory, 17-10 over FIU, in front of 16,262.

We had a great run with that senior-laden team. Now we were going to have to retrench and build again. The natives were restless after our first two seasons and they would no doubt grow restless again, but we were going to ramp up the schedule and improve the only way I know how. Anybody concerned about us not winning right away at the 1-A level would have to learn this is not an overnight thing.

The goal now was to win our conference and get to a bowl as fast as we could. We were going to prepare for that by playing some tough games and getting some experience that would help us later. I preferred that we play teams that were better than us. If we got a lot out of those games, the results would be plain to see. Losses wouldn't kill us. The whole process is not about going 2-2 outside your conference. I knew we would be a better football team for playing these games.

We elevated Danny Embick to lead the offense in 2005, and we gave our quarterback of the future, Rusty Smith, a red-shirt season as we opened our first official year in 1-A ball by facing two Big 12 teams. We lost 30-19 to Kansas and then met Oklahoma State on a Thursday night in front of an ESPN audience. We were the only game in the country that night and my young squad hung in there. We were down 13-3 at the half and lost the game 23-3. Anytime you can get on television it validates you to a degree. Our thinking was it is better to be on television and not win than it is not to be on television at all. The exposure justified what we were doing, proved it was not just a dream.

We followed up with games against Minnesota and Louisville as preparation for a full Sun Belt schedule.

Three years after I left the University of Louisville, the school completed the stadium I had fought to build. Seven years after it opened, I would lead my new team into town for a game at Papa John Stadium.

It was a memorable trip back home. The night before the game, they inducted me into the University of Louisville Athletic Hall of Fame. Then, just before the game began, I received the biggest surprise of my life when they dropped a curtain and announced the naming of the football complex in my honor. The unveiling of the Schnellenberger name on the athletic building that stands in the end zone at the open end of the horseshoe stadium was totally unexpected. Beverlee was in on the secret, but I was overwhelmed by the sentiment.

And then there was the little matter of a football game to be played in front of that giant sign proclaiming the facility the Howard L. Schnellenberger Football Complex. The Cardinals were No. 14 in the country when we played them and although we were 20-6 over the previous two seasons, this was not the same FAU team. We had 15 underclassmen in our starting lineup. We had just two seniors starting on offense and one on defense.

We hung around until the intermission, but a 21-10 halftime score soared to 61-10 before we could go home. Eventually we would have a legitimate chance against these teams. For now we were preparing players to compete in our conference, and we were taking home checks that helped pay for our program.

We finished that season 2-9 and then went 5-7 in 2006 as we continued the tough scheduling that I called advance training. We started the 2006 schedule with five road games in 28 days. Clemson, Kansas State, Oklahoma State and South Carolina were serious tests. I'll admit the schedule was a monstrosity, but we took in $1.8 million in game fees, and we let the players and our fans see the environment we wanted to play in at places like Clemson's Death Valley and the Gamecock's 80,000-seat Williams-Brice Stadium in Columbia, S.C.

By the end of the 2007 season, my detractors would cancel the reservation they had made for me at the loony bin. By then we would be the first Sun Belt representative to knock off a Big 10 team, and we would be flexing bigger muscles during our conference schedule.

The Big 10 win came against Minnesota. Rusty Smith, my 6'5", 212-pound sophomore quarterback out of Jacksonville, introduced himself on the national scene with five touchdown passes. He was 27-44 for 463 yards through the air in a 42-39 victory. With a season-opening win over Middle Tennessee and another win at North Texas, we were 3-1 at the end of September. The one loss was to Oklahoma State.

That brought me to yet another homecoming, this one in Lexington, Kentucky. I was already in the University of Kentucky Hall of Fame as an All-American, but they honored me on this visit by retiring my jersey. They feted my playing days, credited me with bringing back the Kentucky-Louisville rivalry games on the gridiron and celebrated my part in improving the quality of high school football in the state. I had lobbied the high school association to hold spring practices while I was at Louisville. It's hard to get good players if they don't have spring ball, because that's where you learn football. Fall practice is more about getting ready for specific opponents.

Going back to your alma mater as coach of a seven-year-old team you started is a thrilling thing. Winning was the only thing that could have made it more special. They walked over us 45-17.

We also marched into the Swamp in Gainesville to play the Gators in this, Tim Tebow's Heisman year. They sent us home on the losing end of a 59-20 score, but Smith looked like the better passer while completing 18 of 33 throws for 290 yards. He had one touchdown and no interceptions. The game meant a lot to me because all but eight of the players on our roster were from the Sunshine State, and I had promised them we would be competing with Florida, Florida State and Miami. The score wasn't what I wanted, but it was the same score they beat Tennessee by that year.

We were sticking with a plan that traced back to my childhood. When I was 10 years old, I remember playing out in the school yard against 14- and 15-year olds. I got the stuffing beat out of me, but it wasn't long before I was a pretty good player. You can't be the best if you don't play the best. Just to get in the same ring with Muhammad Ali gives you a certain amount of credibility that you don't have before you do that. You might get knocked out, but there's an opportunity to win.

We were young, but we had a remarkable year with four seniors, 18 juniors, 15 sophomores and 30 freshmen on the squad. Smith would be named conference player of the year. He finished with league records of 32 touchdowns and 3,688 yards in one season. He led us to three come-from-behind wins.

Smith was as smart as Kosar and he had great leadership skills. He was another tall, skinny kid with an unusual delivery. That never bothered me. When I analyze a throwing motion, the important thing isn't whether or not it looks like the ball is coming out of his ear or two inches above the ear. There are three important questions: Does the ball start out of his hand prior to the receiver getting open? Does it get there as the receiver is open? Does it get there with velocity and with a tight spiral?

Photo courtesy of FAU Athletics, Ralph Notaro

Smith could do all that and he mastered my pro-style offense. He knew how to find his 6'3" tight end, Jason Harmon. They connected 63 times for 825 yards that year. He hooked up just as often with wideout Cortez Gent and picked up over

Rusty Smith led FAU to a Sun Belt Conference championship and two straight bowl victories. He was Conference Player of the Year in 2007 and was the first Owl player drafted by an NFL team.

1,000 yards that way. And before the season was over, Smith would discover another favorite wide receiver, a 6'3" true freshman named Lestar Jean.

There was more to this Owl team than our offense. Our defense was led by linebackers Frantz Joseph of Fort Lauderdale and Cerge Sincere of Belle Glade.

Joseph, who came to us after one year with Boston College, set a new FAU career record in tackles in the three seasons he was with us. He played middle linebacker at 6'1", 229 pounds, and he led the Sun Belt with 131 tackles in 2007 and made the All-Conference team.

Sincere was a born leader from a dominant high school program where he was part of three state championships. He walked onto our team at 5'11" and 190 pounds but earned a scholarship with his hard work. He played four seasons and became our defensive captain. He was second on the team in tackles and went to the Senior Bowl with the Top 100 players in the country in 2007.

I have always had a soft spot for walk-ons. They make great examples for the rest of the team. Not every walk-on succeeds, but if they weren't recruited or were told they are not good enough, they often respond by practicing longer and harder to prove everyone wrong. Sincere certainly did.

That unit was fourth in the nation, chalking up 33 turnovers. Sincere forced six fumbles. A red-shirt freshman, Tavious Polo, was among the leaders nationally with seven interceptions, most of them early in the season before teams starting throwing to the other side of the field.

We made the most of that with a turnover ratio of plus 19. Smith had just nine interceptions, and the running backs understood John Heisman's theory that it would have been better to have died a small boy than to fumble the football.

We were 5-5 with our big-time schedule, but a 4-1 record in the conference meant we had a chance at the post season as we headed into our final two games.

We took the Shula Bowl 55-23 with Smith completing 20 of 30 passes for 330 yards and four TDs. With FIU in the Sun Belt conference alongside us that game was now doubly important.

The win set up a final game with Troy in Alabama. The conference title and an automatic bowl bid were on the line. We had played them four times without any success. They were the defending conference champs and 15-point favorites.

We took heart in students walking across our campus wearing shirts that embraced our mantra. The front of their shirts proclaimed "To believe is to be strong." The backs said simply, "I believe." Belief is the basis of religions and the basis of all the football programs I have built.

We started fast and never trailed in a close match with Troy. Our junior running back, DiIvory Edgecomb, set up a couple of scores with kickoff returns of 42 and 62 yards. He added a four-yard touchdown in the fourth quarter. Smith was 23 of 34 for 291 yards and two touchdowns. The final score was 38-32.

We were now the youngest program in NCAA history to earn a bowl bid. The New Orleans Bowl would be the prize. The game would be played in the Louisiana Superdome. We were in the spotlight 17 days before the national championship was decided at the Sugar Bowl game on the same field.

The first bowl is very important to any program. There is something pure about it. It opens you up to a level of acceptance that you didn't have before. The first bowl milestone is like a bar mitzvah or a confirmation, whatever is your pleasure. It is a coming of age and we were doing it at the age of seven.

It was a proud moment. Three thousand fans from Boca Raton came to New Orleans for the game. We had a 60-member marching band traveling with us thanks to bowl proceeds. The band was one more sign of our continuing development as a program. They started in 2002 on a shoestring and wore Hawaiian shirts because there was no money for uniforms. By 2005 we had raised $240,000 for equipment and uniforms. Now they were traveling and performing at a bowl game and measuring themselves against a 200-member Memphis band called the Marching Sound.

It was only the third time we would play in a dome. We had done it in Flagstaff during our 1-AA playoff run and again against Minnesota. I arranged for us to prepare at the Saints' domed practice facility in the suburb of Metairie. I thought it gave us a slight edge.

Memphis had just one practice in New Orleans. They didn't bother with a curfew except for the night before the game. Their players were downtown at 2 a.m. during the week. We had a different approach.

I was intent on keeping a young team from being distracted—and keeping an old coach perfect in bowl games. It wasn't my first rodeo, but it had been 14 years since my Liberty Bowl trip with Louisville. I assured the players they wouldn't remember what they did Monday through Thursday, but they would never forget what happened on the field Friday night. I kept them focused on the game. It made no sense to work as hard as we did all season to get there and not follow it up with a valiant effort.

We played like we had been there before. Rusty Smith was the MVP, throwing a record five TD passes. He was 25 of 32 for 336 yards, another bowl record. Jason Harmon caught seven of those passes for 97 yards and Lestar Jean grabbed four for 73 yards. DiIvory Edgecomb opened the game with a 42-yard kickoff return and had another for 62 yards later in the first quarter. He had a record 151 return yards in the game.

It was 30-20 at the half and we won the game 44-27. I got another victory ride on the shoulders of players.

We would be the only Florida team to win a bowl game that year, and we did it with 98 of 104 players on our roster hailing from the Sunshine State. We were second in the nation in the percentage of players coming from the home state. San Jose State was just a tad better.

With the bowl success in our rear pockets, we knew we couldn't rest. You can't ever stand still. That is the first unwritten law of team sports. If you are not going forward, you are going backward.

We had 18 starters and a lot of talent coming back and we would prove our bowl success was not a fluke, but once again we did it the hard way.

Our 44-27 victory in the New Orleans Bowl in 2007 lifted the program to a new level. (left to right: Craig Holly, Officer Delancy, Jarred Smith, Javonte Jackson, David Matlock)

We started 2008 in front of 98,053 fans at Royal-Texas Memorial Stadium in Austin. Texas was led by Colt McCoy and in an electric atmosphere he was 24 for 29 passing for 222 yards against us. McCoy also rushed for over 100 yards. We were competitive until Rusty Smith hurt his shoulder early in the third quarter.

On the opening drive of the game, Smith moved us to the Texas 16-yard line before a shotgun snap sailed over his head. On our next opportunity with the ball, Smith completed a 62-yard pass to Jamari Grant. That threat ended when a pass was deflected as it came out of Smith's hand and Texas intercepted in the end zone.

Texas established order at that point and pushed to a 28-10 halftime lead. Smith was unbowed in the locker room. He still believed we had a chance. They hadn't been able to sack him, and he was 15 of 31 for 253 yards with one touchdown and one interception. He was frustrated he didn't get the ball into the end zone early, and I would love to have seen what he could have done in the second half. Without him, we fought the good fight until the closing whistle, but we couldn't move the ball and we went down 52-10.

We settled for experience, exposure and financial gain. It was our biggest money game yet. Texas paid us $900,000 to play there.

We won at Alabama-Birmingham, 49-34, but lost 17-0 at Michigan State and 37-3 at Minnesota. Middle Tennessee broke our hearts, 14-13, on a fourth down touchdown pass with no time left on the clock. Then we looked like chumps when we lost to Troy, 30-17, at Lockhart.

We were 0-2 in the league and 1-5 overall. Smith had dislocated his shoulder in the Texas game and it hurt his mechanics. That might have explained his rash of interceptions that nearly had us in the tank, but there was more to our season on the brink than that. I snapped and threw a little tizzy worthy of Bobby Knight. It was time to treat these players like a big league football team. They were defending champions in this conference. They had enough ability to be winning and they weren't.

My rant brought about a seniors only meeting. I looked to them for leadership and they came out intent on winning the rest of our games. They nearly did and some of it was in spectacular fashion.

We rallied from 10 points down to beat Western Kentucky 24-20 at Bowling Green. One of our seniors, Charles Pierre, rushed 24 times for a single game record 192 yards. He had two touchdowns on the ground and one through the air. Smith was 15-23 for 174 yards.

The following week Smith hit Cortez Gent from 22 yards out with 20 seconds left to win 29-28 at Louisiana-Monroe. Smith was 7-8 on that closing 72-yard drive and 28-39 in the game for 267 yards and two touchdowns.

Smith had four touchdown passes as we won 46-13 at home against North Texas.

We climbed back to 5-5 and 3-2 in the league by beating the conference leaders from Louisiana-Lafayette, 40-29. Then we put it all at risk by losing 28-14 to Arkansas State at Jonesboro.

We were going to close the regular season against Florida International with stakes even taller than the three-foot Shula Trophy. Each of us needed to win to be bowl eligible and everyone played with that level of intensity. We were tied 22-22 after three quarters. Each team got into the end zone four times in the final quarter. We rallied from two touchdowns behind twice in the final seven minutes.

We scored our last two touchdowns in the final two minutes and eight seconds to force overtime. Then we celebrated like nobody has ever celebrated when Smith threw his fifth touchdown pass of the day to win it 57-50.

The crazy scene on the field culminated with Don Shula walking to mid-field and presenting his trophy.

Within the week, we would learn that the win earned us a trip to the Motor City Bowl to face Central Michigan in the dome at Ford Field. It was the third straight appearance in that bowl for the Chippewas.

The game was tied 10-all when we started our first possession of the second half on our own 2. The eighth play of the drive was a 52-yard scoring pass from Smith to Chris Bonner. We got some breathing room when Smith hit Cortez Gent from 18 yards out with 10 minutes left in the game. Central Michigan climbed back to within three, but we sat on the ball and ran out the clock for a 24-21 final score in front of 41,399 fans and our prized TV audience.

This second generation of players at Florida Atlantic had established us as a legitimate Division 1-A program. They put up a lot of numbers I could look back on and marvel over at the end of our second straight bowl season.

Frantz Joseph finished second in the nation with 154 tackles. He put up double digit numbers in 12 of 13 games and was an honorable mention All-American.

Charles Pierre became the first FAU back to rush for more than 1,000 yards in a season. He had 77 in the bowl game for 1,014 in 2008 and 3,069 in his career with us.

Cortez Gent had seven catches in the bowl to finish the year with 60 receptions for 935 yards.

Tight end Rob Housler had 32 catches for 519 yards.

After a slow start to the season, Rusty Smith passed for 3,225 yards. He completed 234 of 435 passes with 24 touchdowns and 14 interceptions.

Smith would reopen my pipeline to the pros after an injury-shortened season in 2009. He would accumulate more than 10,000 yards passing at FAU and throw 76 touchdown passes for us. We had more than a dozen players sign professional contracts but Smith became the first FAU player to be selected in the NFL draft. He was taken by the Tennessee Titans.

Lestar Jean would be right behind him. Jean caught 25 passes for 257 yards in 2008 and followed that with 38 catches for 501 yards and 64 catches for 988 yards. That led him to the Houston Texans.

Housler, who would sit out a year and then have another standout season in 2010 with 39 catches for 629 yards, went on to play for the Arizona Cardinals.

And Alfred Morris, who was a red-shirt freshman getting limited action behind Pierre in 2008, would bust out as the new face of our offense the following three seasons. He ran for 3,529 yards and 27 touchdowns at FAU and then jumped to the NFL. Morris set the Washington Redskins single season rushing record with 1,613 yards on the ground in his 2012 rookie season.

I am like a proud father watching all of them still play on Sundays. Having our alumni in the NFL is more than a point of personal pride, though. It nurtures the fan base and it pays dividends in recruiting.

NUDGING ONE LAST PROMISE ACROSS THE GOAL LINE

Only one critical piece of business remained for me. We still didn't have an on-campus stadium and I believed that was the best way to assure a bright future for this program. I had been talking about it since my first conversation with President Catanese in 1998. It was part of my first presentation to the Board of Regents.

The original timeline that we circulated in our first fundraising efforts called for construction to begin in the summer of 2001. We envisioned playing our 2003 home games in a 40,000-seat stadium on campus.

From the start we kept the stadium dream alive by visiting new facilities. We returned from each trip hungry for a stadium of our own.

There was significant local resistance to overcome. It came in waves.

The first opponents were from the environmental community. They were troubled by any discussion of building on vacant land that was home to two pairs of burrowing owls and 10 gopher tortoises. Each was a species of special concern, meaning they were not endangered but close.

Catanese addressed those worries by agreeing to encroach on just eight acres of an area where students had studied plants and wildlife for 30 years. He promised to manage 87 acres next to the proposed stadium as a preserve, to remove exotic plants and create nature trials to open the property to more students and make it more of a public resource than it had ever been.

The footprint of the football facility was approved alongside the preserve. That put an end to any talk of searching for an alternative stadium site in Fort Lauderdale or on the Jupiter campus.

Construction of the Oxley Center set a very visible marker from which there could be no retreating. The natural progression from there was to build our stadium, but we still had several hurdles.

We went through a lengthy debate over the size of the proposed stadium. After Catanese left his position, an interim president, Richard Osburn, put on the breaks, calling for a no-frills 20,000-seat facility. Apparently we were going to have to prove the program was viable first.

When we made the 1-AA playoffs and then jumped to Division 1-A, those high-profile successes gave us renewed momentum. We announced a new goal of building a quality campus home by 2006.

To help people see what was possible, I commissioned a rendering. The newspapers had some fun with that when the university's vice president of facilities, an architect responsible for all construction on campus, said he had never heard about my stadium.

Tom Donaudy would eventually become an ally and friend, but he wasn't happy to be out of the loop. "I was thinking to myself," he told a reporter, "How did Schnellenberger get a rendering?"

A bureaucracy can slow you down and I simply didn't consult with him at that point. The university wasn't out any money and the rendering didn't commit the school to anything. I thought of it as a sales tool. One I had employed before with mixed results.

My rendering was of a domed stadium that would seat 40,000 fans and serve as a football and basketball facility. We could create a great place for both teams and solve all our problems. Every touring artist in the country would want to perform in there. A dome made sense with our weather, too. You could avoid the rain and lightning and have air-conditioned football.

We pointed critics to a success story in the northeast. When Syracuse built an all-purpose domed stadium, their football and basketball teams immediately went to the top of the Big East Conference.

The next president of Florida Atlantic, Frank Brogan, led city leaders to Syracuse to see their multipurpose building. Spirits were high. In 2006, he put a comprehensive strategic plan in place calling for large-scale physical development of the university.

The improvements Brogan wanted built on the Boca Raton campus would double the amount of on-campus housing while erecting a stadium and a retail complex.

The next obstacle was a more basic resistance to the idea of expanding the Boca Raton campus at all. The faction of the community that wanted to slow the pace of growth in the area opposed more student housing and the stadium because of the potential impact on traffic along busy Glades Road. The local paper referred to the former mayor, who was the champion of this group, as Madam No because of her loud and certain opposition to virtually any development.

Madam No had been replaced by a more open-minded politician in the person of Steven Abrams. We were going to have to win him over and convince a majority on the city council that football was their friend. It was going to take a massive re-education program to get anything done.

The crowds were growing steadily. We would peak at 18,444 in average attendance—more than 90 percent of capacity at Lockhart—before building our own house and leaving the 50-year-old Fort Lauderdale field.

Mayor Abrams made the trip with us to the New Orleans Bowl. He even pledged a parade and then delivered on his promise.

The next mayor would turn out to be a long-time friend of the university, Susan Whelchel. She gave us a decisive advantage and guided us through the permitting process.

With our political problems solved, all we needed to do was finish raising $8 million from private sources. The rest would be generated by selling revenue bonds. It is hard to believe that the money would be the least of our problems in this decade-long quest.

Remember Susan Peirce, my chum-and-fish partner from our founding days? She came back to help shepherd the fundraising efforts. We had already raised about $2 million before our trip to New Orleans. After the back-to-back bowls, construction of a stadium was one of the main topics on campus.

Peirce traveled with various founders to our high-profile away games and they returned with first-hand experiences and insights into the business of stadiums—what worked, what didn't. Copious notes were kept on signage, parking, tailgating, ticketing, restrooms, concessions, and every element of the game-day experience for home and visiting families and fans.

The stadium boosters bused to the University of Central Florida to scour Bright House Stadium before it opened in 2007. They walked through every nook and cranny and reviewed a punch list with the construction foreman.

Our stadium was getting closer. It was going to be all the nicer for their efforts.

There would be one more university president to convert. We would need a newly installed campus leader, Mary Jane Saunders, to pull the trigger and float the mortgage, but there were just enough good things happening to keep everything positive until we could break ground on October 15, 2010.

After all those ebbs and flows, what we eventually built was a $70-million stadium that would host a near capacity crowd of 29,103 for our first home game one year to the day after we broke ground. The stadium seats 30,000, but it is smartly designed for future expansions. The footprint was drawn for 40,000 fans, but segments in the corners of the end zone were left out of the original construction and can easily be plugged in later. The design also anticipates a day when another football generation may desire 65,000 seats.

The residential and retail improvements Brogan wanted were built as well. The stadium sits near towers that house 1,200 students. Another 130,000 square feet of space was devoted to shopping, dining and entertainment venues. And the environmentally sensitive land was preserved as promised.

The stadium itself has the comfort and the feel of a larger facility. Some of the nice touches that our study committee helped put in place include:

— Two suite levels consisting of 25 luxury boxes. Each has 16 theater-style seats and windows that can be opened;

— Even in the general admission bleachers every seat has a chairback;

— Our video board is 50 feet tall and 30 feet wide. That's twice the size of the screen at Central Florida's stadium and cost us $1.7 million;

— A tropical theme incorporated into the architecture and almost 200 palms and a few splashes of beach sand inside and around the stadium;

— The only natural grass surface in the Sun Belt Conference.

The stadium turning into a reality over the course of a year was unbelievably special. It thrilled me to see the work progress day by day. It seems almost unreal that my football son, Stuart, worked for the construction company and had a part in building it.

When they dedicated the finished product, a lot of nice things were said about me.

Two of our founders, Pete and Kerry Lobello, were gracious enough to commission that bronze likeness of me to stand sentry outside. The man in the statue is 65 years old. That was flattering. I may have called the image life-sized earlier, but it is actually 10 feet tall and weighs 575 pounds. I like that.

President Saunders called the stadium the House that Howard Built.

I know better. There were a lot of others involved. The night before our first game at the stadium, we invited all of our former players and assistant coaches to a dinner in the Priority Club. I have a large photograph of the stadium over the desk in my office and below the picture is a list of every one of those contributors. They came to FAU on my promise that we would achieve something special. Their sacrifice is the foundation that we built upon.

The stadium was weeks from completion as we approached the start of the 2011 season, and I chose that time to announce my retirement at the end of the season. We had struggled to 5-7 and 4-8 records the last two seasons. I didn't know it at the time, but we would lose at Florida, Michigan State and Auburn and get only one win that season. I was 77 years old and I needed a hip replacement. There are six major joints in the body. I had already replaced a shoulder and a knee. I was well on my way to becoming bionic. It was time for someone else to push the ball the rest of the way up the hill.

My contract was set to expire after the season, and I hoped my early announcement would make a seamless transition possible. There wouldn't be questions all season about whether I was coming back. The search for a new head coach could begin in earnest.

The university offered me the position of ambassador, which I summarily rejected. I said I would require being named ambassador at large, so I wouldn't be confused with those senior students who squire around the freshmen when they come for orientation.

I haven't retired; I have simply stepped sideways. My office is in the administration building. I work with the FAU Foundation in a fundraising capacity. I am a serious friend of the football program, but I don't work in the Athletic Department. Others run the team.

You can still find me roaming the stadium, though, along with other fans on any given game day. Sometimes I'm in the president's suite above the western stands. I like it there because it's at the top of a 145-foot tower

and you can gaze out across the field and the visiting grandstand to the Atlantic Ocean. They tell me mine is the only football stadium in the country where you can do that.

I sit there with the knowledge that for many years to come FAU fans will be enjoying Football in Paradise.

Photo courtesy of FAU Athletics, JC Ridley

Football in Paradise was a signature phrase we used to promote the start of the program at Florida Atlantic. When we built our stadium within sight of the Atlantic Ocean, I felt like we had delivered what we promised.

CHAPTER 12

RECRUITING AS AN ART FORM

"He has always been a man with a plan. He dreams big. He brings in people who want to live in his dream."

– Cergile Sincere, *Florida Atlantic University linebacker*

Some of my recruiting methods produced pretty good results, but everyone has their own style and the best approach to recruiting is going to be different at every school.

You need to have a vision of where you are going and you need to invite athletes to be part of it. That's the key to the whole damn recruiting thing. You have to recruit to the situation at hand. At Miami the sales pitch was that we could be like the University of Southern California, a private school playing in a prominent stadium and be a championship team. At Louisville it was that we would build a stadium and climb into the elite. At FAU it was that we were going to start from scratch and climb to Division 1-A faster than anyone had ever done it.

Okay, here are some recruiting themes to contemplate and maybe a few universal truths.

1. YOU HAVE TO MARK YOUR TERRITORY AND THEN PROTECT THE HOME FRONT.

At Alabama our goal was to visit every school in the state and bring back the best athletes. We told them it was their birthright and it was where they were going to go to school. A state university can do that.

Lots of other universities target an area within 200 miles of their campus, but that's not always the best plan.

If we took a compass and drew a circle going out 200 miles around Miami, two thirds of the area would be under water in either the Atlantic or the Everglades. We had to try something else—so we took the southern half of the state. We called the area south of Interstate 4 the State of Miami and we made it ours. As with the history of the United States, we began with fewer colonies and gradually expanded our territory. We had the five Miami area counties. Then we took in the Fort Myers area and then Tampa to Orlando.

That approach also worked for us at Florida Atlantic University, which was more centrally located in South Florida. We just renamed the area south of Interstate 4 Florida Atlantic Territory and hit the road.

At the University of Louisville, we were in the middle of basketball country and there wasn't enough local football talent to outfit even the state university up the road in Lexington. I had a city within a day's drive of half the nation's population, so we recruited across the region and in Florida where my staff already had a lot of contacts.

Whatever territory you identify as your own, you can only defend it by smothering it. My assistants would spend more hours in the 400 or so schools that made up our territory than any other staff in America.

Our goal in the spring was to collect information on up to 1,000 athletes. Each of our coaches first met with the principal or assistant principal to let them know the state of our program. The coach did the same thing with the athletic director, but spent most of his time with the head coach and assistant coaches. He identified the best prospects, reviewed tapes of the previous season and then watched a portion of spring practice.

We would also save enough time to have a good, long meeting with the counselors at which time we got transcripts and pertinent academic information, including standardized test scores. We needed insight into each student athlete's desire and ability to handle college-level work.

The entire visitation process would last up to two-and-a-half hours at each school. It was not a one-time thing. We would be back every fall and spring. We made sure not to overlook one school or principal or athletic director.

The same coaches would work the same area year after year and establish relationships in every high school. They had to be on a first name basis with principals, academic advisors and coaches.

We were dedicated to the area schools and determined to improve their lot along with our own. Our staff would share the latest techniques and new professional ideas with each receptive coach they could find. With the cooperation of our friends, there was no possible way for us to overlook or misjudge any potential student athlete.

We were not going to outrun our supply line. We wanted to know everything about every kid; who was maturing and who would get a lot better. This is possible only in a targeted zone and it has to be done in person.

When this saturation approach was working at its best, we were familiar sights in many neighborhoods. I would go into the minority sections of Liberty City or Overtown in Miami to make a home visit and the neighborhood kids knew who I was. They would be on bicycles and ride alongside and shout, "The scholarship man is coming. The scholarship man is coming." When I'd get to the house I was looking for, they would sit on the car and watch it for me. I became the boss man. Other staffs would make an occasional visit, but we were endeared to the community.

2. RECRUITING IS LIKE EVERYTHING ELSE IN LIFE: PRESENCE IS THE MOST IMPORTANT FACTOR. THE MORE THEY SEE YOU, THE MORE THEY LOVE YOU.

I told the story of recruiting Joe Namath for Alabama earlier. His successor behind center, Steve Sloan, says I won him over the same way:

> *"Coach Schnellenberger was a good recruiter. It was the full-court press. He was persistent. I hadn't thought about going to Alabama. I liked Tennessee and Georgia Tech as a kid, but Coach Schnellenberger was there all the time. He loved football and we hit it off pretty well. He made me feel like he really wanted me. He just out-recruited the others."*

While at Kentucky in the '50s I remember camping out, actually sleeping in my car in front of an athlete's house to fend off other suitors, or at least keep them from telling my prospect any lies. I loved the battles we had in the old days.

At Miami and Florida Atlantic, we were fighting off the carpetbaggers who would come down once in the spring and once in the fall. We did it by going to high school basketball games and seeing the players sitting there. We made sure to hug their moms.

Wherever we were recruiting, I had a little plan to get at least two home visits if I was going to need them. The first time I forgot my pipe and had to return to a house to retrieve it, it was probably by accident. It turned out to be a pretty good deal, so I did it more than once (but never twice with the same recruit). You walk into a player's house with a pipe and they are not going to ask you to put it out. Back in the day more people smoked and it wasn't the imposition it is now. I would sit down in the best chair they had in the living room or parlor if you will. I would sit in a cushioned chair and during the conversation, if I thought I was going to need another visit to close the deal, then I would either put my pipe in an ashtray or place a pouch of tobacco on a table and leave the house. It gave me a reason to visit the home again and talk to the kid again if he needed a boost to make up his mind to join us. It worked a time or two.

Today, with smart phones and texting and Facebook, some lazy coaches think they can make it happen without all the work. Those things are just another cheat. It takes effort. You have to work it like any business; that's the most important thing. If you relate well, you can be folksy. If you are articulate, you can do it a different way. But in the final analysis you have to identify the players you are interested in and you have to go meet them. Then you have to get them down to the school, and let them see a game, meet your players and meet the girls and go out after the game. Then you go back and do the closing thing. But before you can close, you have to have a plan and you have to be able to explain it.

If you are not already in the top echelon, you have to communicate how you will get out of the mire and move ahead.

Contrary to what sports writers think, these are not sophisticated people. Some are pretty good students, but they are only 17 or 18 years old. That's why you can get them to enlist in the U.S. Marines; the uniforms are pretty and they can be convinced they can be something special.

3. YOU HAVE TO HAVE SOMETHING TO SELL BEFORE YOU CAN CLOSE.

You sell whatever it is you have. If you are doing your heaviest recruiting on the home front you start with one easy sales point: the opportunity to continue their education and to pursue football aspirations within driving distance of their homes.

At Louisville we were recruiting most of our players within a day's drive of the campus. That was close enough that their parents could see them play—and I could sell that.

At Miami and Florida Atlantic we pressed that point even harder if they were considering a school up north.

We preached non-stop that they shouldn't have to leave mom and dad, brothers and sisters, girlfriends, coaches and these great fans who had cheered for them every weekend.

We told them they weren't looking at all of the costs of flying off to distant lands. They would have to travel thousands of miles many times from home to college and back. The high school senior doesn't know he will need a new wardrobe of winter clothes. He's unable to imagine the difficulties and expense his mom and dad will face driving thousands of miles or flying to see him play on Saturdays.

We remind the family that the opportunities for work will cause him to start his career in that faraway land. When the boy meets the love of his life and the girl's family doesn't want her moving to Florida, the boy's mama and daddy never get to see their grandchildren.

Come to your local school. There will be no need to buy plane tickets. The people who backed you in little league and high school will continue to cheer. Meet your bride in your home state. South Florida will benefit from retaining our best and brightest. Grandparents can choose to babysit at their pleasure.

We were confident we had something to hold their attention and make our next pitch.

Winning is important; good players want to play for winning teams. It is still the best recruiting tool. Some schools can lean on their tradition. If you don't have a proud history, you need to sell the future.

I like to think of the young men who come based on a vision and not a past as givers. Investing their talents in a promise, our players were willing to work harder and longer with less recognition at the outset than if they responded to the football factories from up north. Our crusaders knew they would be cheered only for what they accomplished.

At Miami, Louisville and Florida Atlantic our recruiting posture was nearly identical. We challenged kids to come and take Cinderella to the ball. At all three schools they got there.

Courageous athletes prevailed at each school. They chose to come to us and go on a mission just like Catholic priests and Mormon students. Their mission was to be as good as they could be as fast as they could do it.

The other common theme at all three schools was to sell the pro-style passing attack and NFL defensive schemes we featured. They knew they were going to be trained to play professional ball if they had the talent, the work ethic, and were coachable.

At each school we improved the training facilities and celebrated our vision for an on-campus stadium. We would get two of them built. Miami never got the job done, and they are paying a steep price for their hesitation.

4. YOU NEED THE RIGHT PEOPLE OUT THERE RECRUITING.

Whenever I hired a coach it was my preference to hire someone I already knew and had seen at work. If there wasn't somebody out there like that, then I preferred a coach who had worked for someone I knew and respected. It also helped if they were temporarily out of a job and hungry for football work.

I had a simple method for identifying a good recruiter. This will get me in trouble with the political correctness police but I'll share it anyway. Once I met the potential coach's wife, I could easily assess his recruiting skills. I wanted to see how good-looking, outgoing, gregarious she was. If she was a winner and their kids were well behaved, then I figured he was a pretty good recruiter. He could sell himself to high school athletes if he did well in the most important recruiting job of his life.

I found a lot of people who succeeded with that first big recruiting effort and then delivered for me as well. Christ Vagotis and Gary Nord were two of the best and they came with me to several schools. Bill Trout was exceptional at Miami and Arnie Romero was outstanding as well. Danny Hope was a stellar salesman for me at Louisville.

We don't want lawyers on our coaching team; we want salesmen. People with a self-confident track record of success and experience at the level we're playing at. I didn't hire them and babysit them. I gave them a crash course and put them out there.

I taught them using the model of the Fuller Brush Man. I remember listening to those salesmen who came to the door of my childhood home. They were there as often as the charity fundraisers are today. They had to make 100 calls a day. You have to thrive on it, knock on doors. If you get a sale or a donation the first time, great, but if you don't succeed until the 10th time, that's OK, too.

If you don't get in front of a prospect, you won't get the chance to close. For every kid we got, we recruited 25 or at least looked at 25. My assistants had to be able to make cold calls and accept rejection.

Recruiting is hard physical work. You have to get up early and have a schedule. If you aren't willing to hear "No" 50 times, you are not going to get the five positive answers you need.

We would start with 1,000 names and then analyze the academics and throw half of them out. We would watch them play from their sophomore year on and then throw out half again. We might make another cut to 5 at each position and get it down to three for each scholarship before we accepted visits. We tried not to overload ourselves at any one position, but that doesn't always work out. The NCAA allowed 95 athletes to make official visits to a school. Some would tell us no and some we had to tell no.

5. THE COACHES NEED TO KNOW WHO THEY ARE RECRUITING.

We graded everyone ourselves. We didn't pay attention to the *Parade Magazine* All-America team. We weren't interested in who made an All-star team. We relied on our own evaluations. The recruiting services they have today are the worst thing that ever happened because it has made coaches lazy. I told all my coaches not to look at the scouting services. Those people are not going to get fired if you recruit the wrong kids.

We kept dossiers on players we were interested in from the time they were sophomores. And we made good use of them.

I would make about 80 home visits a year. As we were riding along, I had the assistant coach reading me the dossier on the player so that I was ready to go into the house. You need to know if this is their first mom or second mom, what the dad does, what the mom does. When we get in there, I have a legitimate chance to mesmerize him with how much I know about him and then I can lead the conversation.

You certainly don't want to ask, "What position do you play, son." You really don't want them to have that much time to talk; you want them to listen. It will be their turn to talk when you want them to say, "Yes, I want to come and play for you."

I've recruited and coached young athletes who, for many reasons, could be destined for a rocky path. They come from the inner city, rural countryside and Middle America; they are of every color and race. When it was appropriate, I would sell them on the support system we could provide.

I tell them up front there is a very high price to pay to become a winner. Rules and regulations are to be respected; time is to be used wisely. Pulled together and united by organized team activity, disadvantaged youngsters get the only chance they may ever have to stabilize or change their course.

Every freshman comes to college full of ambition and hope. A student athlete's successes will be measured by earning his college degree, fulfilling his athletic potential, and helping his team reach new heights. Academic ineligibility is the most common cause of failure. The head coach's responsibility is to make certain the support system is in place to keep the athletes eligible if they are willing to do the work. This is essential to graduation and fulfillment of the athletic goals we have. Failure in the classroom derails a young man's opportunity to continue. While I can't guarantee every athlete will be a great player, I can guarantee each player will graduate as long as he doesn't buck the system.

6. YOU NEED TO KEEP SELLING WHEN YOU ARE SOMEONE'S SECOND CHOICE.

If you are the clear second choice, you need to accept that and still make your best effort to sell your program because sometimes they come back to you. Often a kid's first choice doesn't work out. They may not get an offer from that school or they might call you after a disappointing visit to that school or a difficult first year there.

While I was recruiting at Kentucky, we had a top player who wanted to study engineering. He took an official visit to Georgia Tech and the dean of their College of Engineering convinced him there was no other school that was as good at football and engineering. I took a run at him anyway and convinced him to visit us. I wanted to counter his Atlanta visit, and I told our dean we only have one shot at it. He did a great job telling the merits of our school, the accolades we had received and how we were highly rated.

We might have lost the student athlete at the end, though, because the dean told him that Georgia Tech was better for engineering students in one way: they put the engineers in their fight song.

It might be the only time I lost a recruit to a line in a fight song: "I'm a ramblin' wreck from Georgia Tech and I'm a hell of an engineer."

The effort we made even if we were seen as second best was worth it because even though he did go down there, about a year later he wanted to come back home.

7. YOU NEED TO RECRUIT WALK-ONS, TOO.

You have to let hard-working walk-on players win a scholarship. You can't do that unless you are willing to reward their effort with playing time in scrimmages. They can push others to press harder and improve. Or they can outperform the more physically gifted player that isn't willing to put in the work.

You can get a lot out of a determined athlete who has no scholarship offers and has been advised by everyone that they are too small. If you say come on down, walk on, and work hard to get bigger and faster and you may earn a scholarship, they will give you everything you ask for on the field or in the weight room.

Sometimes we had more walk-ons than scholarship players. We had an unlimited number for a while at Florida Atlantic.

A smart coach simply cannot have an ego that requires his prize recruit to play when a shorter, fatter kid with a great heart is actually performing better than the highly touted scholarship player.

I have saluted dozens of walk-ons in these pages because they became major contributors to my teams.

One great source of walk-on talent for all of my teams came in the form of athletes who transferred from another school. It was my practice everywhere I coached to make transferring players walk on and earn scholarships. You might remember I even applied that rule to my son, Stuart, when he left Duke for Miami.

I did the same thing with Julio Cortes, a fine defensive end who went on to play three seasons in the NFL. He was another player we recruited out of Christopher Columbus High School, but he chose to go to the University of South Carolina. When he got homesick, I let him walk on at Miami. He got a little playing time in 1982 and earned a scholarship before helping us win a national championship in 1983.

> *"People know the talented athletes and great teams Coach Schnellenberger was a part of, but they never indicate what made those teams so different. He was always looking for good, mentally tough football players. He overlooked less than ideal physical qualities. He gave chances to smaller guys with heart. Some of his best players and team captains were walk-ons or athletes everyone else passed on because they were a little too short or skinny."*
>
> **– John Bock,** *University of Louisville, six-year NFL veteran and FAU assistant coach*

8. TURN YOUR PLAYERS INTO RECRUITERS.

Once a player accepts a scholarship, he has a vested interest in the success of the program. You need to encourage incoming players to spread the gospel you preached to them. There is no better evangelist for a program than the newly converted.

We got that kind of boost from Olympic Heights running back Anthony Jackson when he committed early to Florida Atlantic and brought several players with him.

Alonzo Highsmith was one of the folks who did that for me at Miami. After he made his decision, he got on the phone and called the other kids who were having trouble making a decision. Michael Irvin did that as well.

When people try to identify the keys to our success at Miami, they often overlook this aspect. This was part of the mystique in our methods. We got the leaders in Dade and Broward counties in our second and third years and they became our community organizers. They got on the phone and said, "We all need to stick together; we're already winning and we need everyone to come here with us." That's how we got Bennie Blades and Eddie Brown and many others on board.

We created the same kind of dynamic by employing a networking approach in the Cuban community.

> *"Coach Schnellenberger came to my house. My parents were not as involved as parents are today. They really learned about my college opportunity when he showed up. There was no media coverage. I went to South Miami High School, right down the street from UM. Coach was a marketing guy. He used that to sell the Cuban community on the team."*
>
> **– Juan Comendeiro**, *University of Miami*

Juan was one of five Cubans we brought in at that time. We took them with us to the parade on Eighth Street during the Calle Ocho Festival and to other events in the Cuban community and celebrated them being on our team. That served to promote the program and to recruit other local kids. It wasn't lost on the close-knit family of future pro Julio Cortes.

9. YOU CAN RECRUIT WELL AND STILL DO IT HONORABLY.

Recruiters are easily separated into two groups: those that do it honestly and those that don't. You can do it honorably and still be successful.

You should start by having a reputation for honoring your commitments. I lost Tom Deming, one of my top recruits for Miami, when he suffered an injury in a North-South high school All-star game in 1981. He was 6'4", 230 pounds, and All-State at linebacker. He committed to me and then tore knee ligaments during the All-star game. He never played for my Hurricanes, but we honored his scholarship for four years.

The staff needs to know how you intend to approach things. You don't have to constantly remind people to do things the right way if you never show a hint of doing it any other way.

I always relied on a recruiting coordinator to do all the paperwork. They were paid according to how good they were, and sometimes they made more than a first-year assistant coach.

My recruiting director at Miami from 1981 to 1983 was Suzy Wilkoff. She was a former cheerleader who studied at Ohio State. She worked at the University of Pittsburgh and Southern Methodist University before coming to work for me. She answered an ad in a newspaper for an opening in sports organization and it turned out to be a job as recruitment secretary at Pitt. The coordinator left and she ended up doing most of his job. I made her the first female recruiting director in the country.

> "On my first day of work in March of 1981, Coach Schnellenberger told me that the University of Miami was under investigation by the NCAA. He had mentioned in the interview that I needed to know the NCAA rule book inside and out. We were going to recruit by the rules. He insisted I call the NCAA every day with a question even if I had to make one up."
>
> – **Suzy Wilkoff,** *University of Miami Football Recruiting Coordinator*

The key was good organization. She sent letters to every high school coach and asked them to tell us who was a prospect and who we should be looking at. We followed that up with visits, but she made sure we didn't send mail to a teenager until we had checked them out. We didn't want to send recruiting mail to a lot of kids and then have to tell them we were not interested.

I never paid anyone to come and play, and I never allowed anyone else to do it for the school. You can debate whether the players deserve a financial stipend, but they don't deserve to be bribed by corrupt coaches and boosters.

Another time-honored and equally immoral (even if legal) recruiting tactic is the offer of a coaching job to the father of a star player. I had that temptation at least twice, but didn't succumb to it.

Alonzo Highsmith's father was a high school coach when I was recruiting his son to come to Miami. He didn't ask for a job, but he mentioned he had been at his school for a really long time and he told me they were pretty good.

At Louisville, I was trying to recruit a nationally known talent, Chris Redman, and his father was a coach who wanted a job wherever his son went.

I didn't offer either one a thing, but their sons still chose those schools.

The closest I ever came to playing that fast-and-loose game was in recruiting Joe Kohlbrand for Miami. He was highly pursued and talented enough to later play in the NFL for five years. It was brought to my attention that he had a brother who would be going to school and would graduate the same year. I told Kohlbrand that if he came with us, I'd help his brother get a job as a student manager. The brother got student aid that didn't count as a football scholarship.

10. THE HEAD COACH IS THE LEAD RECRUITER AND NEEDS TO BE THE CLOSER.

Campus visits by your top prospects are critical to the recruiting game and they need to be well conceived.

My staff did little or no direct recruiting during the athletes' campus visits. We were atypical in that fashion. Our aim on official visits was to use the 48 hours we had to provide a capsulized view of what it was like to be a student athlete.

Athletic ambassadors greeted each recruit and led everyone to dinner on the waterfront. Our prospects met their student-athlete hosts and began to experience the most important aspect of their visit—student social life. The personal relationships that develop between recruits and players are instrumental to success.

We showed them the best that we had. Breakfast was at a posh resort. Our approach to campus was plotted with the mind of a real estate salesman. We made sure the drive showcased our best features. In Florida that meant we arrived by way of the beach.

After a campus tour we would emulate game day and leave for the stadium at noon. We assembled in the home team locker room. Each recruit sat before what could be his locker.

Ambling through the tunnel, nearing the playing field, the young men heard fight songs. Each player transformed into a titan as he heard his name announced over the PA system, ran onto the field, and saw his picture flashing on the big screen. Standing by the playing surface, he felt that he had entered the Grand Canyon, surrounded by tall cliffs. He visualized thousands of cheering fans.

Sleep didn't come easy for the recruits. On the second day of their visit, coaches gave players an introduction to our style of football. My staff met with players by position. A coach occasionally put a player to the blackboard and queried the prospect's depth of knowledge about his position. We were able to observe the players demonstrate confidence on their feet. Don't forget that we were still in the evaluating stages. As the players studied us, we studied them.

If everyone did their part well, our job was a lot easier when we made our home visits.

Some head coaches don't make a lot of home visits, but I learned recruiting from Bryant. My time with Alabama and in the pros and the championships we won were part of our sales pitch, so I had to be the closer.

> *"I will never forget the confidence Coach showed when he entered my home for a visit. Here I am one of the most highly recruited kids in the nation and he made me feel nervous. He told me I could go to any school in the nation, but to come to Miami and build a legacy is something few people get a chance to do. My talent would just add to an Oklahoma, Notre Dame, or Michigan legacy. Building a foundation and dominating college football is what I was interested in doing and Coach told me I could be a key part in turning Miami into a national power. I knew I wanted to be part of something special and to be the first. That would be like Christopher Columbus discovering America to me."*
>
> — **Alonzo Highsmith,** *Christopher Columbus High School in Miami and University of Miami*

Be your own Christopher Columbus; where do you think he heard that? You have to know who you are recruiting.

My rings were a favorite prop. They came off my fingers many times. If you were to examine them today, you would see how they are well worn on the side. You can barely make out the acronym "EDGE" on the Super Bowl ring.

> *"When I went on my recruiting trip to FAU, we were sitting at one of those recruiting dinners. He saw me looking at his Miami championship ring and before I knew it, he threw it across the table like it was nothing. He said, 'Want to try it on?' He promised me we would have that one day."*
>
> — **Nick Paris,** *Florida Atlantic University*

"I was a senior at Bishop Watterson High School in Columbus, Ohio, the day my high school coach interrupted our English class. His face had seemingly lost all color and he was sweating profusely. 'Someone very, very important is here to see you,' he said as we walked down the hall. When we entered his office I met Howard Schnellenberger. He introduced himself, took off his University of Miami National Championship ring and Miami Dolphins Super Bowl ring and insisted I try them on. He removed his ever-present pipe and in the lowest voice I had ever heard asked 'How would you like to have one of these someday? To this day I wear with pride the championship rings we received for defeating Alabama in the 1991 Fiesta Bowl and Michigan State in the 1993 Liberty Bowl."

– Tom Carroll, *University of Louisville*

You have to have something special to sell a high school player. I sold dreams.

"What the University of Louisville program looks like now, that was what coach was talking about when he recruited us. It was the dream he sold us—he started it all."

– Joe Johnson, *University of Louisville*

"Coach Schnellenberger has a way of writing you into his vision. Somehow the part that he sees you playing becomes the biggest part of the dream. Somehow you are drawn into the responsibility of making this vision come to pass. It's contagious. I wanted to be a part of the magic that he spoke of."

– Johnny Frost, *UL player and FAU assistant coach.*

In any event, I had a personal meeting with each player we were prepared to sign. Usually that was when the scholarship offer was extended. On many of those occasions the player would give a verbal commitment. At the very least, we would agree on a schedule for his decision-making. We needed a timely answer because there were others in line.

When we had a quarterback on deck, I liked to get them in my office where they would be surrounded by the memorabilia and artifacts of my career.

I would show them a video we called "The Making of a Quarterback." It took them through all the quarterbacks I had worked with starting with Joe Namath and moving through Roman Gabriel, Bob Griese and Bert Jones.

After the success we had at the University of Miami, I had a four-part poster prepared to display *Sport Illustrated* covers featuring Jim Kelly, Bernie Kosar and Vinny Testaverde. The fourth panel was always reserved for my next prospect.

If the boy's parents were with him, the mother might be crying and the father beaming. In most cases, the boy was going to join us and try to live his dream.

CHAPTER 13

MY LAST PRESS CONFERENCE (MAYBE)

After 18 months working together on my memoir, I sat down for one last interview with my collaborator, Ron Smith. With no subject off limits, we talked about the ups and downs of my career and discussed the state of the great game of American football today.

Q. Why are you writing this book now?

A. People have been asking me for a long time when I was going to write my book. I always said it wouldn't be until the last chapter was done. The last chapter was Florida Atlantic University.

Q. Bobby Bowden once said that after you retire, death is the only big event left.

A. Maybe he shouldn't have written his book until after he retired.

Q. What would you say to someone who suggests you mismanaged your career by leaving places prematurely?

A. I don't choose to look at my career that way. Coach Bryant made his impact at many different places and that's what I've been able to do. How many coaches have the opportunity to be part of building three programs like the ones that I've been a part of, programs that have impacted entire communities, programs that have created something that will last into perpetuity? When you look at what we've tried to do that way, I think it's pretty awe-inspiring.

Q. Any regrets?
A. No.

Q. Okay, but if we could give you a football mulligan would you use it?
A. No.

Q. If you could play one game over, wouldn't you like another try with Joe Namath in the Orange Bowl against Nebraska? I believe that's the only bowl game where one of your teams came out on the losing end of the score. Wouldn't you like to replay that one? Or the Dolphins Super Bowl loss to the Cowboys?
A. Everything works out like it is supposed to. We might not have had our undefeated Dolphins season if we had won the Super Bowl the year before. And Joe Namath went on to some pretty good things.

Q. Do you have a favorite memento from your career?
A. Yes, these two rings. One from the Dolphins perfect season and the other from the University of Miami national championship season.

Q. You have received many honors through the years. You are in the ring of honor at the University of Kentucky, you are in the Hall of Fame there and at Louisville and Miami. They named the football complex after you at Louisville. They erected a statue of you outside the stadium at Florida Atlantic. Does any single honor stand out for you above the others?
A. Not discernibly.

Q. Missing is a place in the College Football Hall of Fame. How do you view that?
A. As temporary.

Q. What was more rewarding, going 17-0 in the perfect season with the Dolphins or going 6-0 as a head coach in college bowl games?
A. That's a gimme really. The perfect season is Don Shula's. The 6-0 includes the University of Miami win over Nebraska. That 6-0 should get me into the Hall of Fame.

Q. If you could only fly one team flag going into the hall, who would you associate yourself with?

A. I am not going to choose one. I don't want to be associated with just one school. I want to be a man for all seasons. It would be like a lifetime achievement award for me to go into the hall that way.

Q. What are your thoughts about all the legal trouble that football players seem to get into at major universities these days?

A. The culture is completely different now. I think one season when Urban Myer was at Florida 30 of his players were arrested. It really didn't happen very often years ago. When I started at Miami, the idea was we're here to play football and to get an education. I can only remember one athlete who got arrested. That was after a fight with someone in a liquor joint who wouldn't leave his girlfriend alone. I got a call telling me he was in the pokey and would be arraigned the next morning. I went down to the courthouse and found my way to the judge who was handling it and asked if I could appear on the boy's behalf. I told the judge the kid had never been in trouble and I'd make sure he got a physical penalty worse than incarceration. And the judge turned him over to me. That doesn't happen today.

Q. A lot of things have changed. What do you make of the world of Twitter and Instagram that athletes live in today?

A. It's out of control. The last few years I was coaching I would collect all the cell phones on Friday night and put them in a gunny sack because they were all talking on their phones on the bus, at our team meals and in the locker room. Hell, they'd use those things on the sideline if you let them.

Q. This season the Bowl Championship matching the top two teams will be replaced by a four-team playoff to crown a champion in Division 1. Have they got it right, finally?

A. No. This will be better than what we have had, but it needs to be a 16-team playoff the same way it is in the other football divisions. I have always believed that, but I became a devoted advocate of a full playoff after taking Florida Atlantic into the Division 1-AA post season in 2003. That format generates tremendous excitement. We need to determine a unanimous No. 1 team in America and the only way we can do it is by giving everyone with a serious chance of winning it all an opportunity to do so. Stripping the top four teams out of the major bowls may finally break that system and force a compromise. We should use the traditional bowl games as part of the playoff.

Q. What are your thoughts on Title IX governing gender equity in college sports?

A. I fully support it. I'm not sure I had much involvement with Title IX early in my career, but I was very conscious of it at Florida Atlantic because we were starting a football program at a school that was widely recognized as a trailblazer in emphasizing women's sports. FAU was first among 78 peer institutions in spending on women's sports. One year FAU was the only co-ed institution in the country spending more on women's athletics than on the men. Dr. Catanese, who brought me in at FAU, was a strong advocate for Title IX. When we committed to raising millions to start the football program, he insisted and I agreed we would raise significant funds for the women's programs in the same drive. When we built the Oxley Athletic Center, we designed it for use by male and female student athletes.

Q. What is your feeling about college players, led by student athletes at Northwestern, submitting a petition to the National Labor Relations Board to create a first-of-its-kind union to negotiate NCAA rules?

A. This is America, so it is their right, but it isn't the players, it's the people who will make money off those players who are driving it.

Q. Do Division 1 football players deserve to be paid a stipend?

A. Being awarded a scholarship, full tuition with room and board to attend the university of your choice is the deal of a lifetime. We used to say after practice that with three hots and a flop, we had it made. I think if we start paying players, it would force some schools to drop football. Title IX says every athlete gets the same treatment, man or woman, no matter what sport. There is not that much money. The income from football supports the other sports.

Q. With all the safety concerns being raised today, do you believe football will be played in 20 years?

A. I think it will be played to infinity. I am not worried about any of the rule changes. This great game is interwoven into our society. We've gone through a purging time, but I think there was a similar problem with people viewing the sport as barbaric back under President Roosevelt. The National Collegiate Athletic Association helped bring the sport back into good graces and it has exploded in popularity. I have played with and coached a lot of players through the years, and I really only know one person with an unnatural early onset of dementia. I know that's unscientific, but there are an awful lot of lawyers on the job, and I have a concern that so many people are bringing these claims in a class action lawsuit against the NFL. We need to get down to the real truth about head injuries and some of the things that are being attributed to football.

Q. What did you make of the bullying controversy involving Jonathan Martin, Richie Incognito and the Dolphins?

A. That has been made so complicated by the layers of bureaucracy involved. That should have been a problem for a coach and two players. They should have known about it when it happened, but now the commissioner and the players' association and Congress are all involved. When we had two guys jawing at each other and distracting the team what I used to do in those situations was call a time out, go get the boxing gloves, form a circle and make them go three rounds. I'd give them the biggest gloves you can find, and after a few minutes they couldn't even lift their arms and they shut up. Then they can shake hands and it's just like fighting with your brother, you end up tighter.

Q. What is your thought on star NFL players like Matthew Stafford, Robert Griffin III and Jay Cutler sitting in on team interviews of head coaching candidates?

A. I don't see anything wrong with that if it will help the owner make the right decision for that team. It might be a plus if it eliminates problems later between the quarterback and the coach. You want a good relationship because they can cost you the job today.

Q. How much satisfaction do you get from the success of your former assistants?

A. I don't claim the successes of my former assistants as my own, but through the years I have certainly rooted for their teams when they became head coaches at the college or pro level. Using the Kevin Bacon formula to the third degree, there are 31 college or NFL head coaches with ties to me. Ten of my assistants went on to become head coaches, and they in turn helped pass the head coaching torch to another 21. Lately I have been keeping a closer eye on the Chicago Bears and the Detroit Lions. Marc Trestman, my former University of Miami assistant, took over the Bears in 2013. Jim Caldwell, one of my assistants in Louisville, became head coach of the Lions this year. I will also be pulling for the Redskins this fall because one of my Louisville quarterbacks, Jay Gruden, is the new head coach there.

Q. When you left Louisville for Oklahoma in 1995, you said part of the motivation was to chase the dream of being the first head coach to lead two different college teams to a national championship. How impressed were you when Nick Saban achieved your dream by winning it all at Louisiana State in 2003 and then leading Alabama to the first of three championships in 2009?

A. He did it where it was almost a given. LSU was a bigger achievement than the Alabama championships. Alabama has such a good set up that it makes all other places in the SEC look inferior.

Q. Are you happy to see Louisville joining the Atlantic Coast Conference this year?

A. Oh, you bet I am. That level of competition is what I wanted for them when I was there. Their decision to join a second tier conference was a big part of why I left.

Q. Did Bobby Petrino deserve a second shot at Louisville?

A. The guy that makes a difference, the Athletic Director, thought he did. I agree. I'm happy to see him back there because he fit in very well when he was there before and the team is more likely to continue on the path we've been on with him there. Falling off his motorcycle with that woman didn't make him a worse coach, just a worse husband.

Q. What was your reaction to the fall of Joe Paterno?

A. I love everything I know about Joe Paterno. I think he was one of the greatest football coaches of all time. He was right there with Bear Bryant. I know that because I saw him recruit, I saw him practice and I saw him coach games. I saw the result of his coaching on his players. I was able to see all that and evaluate all that for myself. I don't know anything about what happened on that campus as it relates to those kids that were abused, so that's where I leave off and Joe's God takes over.

Q. How about Charlie Strong's new challenge leaving Louisville for Texas?

A. Well, Charlie had better be strong. That's a little like Oklahoma for me. They don't seem to be welcoming him like he is from Texas.

Q. Do you think Mark Stoops can win an SEC championship at Kentucky?

A. No, I don't think so. Not unless the administration and the powers that be take a personal inventory of their shortcomings and drill down to bedrock and find out what's wrong with their program.

Q. What do you think of Florida State's Heisman winning quarterback pitching in relief for the FSU baseball team this spring? Would you allow that?

A. Absolutely. It's not that risky. How do you think I got Browning Nagle to come to Louisville? Not everyone has a chance to play two sports. They are not all like Bo Jackson or Deion Sanders. It's one out of a thousand. If they are good enough to start in two sports, they should be able to play both.

Q. Can you rank these big stadium moments in your career for us: the celebrity game you and Don Shula coached as a final salute to the Orange Bowl before they tore it down; seeing the University of Louisville unveil your name on the football complex there; and the opening of the FAU stadium while you were still coaching?

A. The opening of FAU stadium was very personal and has to come first. The naming of the Louisville complex was a very nice surprise. And I have always said I drew energy from the Orange Bowl, and I had big moments there while I was with Alabama, the Dolphins and the University of Miami. We had a great salute to it before they tore it down.

Q. Where did you do a better coaching job, helping Miami beat Penn State in Happy Valley in 1979 or leading Louisville over Alabama in the Fiesta Bowl? You have said that those were the keys to turning around each program.

A. Beating Alabama. Penn State was the first year I was at Miami. I made the decision to get Jim Kelly in as a starter and keeping it under my hat made it double tough for Joe Paterno to adjust on game day when we came out passing on every down. But when Louisville beat Alabama we had gone from a 2-9 and 3-8 and 3-7-1 start. To come back and play well enough to get into the Fiesta Bowl pulled that whole program out of obscurity.

Q. Who was a tougher opposing coach to face, Joe Paterno or Bobby Bowden?

A. I think I was 2-1 versus Joe and 3-2 versus Bobby while I was at Miami. I don't count Bobby beating me at Louisville because that was too big of a mismatch. I had a lot more fun beating Paterno. Bobby was an ally. We were the U.S. and Great Britain fighting Hitler. It was me and Bobby against Charlie Pell and Florida. That was an important alliance because Pell was an overaggressive recruiter.

Q. Who was the bigger villain in your career, Robert Irsay or Tad Foote?

A. That's easy. Irsay. He embarrassed me and did me in on national television while my wife and kids were watching. Foote took me on in private.

Q. Who would you rather beat on the field, Jimmy Johnson or Barry Switzer?

A. Jimmy. Barry is a lot more likable. They were both trained by the same master. They both tried to defrock me and undermine me, but Jimmy did it in my house. He tried to purge me out of what I built at Miami.

Q. What was the bigger stadium success story: Louisville or FAU?

A. We don't know the success of the Florida Atlantic stadium yet because we haven't scratched the surface of what will happen there in the next 20 years. They are in the infant stage but there will be bowl games played there and a whole lot more. The stadium in Louisville has made them into a national power and lifted them to the ACC. What the Louisville stadium did, too, was serve as a big confidence builder for the university and the city. Without it there would be no Yum Center; that's the greatest basketball arena in the country and it's right there on campus in that parochial town of Louisville.

Q. What was the bigger disappointment, the Dolphins losing the Super

Bowl to the Cowboys or FAU getting knocked out of the Division 1-AA playoffs in the semifinal round in 2003?

A. By far the Dolphins. That FAU loss was a win. We went so much further than we could possibly expect just getting into the tournament, let alone being one game away from playing for the championship.

Q. If you had stayed at Miami the rest of your career, would you have won over or under 5 national championships?

A. Only God knows that. I probably would have won as many as the rest of them did. I will tell you this, though, I don't think I would have lost 5 games in 1984 with that great team that I turned over to Jimmy Johnson.

Q. After being called Howard the Mouth, Howard Hyperbole and a lot of other unpleasant things in your career as a coach, is your skin over or under 2 inches thick?

A. Over, but with the heart of a lamb.

Q. What is the toughest football conversation you ever had?

A. Talking my son Tim out of his football dream. Despite his size, he was trying to play quarterback on his high school team. The team's starter was Michael Shula who made it to the NFL. I spoke too much as a coach and not enough as a father. It took Tim a while to forgive me, but he was meant for different success. After a big-time modeling career, he became a professional photographer and his art is in many galleries throughout the United States.

Q. The Long Last Name Club … something or nothing?

A. Something, nothing and maybe something once again. I've been talking with reporters Jim Martz and Gary Long about trying to get some club publicity out there again. When they wrote about it back in the seventies I had people in India, Thailand, Czechoslovakia and all over writing to me, telling me the burden their name had been to them. I knew the trouble with my last name when I got caught smoking in the school yard in first grade and Sister Viola made me write my name on the blackboard 1,000 times.

Q. You've had a lot of fun with your Long Last Name Club over the years. Shouldn't Bo Schembechler have been invited to join?

A. We don't go after people. It's not by invitation; we accept applications. Besides, his first name is way too short.

Q. When did you lose the pipe as part of your identity?

A. I agreed to make a commercial for the benefit of the Cancer Society about 10 years ago and when I went in to do the shoot, I was asked not to smoke my pipe. I asked why and they said you can't be asking for money for cancer research and be smoking a pipe at the same time. I took their challenge and gave it up. I ended up throwing away about 50 pipes. I probably had $10,000 worth of pipes. I had a couple of valuable ones that I had been given as gifts, so I have kept them. They are Meerschaums, made in Greece out of magna.

Q. It's hard to think of you without the pipe. Over the years you gave away a lot of pins that featured that push-broom mustache of yours and the pipe.

A. The idea for those pins came to me in the night. I got the idea from Willie Stargell of the Pittsburgh Pirates. Rather than sign autographs, he used to give out little stars. I gave those pins with the caricature of me to the unsung heroes of my football programs. I still run into people who proudly wear those pins on their lapel and I'm glad because they deserve to be recognized the same way as the big donors to our programs.

Q. You and Bart Starr came out of college the same year and you were both drafted in the late rounds—maybe the 17th round. Didn't they have the combine to evaluate players back then?

A. Bart Starr only won two games his last two years at Alabama (0-10 and 2-7). That confused them on his value. My Kentucky teams had a winning record every year and never lost to Tennessee, but I was always catching the ball in a crowd because I didn't have enough speed to get open. I also had a military obligation to fulfill so I went where I belonged in that draft. Do you know who went at the top of that draft? Hopalong Cassady and Earl Morrall.

Q. If they want to sprinkle your ashes on a playing field one day, what field do you want to become one with?

A. That's going to happen. I told Beverlee I want my ashes spread on all my playing fields. She is going to take me on a final tour.

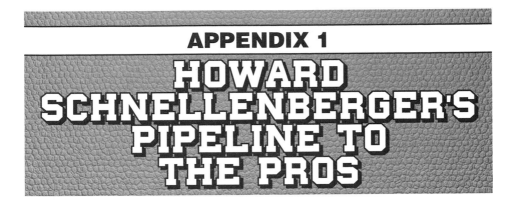

HOWARD SCHNELLENBERGER'S PIPELINE TO THE PROS

Eleven players recruited and coached by Howard Schnellenberger and his staffs became the first selection of their NFL teams.

First Round Selections from the Schnellenberger pipeline:

    Bennie Blades DB Detroit Lions, Seahawks (10 seasons)
    Eddie Brown WR Cincinnati Bengals (7 seasons)
    Jerome Brown DT Philadelphia Eagles (5 seasons)
    Alonzo Highsmith RB Houston Oilers, Cowboys, Buccaneers (6 seasons)
    Michael Irvin WR Dallas Cowboys (12 seasons)
    Joe Johnson DE New Orleans Saints, Packers (9 seasons)
    Jim Kelly QB Buffalo Bills (11 seasons)
    Bernie Kosar QB Cleveland Browns, Cowboys, Dolphins (12 seasons)
    Vinny Testaverde QB Tampa Bay Buccaneers, Browns, Ravens, Jets, Cowboys (19 seasons)
    Ted Washington DT San Francisco 49ers, Broncos, Bills, Bears, Patriots, Raiders (15 seasons)
    Lester Williams DL New England Patriots, Chargers, Seahawks (6 seasons)

More than 100 players recruited and coached by Howard Schnellenberger and his assistants made it to the NFL. Half of them played at least five seasons there. The list includes many names familiar to pro football fans:

    David Akers PK Washington Redskins, Eagles, 49ers and Lions (17 seasons)

Stephen Alexander TE Washington Redskins, Chargers, Lions, Broncos (8 seasons)

Bruce Armstrong OL New England Patriots (14 seasons)

Jaime Asher TE Washington Redskins (4 seasons)

Aaron Bailey WR Indianapolis Colts (5 seasons)

Don Bailey OC Indianapolis Colts (2 seasons)

Rocky Belk WR Cleveland Browns

Rodney Bellinger DB Buffalo Bills (3 seasons)

Albert Bentley RB Indianapolis Colts, Steelers (8 seasons)

Brian Blades WR Seattle Seahawks (11 seasons)

John Bock OL New York Jets, Dolphins (6 seasons)

Deral Boykin DB Los Angeles Rams, Redskins, Jaguars, Eagles (4 seasons)

Melvin Bratton RB Denver Broncos (2 seasons)

Jeff Brohm QB San Francisco 49ers (2 seasons)

Jay Brophy DB Miami Dolphins, Jets (4 seasons)

Selwyn Brown DB Tampa Bay Buccaneers

Willie Lee Broughton DE Indianapolis Colts, Cowboys, Raiders, Saints (8 seasons)

Ray Buchanan DB Indianapolis Colts, Falcons, Raiders (12 seasons)

Jim Burt DL New York Giants, San Francisco 49ers (11 seasons)

Alan Campos LB Dallas Cowboys

Tom Cavallo LB San Francisco 49ers

Martin Chase DT Baltimore Ravens, Saints, Redskins, Jaguars (6 seasons)

Tony Chickillo DT San Diego Chargers, Jets (3 seasons)

Rico Clark DB Indianapolis Colts, Bengals, Patriots (3 seasons)

J.R. Conrad G New York Jets

Charles Cook DE New York Giants

Mark Cooper OT Denver Broncos, Buccaneers (7 seasons)

Julio Cortes DE Seattle Seahawks (3 seasons)

Jerry Crafts OL Buffalo Bills, Eagles (5 seasons)

Wendell Davis DB Dallas Cowboys (3 seasons)

Ralph Dawkins RB New Orleans Saints

Glenn Dennison TE New York Jets, Redskins (2 seasons)

Leon Evans DE Detroit Lions (2 seasons)

Kevin Fagan DT San Francisco 49ers (7 seasons)

Mike Flores DE Philadelphia Eagles, Redskins, 49ers (5 seasons)

Frank Frazier G Washington Redskins

Darrell Fullerton DB Minnesota Vikings, Buccaneers (5 seasons)

Carwell Gardner RB Buffalo Bills, Chargers (8 seasons)

Ernest Givens WR Houston Oilers, Jaguars (10 seasons)

Kelly Gregg DL Philadelphia Eagles, Ravens (6 seasons)

Keith Griffin RB Washington Redskins (5 seasons)

Jim Hanna DT New Orleans Saints

David Heffernan OL Tampa Bay Buccaneers

Rob Housler TE Arizona Cardinals (3 seasons)

Eric Larkin DE Houston Oilers

Lestar Jean WR Houston Texans (2 seasons)

Darius Johnson DB Denver Broncos, Chiefs (5 seasons)

Randell Johnson LB Buffalo Bills

Cedric Jones DE New York Giants (5 seasons)

Joe Kohlbrand DE New Orleans Saints (5 seasons)

Ronnie Lippett DB New England Patriots (8 seasons)

Terry Rice Lockett LB Los Angeles Raiders

Sam Madison CB Miami Dolphins (9 seasons)

Rod Manuel DE Pittsburgh Steelers (2 seasons)

Fred Marion DB New England Patriots (10 seasons)

Tyrus McCloud LB Baltimore Ravens (2 seasons)

Bubba McDowell DB Houston Oilers, Panthers (7 seasons)

John McVeigh DE Seattle Seahawks

Danny Miller PK New England Patriots, Colts

Jerald Moore RB St. Louis Rams, Saints (4 seasons)

Alfred Morris RB Washington Redskins (2 seasons)

Victor Morris LB Miami Dolphins

Winston Moss LB Tampa Bay Buccaneers, Los Angeles Raiders, Seattle Seahawks (11 seasons)

Browning Nagle QB New York Jets, Indianapolis Colts, Atlanta Falcons (5 seasons)

Robert "Speedy" Neal RB Buffalo Bills

Bob Nelson DT Miami Dolphins, Buccaneers, Packers (4 seasons)

Scott Nicolas LB Cleveland Browns, Miami Dolphins

Roman Oben OL New York Giants, Browns, Buccaneers, Chargers (10 seasons)

Paul O'Connor OL Tampa Bay Buccaneers

Daryl Oliver RB Atlanta Falcons

Matt Patchan OT Philadelphia Eagles

Brett Perriman WR New Orleans Saints, Lions, Chiefs, Dolphins (10 seasons)

Carl Powell DL Baltimore Ravens, Bears, Redskins, Bengals (7 seasons)

Greg Rakoczy C Cleveland Browns, Patriots (6 seasons)

Keith Reaser CB San Francisco 49ers

Alfredo Roberts TE Kansas City Chiefs, Cowboys (5 seasons)

Fred Robinson DE San Diego Chargers, Dolphins (3 seasons)

Ed Rubbert QB Washington Redskins

Mark Sander LB Miami Dolphins

Stanley Shakespeare WR Tampa Bay Buccaneers

Randy Shannon LB Dallas Cowboys (2 seasons)

Rusty Smith QB Tennessee Titans (3 seasons)

Travian Smith DL Oakland Raiders (7 seasons)

Willie Smith TE Miami Dolphins

Harry Stamps T Arizona Cardinals

Danny Stubbs DE San Francisco 49ers, Cowboys, Bengals, Eagles, Dolphins (10 seasons)

Reggie Sutton DB New Orleans Saints (2 seasons)

John Swain DB Minnesota Vikings, Dolphins, Steelers (7 seasons)

Barron Tanner DL Miami Dolphins, Cardinals (6 seasons)

Leland Taylor DT Baltimore Ravens

John Turner DB Minnesota Vikings (9 seasons)

Rick Tuten PK Philadelphia Eagles, Bills, Seahawks (11 seasons)

Sammy Williams T Kansas City Chiefs, Ravens, Chargers (4 seasons)

Warren Williams RB Pittsburgh Steelers, Colts (6 seasons)

Klaus Wilmsmeyer PK San Francisco 49ers, Saints, Dolphins (6 seasons)

APPENDIX 2

THE SCHNELLENBERGER RECORD

(53 seasons, 641 games as a college or pro player or coach, 371-257-13)

HOWARD SCHNELLENBERGER'S RECORD AS COLLEGE HEAD COACH

Record as Head Coach in College Bowl Games 6-0 – Best in Division 1 History

1981 Peach Bowl – Miami defeated Virginia Tech 20-10
1984 Orange Bowl – Miami defeated Nebraska 31-30 to win the National Championship
1991 Fiesta Bowl – Louisville defeated Alabama 34-7
1993 Liberty Bowl – Louisville defeated Michigan State 18-7
2007 New Orleans Bowl – Florida Atlantic defeated Memphis 44-27
2008 Motor City Bowl – Florida Atlantic defeated Central Michigan 24-21

College Head Coaching Record By School

University of Miami (5 seasons, 41-16)

1979	5-6	Division 1 Independent	
1980	9-3	Division 1 Independent 18th in Final AP Poll	Peach Bowl Win
1981	9-2	Division 1 Independent	8th in Final AP Poll
1982	7-4	Division 1 Independent	
1983	11-1	Division 1 Independent National Coach of Year –	Orange Bowl Win – National Championship

University of Louisville (10 seasons, 54-56-2)

1985 2-9   Division 1 Independent
1986 3-8   Division 1 Independent
1987 3-7-1 Division 1 Independent
1988 8-3   Division 1 Independent
1989 6-5   Division 1 Independent
1990 10-1-1 Division 1 Independent   Fiesta Bowl Win
             14th in Final AP Poll
1991 2-9   Division 1 Independent
1992 5-6   Division 1 Independent
1993 9-3   Division 1 Independent   Liberty Bowl Win
             24th in Final AP Poll
1994 6-5   Division 1 Independent

University of Oklahoma (1 season, 5-5-1)

1995 5-5-1 Division 1 Big Eight Conference

Florida Atlantic University (11 seasons, 58-74)

2001 4-6   Division 1-AA Independent
2002 2-9   Division 1-AA Independent
2003 11-3 Division 1-AA Independent
             NCAA Division 1-AA Semi-final Loss
2004 9-3   Division 1-AA Independent
2005 2-9   Division 1-AA Independent
2006 5-7   Division 1 Sun Belt Conference
2007 8-5   Division 1 Sun Belt Conference
             New Orleans Bowl Win – Coach of Year – Conference
             Champions
2008 7-6   Division 1 Sun Belt Conference
             Motor City Bowl win
2009 5-7   Division 1 Sun Belt Conference
2010 4-8   Division 1 Sun Belt Conference
2011 1-11 Division 1 Sun Belt Conference

Overall College Head Coaching Record (27 seasons, 158-151-3)

HOWARD SCHNELLENBERGER'S RECORD AS COLLEGE ASSISTANT COACH (7 SEASONS, 58-15-2)

University of Kentucky (2 seasons, 9-10-1)

1959　4-6　　Division 1 Southeastern Conference

1960　5-4-1　Division 1 Southeastern Conference

University of Alabama (5 seasons, 49-5-1)

1961　11-0　　Division 1 Southeastern Conference

Sugar Bowl win – National Championship

1962　10-1　　Division 1 Southeastern Conference

Orange Bowl win – 5th in Final AP Poll

1963　9-2　　Division 1 Southeastern Conference

Sugar Bowl win – 8th in Final AP Poll

1964　10-1　　Division 1 Southeastern Conference

Orange Bowl loss – National Championship

1965　9-1-1　Division 1 Southeastern Conference

Orange Bowl win – National Championship

Overall Record As College Coach (34 seasons, 216-166-5)

Overall Record in College Bowl Games 10-1

HOWARD SCHNELLENBERGER'S RECORD AS NFL ASSISTANT COACH

Los Angeles Rams (4 seasons, 40-13-3 regular season, 0-2 post-season)

1966　8-6

1967　11-1-2　Playoff loss to Green Bay

1968　10-3-1

1969　11-3　　Playoff loss to Minnesota

Miami Dolphins (7 seasons, 71-28-1 regular season, 5-3 post season)

1970　10-4　　Playoff loss to Oakland

1971　10-3-1　Playoff wins vs. Chiefs, Colts; Super Bowl loss to Cowboys

1972　14-0　　Playoff wins vs. Browns, Steelers; Super Bowl win over Redskins

1975　10-4

1976　6-8

1977　10-4

1978 11-5 Playoff loss to Houston
Total record all games as NFL assistant (11 seasons, 116-46-4)

HOWARD SCHNELLENBERGER'S RECORD AS NFL HEAD COACH

Baltimore Colts (2 seasons, 4-13)
  1973 4-10
  1974 0-3
Overall Professional Head Coaching Record (2 seasons, 4-13)
Overall Record As Professional Coach (13 seasons, 120-59-4)
Overall Record As College and Professional Coach (47 seasons, 336-225-9)

HOWARD SCHNELLENBERGER'S RECORD AS A PLAYER

University of Kentucky (4 seasons, 25-12-4)
  1952 5-4-2 Division 1 Southeastern Conference
  1953 7-2-1 Division 1 Southeastern Conference,
          Receptions 2 Yards 5 TDs 0
  1954 7-3   Division 1 Southeastern Conference,
          Receptions 19 Yards 254 TDs 3
  1955 6-3-1 Division 1 Southeastern Conference,
          Receptions 20 Yards 287 TDs 6; AP All-American
Canadian Football League (2 seasons, 10-20)
  1956 Hamilton 7-7
          Receptions 14 Yards 184 Avg. 13.1 Long 30 TDs 2
  1958 British Columbia 3-13
          Receptions 10 Yards 172 Avg. 17.2 Long 41 TDs 1
Overall Record As College and Professional Player (6 seasons, 35-32-4)
Lifetime Record in 53 seasons of football from 1952-2011
641 games as a college or pro player or coach 371-257-13

ACKNOWLEDGEMENTS

When we started this project, I wrote to hundreds of the former players, assistant coaches and professional staff members who supported me throughout my career. I asked them to share comments, observations and memories of our time together. The response was tremendous and I could not have written this book without that help. Those quiet contributors are too numerous to name here, but hearing from each of them again made this a tremendously enjoyable process.

I am also greatly in debt to all the sports information and marketing people working for the university and pro teams I coached. It is possible I leaned the most heavily on Rick Remmert, who served with the University of Miami Athletic Department for years and is now the Director of Alumni Programs. He was gracious enough to respond to my many requests for assistance locating people and verifying facts.

Roy Hamlin, president of North Star Visions in Knoxville, Tennessee, dug deep into his archives to assist me in this effort. He played an important role promoting my teams at the University of Miami and in Louisville and he took an interest in helping me recall many details.

Ron Steiner was an important aide in my career. He was an invaluable scribe who took my disjointed writings and turned them into very powerful and understandable thoughts. Ron died well before the work on this book began. A collection of his writings, found after his death, provided a wealth of memories and facts about our days with the Miami Hurricanes, Louisville Cardinals, and the Oklahoma Sooners.

I would also like to thank my collaborator, Ron Smith. I befriended him 15 years ago when I was starting the football program at Florida Atlantic. I wrote a Sunday column for his newspaper. He offered to help me write my book back then, but I needed to wait until I left the sidelines for the last time. We have been full partners in this project for 18 months. For many of our all-day interviews he brought along three big-time football fans: Dennis Wallace, Spencer Cordell and Dan Hanuka. They asked compelling questions that improved my storytelling.

Hayden Trepeck deserves a special shout out. He is the managing partner of AOR Global and assists me with my speaking engagements and many personal matters. Hayden led me to the folks at Ascend Books.

I am grateful for my association with Publisher Bob Snodgrass. He employs a dedicated and professional staff that takes a personal interest in their authors. I commend the company to others with similar projects.

ABOUT THE AUTHORS

Howard L. Schnellenberger learned his trade from two of the all-time greats, Paul "Bear" Bryant and Don Shula, winning championships with each mentor. Schnellenberger then took the torch that was passed to him and won a championship of his own. He became a transformative head coach at three universities and all three schools have nominated him for the College Football Hall of Fame.

His career brought him into combat alongside or across the field from all the greats. He recruited or coached a stunning array of quarterbacks, including Joe Namath, Kenny Stabler, Jim Kelly, Bernie Kosar, Vinny Testaverde, Bert Jones, Bob Griese and Earl Morrall.

Schnellenberger served as offensive coordinator while helping Alabama and Bryant claim national championships in 1961, 1964 and 1965. His early career also included serving as offensive coordinator for Don Shula and the Miami Dolphins in 1972 during the only perfect season in NFL history.

Schnellenberger is best known, though, for delivering on a bold promise to win a national title at the University of Miami within five years. He won it all on schedule in 1983 and was named national coach of the year as he set Miami on a path to five championships in two decades.

In 1985 he returned to his hometown and took over another struggling program at the University of Louisville and built them into a football power. His time there was capped by a 10-1-1 record in 1990 that included a Fiesta Bowl victory over Alabama.

For an encore, the coach came out of retirement in 1998 at age 64 to start a football program at Florida Atlantic University. His team became the youngest program ever to go to a bowl. The Owls made Schnellenberger 6-0 and the winningest undefeated coach in bowl history.

A statue of the coach stands guard outside the stadium he built at FAU. In Louisville, the football complex that he fought to have constructed is named in his honor.

He retired from the sidelines in 2011 after 29 years as a head coach and 18 more as an assistant coach. He continues to work at Florida Atlantic as an Ambassador At Large. He and his wife, Beverlee, live in Boynton Beach with their Brussels Griffon affectionately named Safety Blitz.

Ronald C. Smith has a journalism degree from Boston University, a master's in education from Converse College and a law degree from Florida State University. Ron was executive city editor of the *Sarasota Herald-Tribune*, managing editor of the *Chattanooga Times* and editor in chief of the *Boca Raton News*. He now lives in Southwest Florida with his wife, Jean, who is an award-winning quilter. Ron is a prosecutor working for the State Attorney's Office; his daughter, Alexandra, is an Assistant Public Defender.

Visit www.ascendbooks.com for more
great titles on your favorite teams, coaches,
athletes, and celebrities.